Worker Cooperatives and Deep Democracy

'A book for our times, highlighting the planetary nature of the contemporary capitalist crisis and demonstrating that emancipatory ways of living, working, and consuming exist all over the world. Drawing on Marxist feminism and several years of in-depth research, care-based alternatives are highlighted for us to learn from to build the next society. Read this compass for grounded hope.'
—Thomas Isaac, former finance minister in the Left Government of Kerala, and author of *Kerala: Another Possible World*

'Grounded in research across continents, this remarkable book reveals how ordinary people are building cooperative and solidarity-based alternatives to capitalism. These real-world experiments show that a radical, justice-centred politics is not only necessary but possible in the face of the global polycrisis.'
—Ruy Braga, Professor of Sociology, University of São Paulo

'As social democratic politicians do their best to prove in practice that there is no alternative, Satgar and Williams provide a timely map of the transformative experiments that are daily seeding feasible systemic alternatives. This is a remarkable book in which the documentation of innovation in ethical economics drives the development of an original theory of a solidarity based political economy just when it is most needed. A very useful resource for immediate use, rather than simply a book to add to your bookshelves!'
—Hilary Wainwright, co-editor of *Red Pepper* and co-author of *New Politics from The Left*

Worker Cooperatives and Deep Democracy

Transformative Politics and Planetary Care from Below

Vishwas Satgar and Michelle Williams

PLUTO ⚓ PRESS

First published 2026 by Pluto Press
New Wing, Somerset House, Strand, London WC2R 1LA
and Pluto Press, Inc.
1930 Village Center Circle, 3-834, Las Vegas, NV 89134

www.plutobooks.com

British Library Cataloguing in Publication Data
A catalogue record for this book is available from the British Library

ISBN   978 0 7453 5157 5   Paperback
ISBN   978 0 7453 5159 9   PDF
ISBN   978 0 7453 5158 2   EPUB

This book is printed on paper suitable for recycling and made from fully
managed and sustained forest sources. Logging, pulping and manufacturing
processes are expected to conform to the environmental standards of the
country of origin.

Typeset by Stanford DTP Services, Northampton, England

Simultaneously printed in the United Kingdom and United States of America

EU GPSR Authorised Representative
LOGOS EUROPE, 9 rue Nicolas Poussin, 17000, LA ROCHELLE, France
Email: Contact@logoseurope.eu

To Michael Burawoy, beloved friend, mentor and comrade,
who tragically left us without finishing the conversation

and

to Martha Harnecker, Paul Singer and Erik Olin Wright,
kindred spirits, inspirational thinkers and committed comrades,
who were fellow travellers to realise emancipatory utopias

Contents

List of Abbreviations

ADS	Agencia de Desenvolvimento Solidario (Agency of Development of Solidarity)
AGM	annual general meeting
AIDS	acquired immune deficiency syndrome
BCE	before the Common Era
BLM	#BlackLivesMatter
Cecosesola	Central Cooperativa de Servicios Sociales del Estado Lara
COP	Conference of the Parties
CPI	Communist Party of India
CPI(M)	Communist Party of India (Marxist)
CUCI	Cincinnati Union Co-op Initiative
CUT	Central Única dos Trabalhadores (Unified Workers Central)
DGRV	Deutscher Genossenschafts Raiffeisen Verband
EU	European Union
EQI	European Quality Index
FEP	Fund for Education and Promotion
FSI	Inter-cooperative Social Fund
GCM	Mondragón Cooperative Group
GDP	gross domestic product
HIV	human immunodeficiency virus
IAD	Institutional Analysis and Development
ICA	International Cooperative Alliance
IMF	Internation Monetary Fund
ILO	International Labour Organization
LCCS	Udayapuram Labour Contract Cooperative Society
MCC	Mondragón Cooperative Corporation
MPI	Multidimensional Poverty Index
MST	*Movimento dos Trabalhadores Rurais Sem Terra* (Landless Workers Movement)

NAFTA	North American Free Trade Agreement
NGO	non-governmental organisation
NRECA	National Rural Electric Cooperative Association
OCB	Organisation of Brazilian Cooperatives
OECD	Organisation for Economic Co-operation and Development
OPEC	Organization of the Petroleum Exporting Countries
PODEMOS	left-wing political party in Spain
PT	Partido dos Trabalhadores (Brazilian Workers' Party)
SEQI	School Education Quality Index
SPI	Social Progress Index
TiVA	trade in value added
UK	United Kingdom
UN	United Nations
UNDP	United Nations Development Programme
ULCCS	Uralungal Labour Contract Co-operative Society
USA, US	United States of America
USFWC	US Federation of Worker Cooperatives
USW	United Steelworkers Union
WEF	World Economic Forum
WP	Workers' Party
WTO	World Trade Organization

Figures and Tables

FIGURES

TABLES

Introduction

As Mark Zuckerberg completes his $400 million compound on the island of Kauai with macadamia orchards to feed his cattle and an underground bunker to protect his family from a dystopian future, residents of the mountainous Wyannad region in Kerala pick up the tattered pieces of their lives after landslides killed over 400 people and another 118 disappeared on 30 July 2024. Despite weeks of heavy rain, there was no warning that entire villages would be erased in one fateful night. The weeks after the tragedy witnessed an outpouring of human solidarity, public support, concrete interventions from civil society and state and government agencies, and the activation of a care economy to help the survivors deal with their pain and rebuild their lives. Within days, the weeklong Onam[1] festivities that were scheduled to start a few weeks after the tragedy were cancelled out of respect for all those who lost their lives. The pain resonated across Kerala.

Across the Pacific Ocean, stretching over 5.5 million square metres of pristine land in Kauai, the Zuckerberg compound exemplifies a very different ethos from what we see in Kerala. With similar elite compounds built across Hawaii, local residents are priced out of the property market and sometimes forcibly removed from their land due to the failure to recognise indigenous land rights. In contrast to myriad acts of care and kindness in the face of climate catastrophe, the latest craze of billionaire bunkers reflects the fantasies of the plutocratic class that resemble a twenty-first-century feudal system where the lords try to control their entire ecosystem by ensconcing themselves (and their servants) in massive fortresses. Fearing climate disasters, cyber-attacks, civil wars, global conflagrations and nuclear detonation, and the rebellion of the poor, the billionaires live in a world in which their extraordinary economic power has disassociated them from the socio-ecological world and given

1

them licence for deeply anti-social behaviour. Their enormous wealth translates into incomprehensible power to do as they please wherever they please.

These two vignettes capture the countervailing tendencies that shape our world today. On the one hand, the economic and political elite have amassed so much power and wealth that they shape reality in their interests with little care for the vast majority of humanity. On the other hand, people are coming together to build a different world based on care, solidarity and socio-ecological relations. This book tells the stories of concrete attempts to build a different world, one based on ethical values of life-enabling commons systems to find a way beyond the planetary polycrisis that capitalism is hurling us into.

It is also against this backdrop that this book takes on special relevance. Based on 368 interviews and visits to 146 cooperatives and initiatives, including field visits in 15 countries, in this book we show that there is a plethora of creative generative experiments seeding systemic alternatives that attempt to create a better, more just and transformed world through constructing democratic economic relations, commoning practices and transformative politics. We focus on worker cooperatives and solidarity economy-based cooperative systems, and we show that they are prefigurative, counterhegemonic experiments rooted in democratic, ecological, just and eco-social(ist) practices and are found in the global south – from Brazil, Argentina, Venezuela and Bolivia to Mauritius, South Africa and India – and the global north, for example, Spain, Italy, USA, Canada, Germany, Denmark and Japan, despite the right-wing shift in some of these societies. The experiments show that ordinary people are engaging in concrete attempts to build anti-capitalist systems and forge new ways of living within societal and ecological boundaries.

Turmoil and uncertainty have been a consistent part of human history. Indeed, capitalism's history is, in part, a history of crises that sometimes become a 'polycrisis' leading to fundamental changes to the system.[2] The Great Depression culminating in World War II was one of those moments of polycrisis. The rise of neoliberalism came out of the polycrisis of the 1970s and was a ruling-class response to the crisis. Today is another one of those times of polycrisis. Even the World Economic Forum (WEF) – the citadel of capitalism – recognises the polycrisis highlighting that 'the overall impact exceeds the sum of each part' (WEF 2023, 57). The convergence of 'parts' includes economic instability and extreme inequality, the climate crisis, fraying social bonds, weakened democratic institutions and geopolitical conflagrations; in other words, the polycrisis is economic, social, ecological, political and global. However, today's polycrisis has an important difference to past polycrises. The central contradiction of capitalism today – its inherent tendency to exploit and destroy nature (O'Connor 1988) – faces an insurmountable problem. For the first time in its history, capitalism's solutions are not resolving the polycrisis because the prevailing capitalist logic of more extraction, overproduction and mass consumption have planetary consequences that could end in our extinction. It is an understatement to assert that the stakes are very high.

As the planetary polycrisis induces uncertainty, precarity and fear, it deepens polarisation. Twentieth-century hegemonic liberal values that centred polities and economic orders are losing legitimacy. With the waning certainties in the prevailing capitalist worldview, there are many possible futures. Some bad: rising religious fanaticism, scepticism about fact-based science and information, a growing number of people excluded from the formal economy, rising temperatures, extreme weather events, biodiversity loss, the return of authoritarian-populist leaders and unaccountable states, invasive and high-risk artificial intelligence and the unravelling of weak market democracies that privilege the power of capital over the demos. Some good: growing recognition of a plurality of knowledges including traditional and indigenous knowledges, attempts to build inclusive economic systems, communities coming together to collectively meet their needs, mainstreaming the climate emergency to mitigate and adapt to climate change, expanding regenerative agricultural practices and struggles for more democracy and accountable, capable states grounded in human- and nature-centred values. Which trend will become dominant depends on many things. It is no doubt an uncertain time, but it is also a time that harbours within it the possibility for epochal change.

While we may agree that today's capitalism and its polycrisis destroys our capacity to lead healthy, dignified lives, viable alternatives are far from obvious. In the twentieth century, debates were not about whether alternatives were possible, as the Soviet Union, China and Cuba, as well as social democracy in Scandinavia and short-lived experiments of African and Nehruvian socialism all demonstrated their existence. Rather, the debates were about how to make them better, more democratic, more vibrant, less austere, less authoritarian, as well as how to transform capitalism. Socialist experiments in countries in Africa, Eastern Europe, the Soviet Union, Vietnam and China failed to achieve democratic and egalitarian societies in which people flourished and human, social and ecological well-being were prioritised. Nevertheless, there was a deep confidence that alternatives to capitalism were possible, even if these alternatives were not perfect models to replicate. Despite the many shortcomings, they served as an important counter-pole to capitalism's claims of superiority. As these alternatives disappeared with the collapse of the Soviet Union, China's turn to authoritarian state capitalism, Cuba's fragile location in the global political economy and the coopting of social democracy, so too has the confidence that alternatives can exist in our lifetime. The anti-colonial struggles, including the anti-apartheid struggle in South Africa, failed to achieve transformative national political projects or to secure breakthroughs from imperial control. The degeneration of anti-colonial movements tells a tragic tale of broken promises, criminalised politics and authoritarianism. The effects of the paucity of positive socialist experiences have registered profoundly in the ideological arena. The idea of alternatives to capitalism still captures the imagination of many, but the confidence of what this would look like or how we get there has withered. Put more starkly, the imaginary of twentieth-century social democracy, Soviet socialism and national liberation politics is in crisis. But is this the end of history?

In this book, we show that alternatives to capitalism, pathways out of capitalism, are being created by emancipatory utopian imagin-

.ings and actual transformative and prefigurative practices of worker cooperatives and solidarity economy-based cooperative systems around the world. This is merely one dimension of a larger pattern of the commons (land, water, biodiversity, creative labour, renewable energy, public infrastructure and goods, cultural heritage, knowledge and the earth system) and commoning (the practice of making the commons). However, the commons pattern is not self-evident and, in the noise and haze of a dying capitalist landscape, the metaphor of a transformative compass seems especially apt as an instrument to help us find our way. In a world in which we are destroying our planetary existence and its life-enabling commons systems, corporations have more power than whole nations, states pass laws that hurt their citizens in order to make more profits for private companies, people die of starvation despite enough food being grown, a few have more money than they can spend in a hundred lifetimes while others struggle to eke out an existence daily, and hate, fear and intolerance are the new moral code for politics; we need a compass that helps save us from a system that is devouring everything. We need a transformative compass that can map next world making, highlight the politics of this new subjectivity and give us a fine-grained understanding of transformative change. In other words, there is a way to reproduce life in the everyday while engendering planetary care from below that ends the war with nature and among ourselves. We hope this book serves such a purpose to renew hope by providing a glimpse of the future struggling to be born in the present.

THE NEED FOR TRANSFORMATIVE ALTERNATIVES AND CHANGE

In a time when neoliberal rationality orders the ideational, economic, political, social and natural world, emancipatory utopian imaginaries and transformative alternatives take on an especially apposite relevance. They demonstrate that humanity can live outside the domination of economic metrics, produce goods and services that meet social needs, live with care for the planetary, relate to others, even those in faraway lands, through solidarity and cooperation, and democratise public power, the economy and society. By bringing economic activity under worker–owner control and promoting commoning of shared time, collective capacity (knowledge, power and culture), finance, creative labour and natural relations, we start to break down the boundaries between waged and unwaged work, the destructive domination of the natural world and the undermining of the social role of states and public power; we start to practise planetary care where we live and work. Unpacking what these emancipatory utopian imaginaries look like in various prefigurative experiments teaches us how we might get to futures different from the destructive fossil-fuel-driven, profit-based trajectory we are currently on. To realise the potential of these alternatives, we must also learn from and further foster transformative politics, new (and return to old) values and ideas that place human society in commons (natural and social) relations and cultures of caring for the human and natural world that nurture and promote the possibilities in these experiments.

There are transformative alternatives being created across the world. Some of these alternatives have antecedents in the deep history of human–earth relations based on solidarity and more recent histories of resistance over the past 500 years since the Columbian moment of 1492. Unlike the dominant alternatives of the twentieth century, today's experiments are not at the behest of states, organised political parties or powerful labour movements. Rather, they are largely created, practised and led by ordinary citizens in local spaces of their daily lives, often through commoning practices and a new transformative politics that rejects the old reform versus revolution binary (Satgar 2024). If the twentieth-century alternatives to capitalism were characterised by a Gramscian 'War of Manoeuvre' that focused on taking over the state, the twenty-first century alternatives are more akin to a 'War of Position' in which the entire edifice of socio-ecological relations is transformed from the bottom up, centring the commons as a commonwealth of life-enabling systems that are ethically and democratically organised. We see resistance to increasingly undemocratic states through attempts to build deeply democratic alternatives in workplaces and communities. While some of these experiments eschew the state, others seek to re-democratise the state to work in the interest of and with the people it claims to represent; all try to challenge the power of corporations and undemocratic states over the lives of people and natural relations. Thus, we see experiments foregrounding the commons – by which we mean commonly held, life-enabling systems ethically and democratically governed (discussed in Chapters 2 and 3) – with, against and beyond the state, market and society. Building transformative alternatives within the current system means that the experiments exist in the liminal space within and beyond capitalism. For most of us, we do not see this clearly and in its complexity because dominant modes of thinking, whether twentieth-century left imaginaries or hegemonic frames of thought that place the market–state relation at the centre of reproducing life and organising society. In this book, we seek to challenge the occlusion of the natural and social commons and locate its materiality in relation to state–market–society relations, as part of a new twenty-first century transformative politics. Transformative politics, expressed through a new political subjectivity, is a necessary condition for transformative alternatives and change to happen, including for worker cooperatives and solidarity economy-based cooperative systems studied in this book.

Scholarship is replete with superficial and provocative ideas such as Hardt and Negri's (2005) 'multitude', which suggests a miraculous joining together of the 'isolated and localized struggles of the disenfranchised, landless, and urban poor' (Chun 2009, 10; Piven and Cloward 1977). In the main, these movements focus on a protest politics aimed at challenging (even destroying) the existing system of political and economic power, often focusing on making claims to and against the state, and do not focus on building the future (Williams 2008). The work that has taken a more in-depth look at alternative class politics has largely focused on the revitalisation of labour movements, the emergence of new forms of worker organisations, the 'rebellion of the poor', and global networks of solidarity (for example, Chun 2009; Evans 2003; Fantasia and Voss 2004; Keck and Sikkink 1998; Sinwell 2023; Webster and Dor 2023).

There is also a vast literature that focuses on isolated cooperative experiences or theoretical models for alternative economies such as 'parecon' and 'real utopias' (Fridell 2007; Gibson-Graham 2008; Gibson-Graham et al. 2013; Grimes and Milgram 2000; Gunn 2004; Isaac and Williams 2017; Jaffee 2007; Rodriquez, Walter and Temper 2024; Wright 2019). There is, however, a dearth of scholarship that focuses on transformative alternatives in relation to the concrete experiences of solidarity economy-based cooperative systems and worker cooperatives, and that builds theoretical linkages to our conceptions of moving beyond capitalism. Unlike the fragmented episodic protest politics of many movements, the cooperatives in this book are not a multitude of discrete subjects divorced from creating an alternative social order. Rather, they are guided by emancipatory visions linked to concrete transformative practices and they work together to create alternatives and aggregate their counterhegemonic power. They are among the forces of socio-ecological reproduction that address harms and that engage in planetary care from below. In other words, such experiences display how transitioning beyond capitalism is possible.

Over the past four decades, cycles of resistance have engendered a new global left imaginary based on experiments in participatory budgeting, reclaiming the commons, rights of nature, deep just transitions, democratic decentralisation, democratising economic relations, degrowth movements, transition towns, eco-villages, local food movements (including food sovereignty movements), solidarity economies, climate justice movements and cooperatives which demonstrate that alternatives to capitalist relations are being created. In all the experiments, we see a renewed politics of democratic civil society participation in which the existing dominant economic, socio-ecological and political systems are engaged, pushed, refashioned, outmanoeuvred and worked around. The experiments attempt to shift power relations in favour of ordinary people, democratic civil society and 'more-than-human life' through deepening and extending democratic practices, opening up decision making, recalibrating and harmonising relations with nature, creating egalitarian redistributive mechanisms, promoting local economic activity, restoring and nurturing the commons, refashioning development planning, (re)valuing indigenous and local knowledge systems and unleashing new forms of agency. Deep democracy is being designed, practised and lived. Across the globe, ordinary people working collectively – including middle and working classes, indigenous peoples, peasantries, marginalised, rural and urban populations, and the precarious subaltern more generally – are attempting to reconstitute the conditions under which they live with the potential for macro-scale transformation through democratic systemic reforms; they are forces of socio-ecological reproduction eroding, taming and exiting capitalism. Their salience for ending the planetary crisis is a crucial theme in this book.

Looking to cooperatives might seem an unlikely place to find inspiration for theorising the constituent elements of transformative politics, a role traditionally assigned to socialist parties and movements. The importance of learning from the real and messy experiences of cooperatives cannot be overstated as many cooperatives are attempting to build new futures in the present through human-to-human, human-to-enterprise, human-to-state/public power solidarities and ultimately human-to-commons relations. In other words, economic activity is reclassified from primarily concerned with profit-maximisation to primarily concerned with socio-ecological reproduction. Cooperatives are central in this.

In this book, we show that the way in which worker cooperatives and solidarity economy-based cooperative systems democratise economic activity *and* embed it within the background conditions of capitalism potentially transforms the system itself. In other words, they reconfigure power relations among the political, social and economic spheres. By integrating economic activity with the 'de-commodified' background spheres – social reproduction, nature, public power and the state, and territorial expansion – worker cooperatives and solidarity economy-based cooperative systems challenge the social organisation of capitalism. The background spheres are the bedrock on which capitalism exists, but they are so intertwined with everyday life that their role in the economy is often unrecognised. Building on Fraser's (2022) critical analysis, social reproduction is the care work, largely done by women, that provides for human development, social bonds and community well-being. Capitalism could not exist without the reproduction of human beings but denies its role. The cooperatives we studied not only recognise the constitutive role of social reproduction but also work to integrate social reproduction into the fabric of the cooperative. The natural world provides the material inputs from which capitalism has been built and is the shock absorber for capitalist pollution and waste. Capitalism underplays its destructive impact and places humans outside of nature. Yet, the natural world and human well-being are integrally intertwined and cannot be bifurcated. The cooperatives in this book seek to reharmonise economic relations within natural relations and place human activity within the natural commons. Public power in state institutions provides the legal underpinnings and social contract, as well as crucial public infrastructure on which capitalist economic relations operate. By creating democratic pressure and active citizens, many of the cooperatives we studied effected positive influence on their local governments and broader political culture. Colonial and postcolonial/imperial extraction and exploitation allowed capitalism to flourish in the centres of capitalism while externalising its ecological and social destruction to colonised lands and peoples. In stark contrast, the cooperatives in this book create relations of solidarity with other cooperatives and progressive movements within their countries and internationally. Unlike capitalist corporations, cooperatives are also place-specific, embedded and generally not expansionary in their logic.[3] Ultimately, capitalism depends on social reproduction, nature and public power as well as colonial and imperial power relations, and has never paid the actual costs of its dependence on these spheres. In contrast, genuine transformative cooperatives, rather than being outside of the background conditions, fundamentally imbricate with them and impact the socio-ecological reproduction of societies. The cooperatives we studied deal with the background conditions of capitalism transformatively and seek to embed the economy into the larger socio-ecological system. Through their transformative praxis, they build worker cooperatives and solidarity economy-based cooperative systems that are actually regimes of socio-ecological reproduction; they engage in life-making and planetary care that provides another crucial condition for defining transformative change.

This framing is important for our work on emancipatory alternatives and transformative politics as it complicates the picture of what activity lies alongside or in the interstitial spaces of capitalism. By embedding economic activity in social reproduction and production, in human and natural relations, in democratic politics and in solidaristic relations with others, we suggest that solidarity economy-based cooperative systems and worker cooperatives are an important arena of anti-capitalist economic activity as they integrate economic activity within broader socio-ecological relations.

RECLASSIFYING ECONOMIC ACTIVITY: THE COMMONS, DEEP DEMOCRACY AND SOLIDARITY

In cultivating new values and redrawing the boundaries between the economy and the background conditions, classification struggles are vital. Essentially, the anti-capitalist experiments engage in a process of reclassification of ownership, economic relations, natural relations and the goal of economic activity. Lying on the margins of the mainstream economy in which worker–owners and commoning are often in a state of 'legal liminality' in which they are neither protected by the legal apparatus nor exempted from it (Chun 2009, 12), worker–owners engage in struggles to gain moral and legal legitimacy. Through bringing dignity, inclusion, quality jobs and social connectedness, worker cooperatives engage in everyday displays of the alternative they are building. At times, these might be public struggles to gain widespread support such as in the recovered factory movement in Argentina (discussed in Chapter 4); the quiet efforts to ensure food sovereignty in their region such as in Cecosesola in Venezuela (discussed in Chapter 5); redefining of the local political field to ensure public officials are accountable and responsive such as in Trentino, Italy (discussed in Chapter 5); achieving some of the lowest levels of inequality in Europe as in Mondragón,

Spain (discussed in Chapter 6); or such as providing construction worker–owners dignity by building some of the best public works projects in Kerala, India (discussed in Chapters 4 and 6). What all of these examples share is their reclassification of economic life to be socio-ecologically embedded in local communities and for worker–owners and community members to be the central beneficiaries of the economic system.

Struggles over naming, defining and categorising the socio-ecological-economic realms either subvert or reinforce the hegemonic order. In effect, waging a war of position that promotes anti-capitalist values and practices simultaneously challenges and possibly undermines capitalism at its core. For Bourdieu (2000), it is the economic elite and the state who typically have the power to determine classifications through the legal apparatus (for example, who qualifies as a worker and is therefore protected by the law). We are suggesting that worker cooperatives and solidarity economy-based cooperative systems also engage in classification struggles that redefine the way work is organised, who makes decisions, but also what is the nature of work itself, what is defined as work, who is a worker, how does work relate to natural relations, rather than 'factors of production' and what constitutes an economy. In other words, as they provide a democratic and ethical institutional framework to common time, creative labour, collective capacity, natural relations and finance, they build counterhegemonic transformative alternatives.

For example, the idea of the commons challenges capitalist economic relations that are predicated upon private ownership, whereas the commons relies on collective sharing of life-enabling systems (discussed in Chapters 2 and 3). Many worker cooperatives are practising (often without naming it) the idea of the commons in their understanding of their work, in their practices and in their visions of alternatives. Hilary Wainwright's work helps us understand this when she highlights the central role of workers' creative capacity in envisioning and creating alternatives (Wainwright 2017). Through their collective creative capacity, worker cooperatives are re-embedding economic relations into the socio-ecological system. The commons comes out of struggles against processes that commodify life-enabling systems which have previously been held in common such as land, water, biodiversity, public transport and even the digital sphere (Bauwens et al. 2025; Satgar 2024). Worker cooperatives are engendering creative labour commons through their individual and collective creativity. This is well demonstrated by Mondragón's knowledge commons, research and development centres, and education and training programmes as well as Cecosesola's collective learning and deliberative ideas sharing. It is also seen in the Timbuktu Collective's dedicated focus on reclaiming and rehabilitating the natural commons of their forests and grasslands in Andhra Pradesh in India. Ultimately, worker cooperatives and solidarity economy-based cooperative systems seek to transform society in such a way that prioritises human development and planetary care through the expansion of the commons (elaborated in Chapter 3).

The route to this is often circuitous. For example, the workers in the Argentine recovered factory movement were not trying to overthrow capitalism – they were trying to secure their futures – but inadvertently engendered a fundamental challenge to capitalism through their rejection of private property and profits vested in an individual owner. While workers may not have been seeking to threaten capitalism through reclassification, the whole idea of 'recovering' a factory from errant private owners fundamentally undermined the idea of private property and private profits. As a result, the recovered factory movement inadvertently unleashed a wave of recoveries based on collective ownership and it inspired hope in an alternative to capitalism. The recovered factory workers did not have preconceived anti-capitalist aspirations to take over the factories but evolved their ideas through their struggles. They were owed money (often many months of backpay and pensions) and many feared that they would not get another job. Therefore, they recovered the factory out of desperation. In several factories we visited, workers had worked in the company for more than 20 years and strongly identified with the company, their jobs and their rightful entitlements. Identifying deeply with their factories was also, in part, due to the Peronist history in which the working class enjoyed job security and a high degree of social benefits.

Through collective ownership and democratic decision making, the recovered factories re-defined the way work is organised, who owns the means of production, how decisions get made, who benefits from surplus/profits and how the cooperative should relate to society. In defining recovery as part of workers' rightful entitlement, the discourse consciously sought legitimacy and socio-ecologically embedded economic activity. The terminology of 'recovered' rather than 'takeover' reinforces the idea that workers had rightful shares in the company, even if this meant taking ownership away from the owners and collectivising it. By collectivising ownership, the workers challenged a foundational feature of capitalism – the idea of private property vested in individual owners based on ownership shares – and therefore were unintentionally eroding capitalism from within. The state's role is paramount as the legal framework underpins capitalism and either closes off or creates the possibility for challenges. For example, expropriation laws can facilitate or obstruct recovery. The recovery struggles turned to symbolic power in order to put pressure on the state. In an effort to gain legitimacy in the eyes of the public, the recovered factory movement invested a great deal of energy in symbolic struggles to popularise its counter-narrative through music, film and art. For example, the iconic Buenos Aires' Hotel Bauen recovery was made into a children's book, *The Dwarfs of Dignity*, with animated characters that tell the story of workers seeking justice and providing a service to society through recovering the hotel from the greedy and extravagant owner.[4] Hotel Bauen is an important beacon for the movement as the struggle was both symbolic and courageous but also showed how workers acting collectively could challenge even one of the most premiere hotels of the elite (former President Menem had a penthouse suite in the hotel) on one of the most prestigious boulevards of Buenos Aires. The struggles no doubt left workers feeling empowered but also garnered public support in their claims for legitimacy in the eyes of the law. On more than one occasion, we heard worker–owners say that the movement has shown that 'workers can run companies without bosses, but bosses cannot run companies without workers'. In effect, they reclassified workers as central to the company *and* the economy; they articulated deep democracy with worker–owners upending power over them in a corporate-controlled market democracy.

One of the important lessons from the recovered factory movement is the way in which solidarity is built and maintained through myriad avenues, such as public demonstrations, films and cultural events, which together helped shore up and solidify a common identity. Engaging the public realm also proved important in legitimating their demands and creating a conducive environment in their legal cases for expropriation. Winning an expropriation claim requires various steps, such as occupying the factory, building support from local communities, organising workers and forming cooperatives, legal framing and state responsiveness, access to capital (either via the state or favourable loans) and tax incentives. In other words, it requires the state to develop a new social contract that redefines access to 'private' property in terms of social criteria rather than wealth.

Solidarity is a foundational principle of transformative alternatives. But as history vividly demonstrates, solidarity can be framed in narrow, exclusionary terms or in expansive, inclusionary terms. Solidarity built on exclusionary categories, such as ascriptive identities of race, ethnicity, gender, nationality, religion, unions and work, reinforces boundaries and works in favour of capitalism's divisions. By hierarchising groups against one another and focusing on difference as bounded categories of exclusion, negative solidarity reinforces powerful institutions, unequal power relations and competitive relations with others that are prevalent across capitalism. The toxic politics coursing through polities in recent times is based on negative solidarities. Anti-capitalist politics sometimes shares some of this when it overemphasises negative solidarities in the sense of accentuating what it is against. In contrast, positive forms of solidarity, while articulating what they are against, also go further and build common understandings based on expansive ideas of well-being, shared humanity, appreciation of humans as part of the natural world, planetary care and democratic practices, and deliberative decision making. Solidarity that builds bridges on the basis of social and ecological justice, human well-being, participatory democracy, worker control and cooperation provides the possibility of connecting the inter-realm boundaries between the economy and nature, social reproduction and public power as well as geopolitical boundaries that divide capitalist centres and peripheries. In other words, class struggle becomes integrally linked to boundary struggles to become socio-ecological class struggle.

THE RESEARCH PROCESS

Some research is not only enriching and informative, but also inspiring and exciting. Through our research, spanning 14 years, we met extraordinary people engaged in many ordinary and extra-ordinary activities in their efforts to shape more just, humane and egalitarian local spaces. We were humbled, inspired and tantalised by what we saw, heard and learnt. The research was a journey into the concrete experiments of human ingenuity and compassion. We saw some of the best of what our species is capable. While we were often amazed by what we witnessed, we also do not want to romanticise the projects. All of them faced hardships, struggles and major setbacks. Some faced internal challenges among participants, others faced external challenges with their states and local conditions, all faced challenges with the global political economy.[5]

In this book, we use the learning from this rich and varied research to theorise and explore various efforts at transforma-tive politics and emancipatory alternatives through the commons, worker cooperatives and the solidarity economy. We combine our theoretical discussions with the empirical material in an iterative process of theory-empirical engagement. The conversation with the rich empirical research is based on 14 years of research in 15 countries between 2008 and 2019 and 2023 and 2024. The countries – South Africa, Mauritius, Tanzania, Kenya, Senegal, Ethiopia, Brazil, Argentina, Venezuela, India, Italy, Germany, Spain, Canada, USA – were chosen based on the experiments with democratic workplaces and transformative politics taking place in the countries. This is not to say that these are the only countries or only experiments within these countries where exciting alternative economic activity is taking place. In fact, it is quite heartening to know that there are many, many more (see, for example, Rodriquez, Walter and Temper 2024). The more we learnt about a place, the more we discovered new and exciting experiments. At some point, however, we had to stop fieldwork and begin the arduous process of making sense of our research material and start writing.

We conducted a total of 337 interviews with cooperative worker–owners, solidarity economy activists, scholars and fellow travellers between 2008 and 2019 and another 31 in 2023 and 2024 for a total of 368 interviews. In Argentina, we conducted 26 interviews and visited nine recovered factories (some a couple of times over a few years), in Brazil we did 19 interviews and had four field visits to cooperatives, and in Venezuela we conducted 29 interviews and ten field visits to cooperatives, making a total of 74 interviews and 23 field visits between 2008 and 2017 in Latin America. In India, we conducted 78 interviews and 43 field visits to cooperatives between 2010 and 2017 and follow up visits in 2023 and 2024 where we did an additional 21 interviews and six field visits. In the USA, we conducted 22 interviews and had eight field visits and in Canada we conducted four interviews, making our North American total 26 interviews and eight field visits between 2008 and 2017. In Africa, between 2008 and 2017 we conducted 86 interviews and visited 37 cooperatives: in Senegal we had eleven interviews and five field visits, in Ethiopia we conducted eight interviews and one field visit, in Kenya we did nine interviews and four field visits, in Tanzania we did 14 interviews and four field visits, in Mauritius we had 17 interviews and seven field visits, in South Africa we conducted 27 interviews and 16 field visits. We completed an additional ten interviews and seven field visits in South Africa in 2023 and 2024. In Europe, we conducted 73 interviews and visited 22 cooperatives between 2009 and 2019: 18 interviews and four field visits were in Germany, in Spain we conducted 20 interviews and five field visits to Mondragón cooperatives and, in Italy, we had 35 interviews and 13 field visits. A number of interviews were with multiple people and sometimes extended over a day or two; we count these as one interview.

In addition to the 368 interviews, we visited 146 cooperatives, recovered factories and solidarity economy enterprises across 15 countries. In a number of cases, we made return visits to the cooperatives over a number of years and conducted multiple interviews with key people. Spending time visiting the cooperatives, recovered factories and solidarity economy enterprises deepened our understanding and appreciation of the work they are doing. In some cases, we spent a few days to a week with them and in others a few hours to a day. These visits introduced us to the physical spaces, the worker–owners and the local environments in which they operate. We came face-to-face with many of the challenges, failures and successes we refer to in this book. In addition, we participated in five intensive multi-day workshops organised with local scholars and cooperative members and activists in five countries: India, Spain, Argentina, South Africa and Italy. These workshops (except for the one in India) were part of Erik Olin Wright's *Real Utopias* project on cooperative economies that we were part of. The last workshop was scheduled to happen in 2019 in Madison, Wisconsin, but never happened due to Erik's untimely death. The workshops introduced us to the latest research on cooperatives in the host countries and provided additional engagements with cooperative members. To give us a better sense of the commons and socio-ecological ways of living, we took three intensive courses in South Africa: a 14-day permaculture course in 2022, a three-day agroforestry course and a two-day wild food foraging course in 2024. See the Annexure of this book for a summary of our research.

This rich research over an extended period of time with such a large number of interviews and field visits, a7s well as intensive multi-day workshops with local scholars and cooperative activists/members, gave us a tremendous feel for the various places, the similarities and contrasts across experiments, countries, regions and continents. It also made patently clear that real alternatives are being practised in various countries, across class, gender, rural/urban, racial and developmental cleavages. Instead of divisive fault lines of competitive neoliberal capitalism and the deeper systemic divides of capitalism, we witnessed human solidarity and cooperation in trying to build a better world.

Our approach was to find breadth and variation across countries, sectors, extant cultures, class histories, historical and economic conditions, and geographical boundaries of global north and south. To do this meant we had to spread our research over many years as academic and activist life gave us limited time every year for dedicated research. We decided early in the project that we would rather take the time necessary for such a project, than try to rush it and only visit a few places. We are very happy we approached it this way and believe the outcome is richer for it. The drawback with this approach meant we had to revisit cases and also rely on online communication and desktop research in order to ensure our data from some of the early visits remained valid. Our approach has allowed us to focus on the big picture. Indeed, it is not the details of any one case that is the strength of this book, but rather the larger trends of transformative alternatives that the concrete experiments demonstrate.

A note about how we draw on the empirical cases: for the three empirical chapters (Chapters 4–6), we chose a few worker cooperatives and solidarity economy-based cooperative systems that exemplified the theoretical ideas, especially boundary-breaking activities. However, we could have chosen other cases or used the cases we chose to highlight other aspects. We have chosen to use some less familiar cases that most readers may never have heard of, while also using some cases that are well known. For the coherence of the book, the cases we chose to highlight are illustrative and often represent practices that are widespread across many worker cooperatives. Choosing what to focus on and what to leave out is always difficult and never a perfect practice, but we have tried to stay true to the cooperatives and their anti-capitalist projects.

STRUCTURE OF THE BOOK

In Part I, 'Beyond the Planetary Polycrisis', we focus on how to think of the current fourth great crisis of capitalism as a planetary polycrisis of socio-ecological reproduction and how the commons (natural and social) is implicated in the everyday crisis of life-making. The current polycrisis is simultaneously a multi-level crisis registering at the systemic, conjunctural (neoliberal class project), imperial and planetary levels. Capitalism's annihilation of its enabling background conditions of reproduction are also at the same time an annihilation of the commons, as part of the last great dispossession of the commons with dire planetary implications. We argue that to overcome the destruction of the planetary conditions that sustain life, there is a need to recentre the commons at the heart of social and ecological thought and how we think social reproduction of capitalism and its background conditions. Moreover, we think through how the commons, worker cooperatives and solidarity economies feature in the current cycles of resistance, as forces of socio-ecological reproduction, elaborating and advancing a new transformative politics. Transformative politics is the first necessary condition to bring about transformative change, which has been embodied by some worker cooperatives and solidarity economy-based cooperative systems for a very long time. It is about a political subjectivity committed to building an emancipatory future in the present. The second condition is the actual practices of cooperatives as transformative forces of socio-ecological reproduction. Drawing on their inherent characteristics, values and institutional orientations to relate to the background conditions of capitalism, they embed the economy in socio-ecological relations. In short, this part of the book clarifies why we need to think the current crisis as planetary crisis, the importance of transformative politics, the role of cooperatives in transformative change and how such change comes about to realise planetary care from below rather than the destruction of everything.

Chapter 1, 'The Planetary Polycrisis of Socio-ecological Reproduction and the Challenge of Commons Ontology', is premised on how life-making for the many has been gridlocked by global capitalism through inequality, unemployment, hunger, lack of access to public healthcare, homelessness, the worsening climate rupture in the earth system and destruction of ecosystems. The chapter provides a systems perspective of capitalism and discusses how the state–market relation takes life-making into a planetary crisis. Capitalism's systems are so tightly entwined with earth relations such that its fourth great polycrisis is a planetary crisis. In this context, reductionist approaches to the contemporary polycrisis of capitalism are not useful to deal with the 'planetary problematic'. How we think about the contemporary crisis is a crucial challenge if we want to find exits and departures. In this chapter, we provide a more expansive framework for locating the crises of contemporary capitalism and its wider relational dynamics by drawing on social reproduction theory, but we ground it in an ontological perspective of the commons. We bring to the fore the importance of the breakdown of socio-ecological reproduction, both as a societal and planetary process. Importantly, this breakdown is being resisted and here we counter-pose 'forces of production' with transformative forces of socio-ecological reproduction, furnishing a historical genealogy of such forces that have resisted the destruction of the planetary commons through 500 years of colonial conquest, imperialism and US-led neoliberal globalisation. Such forces of socio-ecological reproduction have been defending, renewing and championing the commons pattern of life-making and are transformative. The chapter makes a case to centre the commons and commons pattern in how we think the planetary polycrisis socio-ecological reproduction and also transformation. Transformative worker cooperatives, as forms of the commons and commoning practice, are deeply imbricated in the 'boundary struggles' to advance transformation.

Chapter 2, 'The Rise of Transformative Politics and Planetary Care from Below', looks at the emergence of post social democratic, Soviet and national liberation politics on the left. This chapter claims that despite declarations about the 'end of history' and 'capitalist realism', market-centric utopia has not eclipsed left politics. Old left projects that shaped the twentieth century have been defeated but a new transformative left has been rising through three cycles of global resistance with a fourth underway, coming out of the Covid-19 pandemic. We start the chapter by looking at the limits and problems with twentieth-century left and the lessons from this experience that inform the new global left. Crucial in this chapter is the transformation of left subjectivity and imaginaries in the context of championing alternatives to global neoliberal restructuring. In this ferment, forces of socio-ecological reproduction have championed systemic alternatives as part of renewing a new solidarity based counterhegemonic resistance that has defined, as a counter to the old reform versus revolution binary, transformative praxis, emancipatory utopia as method of world making from below, ethics of care as a basis for institutionalising left politics, transformative poly epistemologies and constitutive forms of political power to advance democratic systemic reforms. The new transformative left politics, in confronting the planetary polycrisis, also engages in planetary care as it erodes, tames and seeks exits from capitalism. Deep just transitions are not just about humans surviving but about having a non-antagonistic relationship with earth relations as we reproduce life in the everyday. In this regard, worker cooperatives and solidarity economy systems, as embodiments of transformati7ve politics, are crucial examples of learning to care for human and more-than-human life.

In Chapter 3, 'Cooperatives and Transformative Change', we provide an overview of the state of the global cooperative movement that includes debates about cooperatives as business models, ameliorative forms or transformative alternatives. We show that they can take on any one of these orientations. In this book, we focus on cooperatives that are guided by anti-capitalist principles and values and that consciously engage in transformative praxis.

In Part II, 'Worker Cooperatives and Solidarity Economies as Counterhegemonic Regimes of Socio-Ecological Reproduction', we shift our engagement to explicitly draw on our rich empirical material to highlight the theoretical ideas. These chapters explicitly draw on the interviews and field visits to cooperatives, recovered factories and solidarity economy-based cooperative systems, and the five workshops. This rich research, over an extended period, gave us time and confidence to see the big picture and draw out the transformative possibilities. We show that our case studies not only relate to the background conditions of capitalism differently and provide exits from the planetary polycrisis, but also extend care to these conditions through transformative politics. In this way, these case studies are illustrative of how counterhegemonic regimes of socio-ecological reproduction and planetary care are built from below such that boundary struggles are deeply transformative. Capitalism is being eroded, tamed and exited in these worker cooperative commons and commoning forms that treat time, creative labour, finance, collective capacity and natural relations differently.

In Chapter 4, 'Integrating Socio-ecological Reproduction: ULCCS in Kerala, Chilavert in Argentina and Uniforja in Brazil', we look at the ways in which worker cooperatives have redrawn boundaries between the economy and socio-ecological reproduction. We focus on worker cooperatives that challenge capitalism's boundary between economic activity and the nurturing and sustenance role played by social and natural reproduction. We show how the cooperatives integrate socio-ecological reproduction into their very DNA and, in so doing, contribute to remaking our regimes of socio-ecological reproduction. Despite the centrality of social reproduction, capitalism positions it outside the productive work in the economy and, thus, turns the relationship upside down to appear as though social reproduction depends on production. Worker cooperatives, by contrast, recognise the central life-constituting role of social reproduction and place economic activity within the regime of socio-ecological reproduction rather than in command of it. We chose three pied experiences to illustrate the remaking of socio-ecological boundaries. The experiences of Uralungal Labour Contract Cooperative Society (ULCCS), Chilavert and Uniforja represent different sectors, extant cultures, political traditions and class histories. Yet all are engaged in pioneering ways to internalise socio-ecological reproduction through the way in which they organise work, engage worker–owners and their communities, and remunerate their members.

In Chapter 5, 'Recalibrating Relations with Nature: Cecosesola in Venezuela, Heiveld in South Africa and Trentino in Italy', we shift our attention to look explicitly at the ways in which worker cooperatives relate to the background condition of natural relations. We chose three very different examples to illustrate the ways they have defined their relations to the natural world by embedding economic activity within normative frameworks that recognise human dependence on and within nature and give priority to protecting it. One, Cecosesola (Central Cooperativa de Servicios Sociales del Estado Lara), a solidarity economy cooperative system of markets, farming, health and insurance in Venezuela, another, Heiveld Cooperative, a rooibos tea farmers' cooperative in a remote rural region of South Africa, and the third, Trentino Cooperative Movement, a cooperative system in Trentino, northern Italy engaged in local farming, cooperative banks, consumer cooperatives, social cooperatives and worker cooperatives. We chose such varied examples in order to show how different cooperatives are trying to redraw relations to the natural world on which they depend. They are all acutely aware that the natural world is based on life-enabling commons systems and are trying to upend the destructive and exploitative relations with nature that are hegemonic in capitalism. Capitalism takes from natural commons systems the 'natural resources' and returns to nature the waste products of the production process. In this chapter, we look at the ways these cooperatives, by contrast, embed economic activity within natural relations. We show how worker cooperatives are not only socially embedded but also recognise the importance of finding non-destructive ways of relating to natural relations. Some see it as an ontological question and position themselves with an understanding of humans and all social relations to exist in nature, while others pragmatically approach the importance of protecting nature for future generations. Either way, they relate to nature by valuing its contribution to economic relations and see the importance of operating within the natural boundaries of the planet and with care.

Chapter 6, 'Engaging Political Power and Creating Solidarities: Mondragón in Spain, State–Civil Society Synergies in Kerala and the Solidarity Economy Forum in Brazil', looks at the relationality of solidarity economy systems and worker cooperatives to democracy, public power and the state, which necessarily takes us beyond the enterprise. The separation of politics from the economy has been a central feature of capitalism, carefully orchestrated so that good governance requires separation from economic activity. Ironically, its very existence depends on the public goods (including education, healthcare and transport systems), legal contracts and legislative frameworks, property relations, law and order, and public infrastructure that the state ensures. In other words, the public infrastructure commons are at the core of what the state provides to enable capitalist accumulation. In this chapter, we focus on the way in which solidarity economy-based cooperative systems and worker cooperatives operate on a fundamentally different rationality from capitalism in relation to democracy, public power and the state, as well as the relations beyond the enterprise. We look at the ways worker cooperatives internalise democratic decision making and collective ownership into their quintessence, as well as redraw boundaries between the economy and the state and inter- and intra-national and interenterprise expansion.

In the concluding chapter, we highlight the importance of a new politics for the world in permanent crisis and for life-making and flourishing as we live through the polycrisis. Given what is at stake, there is a real possibility of worker cooperatives and solidarity economy-based cooperative systems that engender counterhegemonic resistance to reset – and possibly fundamentally remake – modes of living to become human and nature-centred regimes of socio-ecological reproduction. In this context, finding anti-capitalist experiments is essential for the survival of all species on earth. Despite living under the yoke of capitalism for centuries and waves of accumulation attempting to commodify all forms of life, capitalism has proven incapable of subsuming all life. Highlighting these spaces of resistance is part of strengthening struggles for transformative alternatives. Hence, in this book, we focus on the politics of possibility that these transformative alternatives represent. In other words, finding anti-capitalist experiments provides a compass to navigate new ways of organising socio-ecological relations. Historians tell us that great leaders emerge in times of peril. This is a story about the great many leaders, not any particular leader. In an era of uninspiring and corrupted leaders, we tell a story of the ordinary people doing extraordinary experiments to create a new history and advance planetary care from below.

CONCLUSION

The cooperative experiences covered in this book are not miracles, but are the result of the hard, often unglamorous, work of building alternatives in the everyday lives of members, communities and society through democratic deliberation, engaged worker–owners and a collective interest in creating a more just, equal and caring planet. They show the limitless possibilities the experiments contain through extraordinary acts of imagination and creativity to think beyond our current conditions, even if the path is circuitous and long. Indeed, the metaphor of a compass illustrates not the kind of compass that points to the most efficient way to get somewhere, but one that shows the possible pathways and points out the challenges, the roadblocks, the mountains to climb, oceans and rivers to cross, and the verdant green pastures. A compass that shows true south, and reminds us that making history is a journey and not an end.

PART I

Beyond the Planetary Polycrisis

1

The Planetary Polycrisis of Socio-ecological Reproduction and the Challenge of Commons Ontology

Life-making for the many has been gridlocked by global capitalism. A catalogue of suffering persists everywhere: inequality, unemployment, hunger, lack of access to public healthcare, homelessness, the worsening climate rupture in the earth system and destruction of ecosystems. Desperation marks the everyday biological reproduction of the many while ecosystems and earth relations are undermined. Capitalism won after the Cold War. Yet, over four decades of neoliberal restructuring of the global economy merely made life unliveable on a planetary scale. With capital dominant across the planet, these realities have been treated as market failures and the solutions have always been the same: more power to markets and capital. It is a tautological nightmare for humans and ecosystems. Despite these inherent failings of the neoliberal class and imperial project, financialised market dogma is not being rethought. The logic of unbridled capitalist accumulation, on a fragile and finite planet, seems unstoppable and prompts the question: will capitalism end habitability on earth?

This chapter explores where the dyad of market–state is taking human and non-human life. Paradoxically, while growth-centred accumulation of capitalism assumes an endless process, for which it ensures the necessary conditions, capitalism has an end. Indeed, capitalism is quickening its own end as it organises social and earth relations into a deep general crisis – the fourth great polycrisis of capitalism – in which the commons of water, land, biodiversity, renewable energy, creative labour, knowledge, cultural heritage, public infrastructure and goods, and the earth system is being anni- hilated as part of its background conditions. Beyond the everyday, this crisis exists at several levels: the systemic, the neoliberal class project, the disciplinary imperial and the earth system. Social theory and economics, more generally, do not appreciate the dynamics of this crisis and its scalar interconnections. Reductionist explana- tions do not capture the complexity, depth and scale of crisis. How we think about the contemporary crisis is a crucial challenge if we want to find exits and departures, given how high the stakes are. This chapter challenges reductionist modes of thinking contem- porary capitalist crisis and provides a more expansive framework for locating the crises of contemporary capitalism and its wider relational dynamics. Drawing on a planetary commons perspec- tive, social reproduction theory and polycrisis systems thinking, this chapter brings to the fore the breakdown of socio-ecological reproduction, both as a societal and planetary process, driven by the ecocidal (mass-scale destruction of human and non-human life) logic of globalised capitalism.

While current forms of class rule are engulfing the planet in life-making crises, there is a crucial exit. This exit was central to reproducing the web of life before capitalism and continues to exist at its margins, interstitially and within socio-ecological reproduc- tion processes. Despite enclosures of the commons underway, the commons and commoning (the practice of making the commons) still provides a way forward for human and non-human life. This means revisiting, defending and renewing the centrality of the life-centric ontology of the commons and its pattern of life-mak- ing. As a counter conception of liveability, the commons provides a different conception of how relationality, particularly humans-in- earth relations, needs to be conceived, understood and storied. In this chapter, we elaborate the ways in which a commons ontology fundamentally challenges the dualistic ontology that underpins capitalism and lays the basis for transformative alternatives. Such a systemic alternative is part of an emancipatory pattern of resistance, driven by transformative forces of socio-ecological reproduction.

Transformative forces of socio-ecological reproduction have resisted the destruction of the planetary commons perpetrated by 500 years of colonial conquest, imperialism and US-led neoliberal globalisation. The patterned agency of such forces is highlighted. These forces are now imbricated in resistance to the historically specific fourth general crisis of capitalism (mid-2000s to present). There is a rich canvass of commoning underway in the shadows and beyond the life-destroying rationalities of ecocidal capitalism. This pattern of thinking the commons is explored further in the next chapter in relation to conjunctural cycles of resistance to remake left politics as transformative politics and in subsequent chapters dealing with actual case studies of worker cooperatives and solidarity economy-based cooperative systems. Situating the practices of such systems within a commoning framework places these cooperatives centrally within transformative politics. Worker cooperatives and solidarity economy-based cooperative systems and their deep democracy commoning practices are one instantiation of a richer palette of ethical commons relations, provisioning to meet needs and modes of democratic governance. They highlight what is possible in the present to build the next world now.

CAPITALISM, THE PLANETARY AND THE END OF LIFE

Capitalism organises, exploits and destroys natural and social relations. It is a system of systems – extractive, production, exchange, financial, infrastructural and logistical – with a metabolic process that constantly uses resources and energy (Biel 2013). It is dependent on earth relations and bounded by its commons systems (land, water, biodiversity, creative labour, renewable energy, public infrastructure and goods, cultural heritage, knowledge and earth systems). Yet it seeks to commodify all natural and social relations and assumes the earth does not have any limits. Today the commons systems that capitalism cannibalise are registered in the systemic, neoliberal class project, imperial and earth dynamics of crisis. One way to characterise this historically specific form of general crisis that is engulfing our lifeworlds is as the 'last great dispossession of the commons' (Satgar 2022a, 182). It is expressed through the search for complex hydrocarbons (after the oil peak of the mid-2000s); rupturing the earth climate system with more oil, coal and gas use; destroying biodiversity in terrestrial and ocean ecosystems at an unprecedented rate; doubling urban land surface areas; surrendering a third of land surface area and 75 per cent of fresh water resources to industrial agriculture; contributing to a tenfold increase in plastic pollution on a planetary scale; privatising state commons infrastructure; increasing precarity of labour; and extinguishing cultural heritage commons systems as part of Americancentricism, among other dramatic signals of crisis.[1] In other words, capitalism's squeeze on the background conditions of capitalist accumulation that are causing a general crisis (reproduction, nature, public power and imperial expansion) is also destroying the commons.

Capitalism's ubiquity and power over lifeworlds is the result of conquest. Over the past four decades, it has been pushed into overdrive through unleashing ambitious and grand-scale restructuring through market reason of earth relations and social life. As a result, capitalism is a planetary system with planetary consequences; it is a planetary civilisation. Nevertheless, it has not been able to subsume everything in its uneven geographies of accumulation and neither has it annihilated cultural difference or the last vestiges of life-enabling commons systems, but it certainly has a conditioning and determining presence on a planetary scale. This is very different from previous modes of production that organised natural relations and established social structures to manage commons systems within earth limits. Chakrabarty (2021) argues that our conceptual categories are not adequate to capture this planetary turn and hence argues for a greater distinction between the global and the planetary in order to better understand the current crisis. Put differently, 'the global is a humanocentric construction; the planet decenters the human' (Chakrabarty 2021, 19). However, the Cascade Institute, a leading thinktank on the polycrisis based in Canada, continues to use the global as its framing when talking about contemporary crisis, neglecting to appreciate capitalism and the planetary.[2] By working with human-centred notions of the global, it misses crucial interconnections of the contemporary crisis. The human-centred approach leads them to see the great harms to humans but miss the interconnected planetary harms: 'a global polycrisis [is] the causal entanglement of crises in multiple global systems in ways that significantly degrade humanity's prospects. The causal interactions between constituent crises are significant enough to produce emergent harms that are different from, and usually greater than, the sum of the harms they would produce separately' (Lawrence et al. 2024, 4).

World systems scholars take the analysis of the relationality of socio-ecological systems further than Chakrabarty and the Cascade Institute by integrating earth science perspectives with world systems perspectives (Hornborg and Crumley 2006). More recently, Albert (2024) looked specifically at the relationship between earth science, world systems and contemporary capitalism, which he calls the 'planetary problematic'. The planetary problematic, for Albert (2024, 94),

> allows us to develop a 'vector map' that illuminates the crises, stressors, and feedbacks working to destabilize current structures. The planetary problematic is the nexus of intersecting problems that impels and constrains the self-organization of the world-earth system, creating a possibility space composed of not-yet-actual trajectories, attractors, and bifurcations between them. It represents the totality of relations and feedbacks between ecological, energy, food, political-economic, technological, and existential parameters – a much broader version of the Club of Rome's World Problematique.

Albert's conceptualisation overcomes some of the weaknesses in Chakrabarty and the Cascade Institute and resonates with the analysis we develop in the book.

One of the crucial master categories attempting to make sense of the planetary presence of capitalism is the notion of the Anthropocene. The concept was developed by natural scientists and brings to the fore the human-earth relationship.[3] Within multilateral climate negotiations, it has become part of official discourse. The Anthropocene suggests all humans are a geological force shaping conditions on planet earth, which began over 250 years ago with the development of coal, oil and gas as the energy basis for the metabolism of carbon capitalism. From the 1950s, there has been a great acceleration with increasing emissions and resource use. Ultimately the *anthropos* – that is, all humans – are responsible for resource depletion and the rupture in the earth system causing the worsening climate and general ecological crisis. Based on the current business-as-usual trajectory of greenhouse gas emissions, humans face an unliveable earth. Existence, liveability and life-making as we know it is poised to end. The Anthropocene tells us that we all brought about our demise.

If human life is on a trajectory to end, the Anthropocene master narrative has serious limits in explaining this grave existential risk. Decolonial scholars provide some important critical engagements to interrogate the claims and ontological assertions of the Anthropocene narrative by highlighting what the Anthropocene narrative occludes, validates and excludes. First, its understanding of history is abstracted from the history of capitalism, and therefore 500 years of capitalist conquest and domination is occluded (Moore 2015a, 2015b); accumulation through ecocide, the mass-scale destruction of human and non-human life, is ignored. We are meant to think of the end of human life decoupled from the dominant social system that constructed capitalist civilisation. Put differently, abstracting the *anthropos* from this historical record of capitalism is not a compelling explanation for our imminent demise.

Second, the master narrative of the Anthropocene validates a problematic binary at the heart of the discourse: humans versus earth. This binary is an extension of the human–nature binary that has been imbricated in the making of colonialism and ecocidal capitalism in which women, nature and the racial other were dominated (Merchant 1983). In some instances, the violence of capitalism was so extensive that it conquered and wiped out entire peoples and lifeforms through genocidal violence, 'witch' hunts and species extermination. There is continuity in US-led western coloniality that expresses a more contemporary version of the human supremacy approach to earth relations. In this regard, ecological modernisation and earth management, integral to this supremacist discourse, are proffered as solutions. A conquered earth should be managed, engineered and brought to heel according to the whims of imperial power, transnational corporations and ruling classes, the real embodiments of Anthropogenic power prevailing over capitalist civilisation.

Third, this master narrative excludes two important issues. First, as Barca (2020) argues, the 'forces of reproduction' do not feature. Ignoring how life is reproduced in capitalist relations tells us that the discourse does not find it important. Negating issues of the relations of race, gender, class and species (non-human life forms), of who dominates life-making and the conditions under which life-making happens, hides from view the actual relations that make life possible. The inequalities, hierarchies and power relations of capitalism are ignored. In other words, planetary care labour is rendered invisible – care for oceans, forests, topsoil, riverine systems, for instance, by indigenous peoples, grassroots women, small-scale fishers, rural communities and small-scale agroecology farmers (Satgar and Ntlokotse 2023). Thus, the abstract *Anthropos* blames all but the powerful. Second, an additional exclusion of the Anthropocene narrative is the failure to see the agentic role of the earth. The earth is not static wallpaper in the background of capitalist civilisation, but an active force that has the power to destroy conditions of liveability. With the deepening rupture in the earth system through more investment, extraction and use of fossil fuels, the earth is responding with climate extremes and unmatched power. An asymmetrical earth–capitalism power dynamic is in the making. Capitalist civilisation will not prevail over the earth. The great harms this is bringing through climate shocks, while tragic, will also unhinge imperial control, ruling-class power structures and create space for new transformative forces of socio-ecological reproduction to sustain, reproduce and enjoy life. The challenge in this regard is to end ecocidal capitalism before it ends life. This requires an appreciation of the nature of contemporary capitalist crisis and the openings it affords transformative forces of socio-ecological reproduction.

Thus, the Anthropocene narrative does not help us understand the actual causes and consequences of humans as a geologic force. It is not all humans and not all human activity that has led to the crises. Rather it is capitalist civilisation that has caused the planetary problematic.

CAPITALIST CRISIS IS PLANETARY POLYCRISIS

The social sciences generally are not equipped to study the crisis dynamics of capitalism. Political science, for instance, offers up explanations of legitimacy crises. Mainstream neo-classical economics understands disequilibrium as an aberration and hence the self-equilibrating market economy is the norm. In other words, crisis is unimportant. The neoliberal version of this kind of economics merely reduces economic crises to market failure and proposes more market solutions as the answer. Even more critical approaches to capitalist crisis tend to provide reductionist explanations. For instance, the crisis that began in 2007 has been reduced to the 'great financial crisis', with an overdetermining role given to financial over-accumulation and the global financial system crashing (Foster and Magdoff 2009). Another approach emphasises that increasing costs to capitalism explains crisis (Patel and Moore 2018). Monocausal and reductionist explanations have become standard approaches to explaining capitalist crisis. This is not to deny the validity and importance of these approaches and the insights they provide, but they are not adequate to understand a planetary capitalist system, operating on a civilisation scale and engendering total crisis. Capitalism is made up of interconnected and fragile systems, spanning globalised circuits and based on extractive relations with ecosystems; capitalism and earth relations are intertwined as emphasised above. This means contemporary crisis involves interconnected socio-ecological systems. A crisis in this system means it has wider systemic scope, reaches beyond economies and has

36

effects and feedbacks on a planetary scale. More sharply, the current general crisis of capitalism is a planetary polycrisis.

The reductionism of these explanations also limits capitalism to the economy. A Marxist feminist approach, by contrast, thinks about the economy beyond the realm of production and extends to social reproduction. For Nancy Fraser (2022), social reproduction provides the background on which production occurs, which enables societal-level social reproduction. The care labour of women and families, public policies to support households, community solidarity networks and supports, for instance, are all implicated in reproduction of the worker and also the reproduction of human life. The articulation between production and reproduction provides a more expansive and holistic understanding of how life is made under capitalism. In short, capitalism is more than the economy and is, rather, the conditions of social reproduction of all life. Reductionism misses this.

Ironically the World Economic Forum (WEF), made up of the world's most powerful transnational corporations, now sees some of the risks of contemporary capitalist crisis. As a 'modern prince' of contemporary global monopoly capitalism and global stakeholder capitalism, the WEF issued a report in 2023, *The Global Risks Report*,[4] in which it asserts: 'The analysis focuses on a potential "polycrisis", relating to shortages in natural resources such as food, water, and metals and minerals, illustrating the associated socio-economic and environmental fall-out through a set of potential futures' (WEF 2023, 4). As a result, the notion of the polycrisis became a global buzzword, editorialised by most business media, policymakers and politicians in lockstep with WEF speak. While this might seem novel and profound, WEF's realisation was rather late. Several thinkers on the left have elaborated a more complex understanding of crisis for over a decade.[5] Since the aftermath of the 2007–2009 financial crash, notions of 'their crises', 'disaster capitalism' and the 'crises of capitalist civilisation' have come to the fore.

Building on work on the crises of capitalist civilisation, we argue that we are living through the polycrisis of socio-ecological reproduction of countries and planetary capitalism. For our analysis, there are four important areas of departure from the WEF understanding of polycrisis. First, the WEF approach is ahistorical in terms of appreciating the history of general crises endogenous to capitalism. The WEF does not recognise that capitalism has previously experienced three great polycrises – late nineteenth century, inter-war years and the 1970s – and from which capitalism has not learnt lessons about how it destroys lifeworlds. Today capitalism is experiencing its fourth great crisis in the context of the deep expansion of globalising monopoly capitalism, which began in the 1980s with the rise of Reagan and Thatcher and the mainstreaming of neoliberal dogma, imposing the primacy of market and transnational corporate power over states, peoples and nature. Since the financialised over-accumulation moment of 2007–2009 (with its limited attempts to tame global finance and its debt squeeze on states, households and corporations), most economies have not recovered and several systemic crisis tendencies have converged: resource peak (including oil peak in the mid-2000s), climate overshoot of 1°C in 2015, several shocks on globalised food systems, biological disasters and the morphing of fragile market democracies into authoritarian and, in some instances, neofascist orders. Put differently, the polycrisis of contemporary capitalism is not prospective, something to be forecast to happen over the next ten years, as the WEF suggests, but arrived in the mid-2000s and is intensifying.

Second, there is a static holism implicit in the WEF understanding of polycrisis. It understands the crisis dynamics it identifies as deviating from a pre-pandemic global economic trajectory that was on course to solve many short- and long-term risks. In other words, globalising capitalism was normatively the best trajectory and these new risks are a disruption. This way of thinking capitalism's crises is informed by an idealism about the past few decades of deep globalisation and restructuring. It also betrays a lack of understanding of the contradictions, contingencies, structures and processes of deep globalisation that brought planetary capitalism into this polycrisis; the systemic crisis tendencies and dynamics it unleashed. More precisely, if more neoliberal globalisation were to prevail, even its stakeholder version advocated by the WEF, systemic polycrisis would not only continue, but would amplify.

Third, and flowing from the previous point about the failure of the WEF approach to recognising the polycrisis as systemic crises of global capitalism, is the wider ramifications. Not only does the WEF approach fail to recognise the crises of capitalism as systemic crises imbricated in the expansionary logic of globalising capitalism, it also fails in terms of levels of analysis more generally to situate these crisis dynamics – that is, from the systemic to the conjunctural to the everyday. The historical specificity of this general and polycrisis registers also at the level of the neoliberal class project. Such a class project has advanced deep globalisation, financialised accumulation, the remaking of states subordinate to the market–state dyad and has securitised market democracies to protect the risk to transnationalising capital (Klein 2007). Four decades of such a class project have entailed policy agendas of liberalisation, privatisation and deregulation. Every short-term cyclical crisis has brought the same neoliberal dogma imposed as the solution. However, the fourth great crisis of capitalism and its polycrises has disrupted the neoliberal hegemonic mode of rule and has shown up its irrationality and limits. Neoliberal reason and its obsession with marketising our lifeworlds reflects an epistemological crisis as well. Put more sharply, neoliberal dogma led to the polycrisis and this class project is *the* problem. The WEF has not reached this conclusion. While the WEF talks about the cost-of-living crisis, polarisation and forced migration in its analysis of polycrisis, it does not fully appreciate the everyday squeeze and suffering in societies. Beyond quantitative trends, the lived experience of hunger, precarity and exclusion by millions is not within the analytical remit of the WEF; there is a limited appreciation of how the polycrisis is part of everyday life.

Fourth, the WEF analysis occludes the hegemonic role of US-led western imperial power and the asymmetric coloniality of its relations with the peripheries. The planetary polycrisis is also about how the peripheries have been disciplined and controlled. Despite the crisis of US hegemony, imperial control is still very much about unequal ecological exchange and extracting the commons of the global south. The WEF's analysis of polycrisis does not dare venture into this necessary background condition of capitalist accumulation. According to Hickel et al. (2022, 1), 'unequal exchange theory posits that economic growth in the "advanced economies" of the global north relies on a large net appropriation of resources and labour from the global south, extracted through price differentials in international trade'. This asymmetrical relationship is expressed in various empirically verifiable trade indices. Dorniger's (2024, 91–104) recent study finds the following dynamics of drain in terms of raw materials (measured in tonnes), labour (person year requirements), energy supply (joule) and land use (hectares):

- From 1990 to 2020, his results show a constant net flow of resources from the global south to the north. For raw material equivalents the global south provided about seven gigatons (exports minus imports per year), in terms of primary energy it was 107 kilojoules and labour 240-million-person year equivalents over the same period. For embodied land for final northern consumption, this amounts to about 430 million hectares. From 2011 to 2020, it dropped to 160 million hectares per year. These indicators make patently clear that there is a net flow of natural resources from the global south to the north. Unequal ecological exchange is inherent to this relationship.

- From 1990 to 2020 using the TiVA (Trade in Value Added) indicator in constant 2015 US dollars, he further reconfirms unequal ecological exchange and the pattern of drainage. The monetary drain from the south in terms of northern prices increased from around US$6 trillion in 1990 to more than US$17 trillion in 2008, after which it decreased again to more than US$8 trillion in 2020. The windfall scored by northern economies during this period and in aggregate adds up to US$343 trillion.

Clearly, the WEF's understanding of polycrisis is a descriptive term that captures multiple prospective risks that worsen challenges across different social and economic spheres. However, it fails to provide an analytical perspective and tool given its ahistorical understanding of capitalism. For our purposes, polycrisis is a powerful explanatory concept because we anchor it at the planetary level. We appreciate the agentic power of the earth, understand capitalism and its civilisation are the problem and recognise the fact that the global south continues to bleed resources to the global north due to imperial power relations.

FROM SOCIAL REPRODUCTION TO THE PLANETARY POLYCRISIS OF SOCIO-ECOLOGICAL REPRODUCTION

Social reproduction refers to the biological reproduction of our species and working class. This involves making babies, childrearing, nurturing and care, cooking, cleaning, learning support, sports and everything that makes humans grow and thrive. In short, care labour shapes our life world. Social reproduction happens not only within the household, but also at the level of society by creating gender orders, production and society. It also happens at the level of the production/social reproduction relationship in which social reproduction provides the care work within households and communities. Marxist social reproduction theory is making a return as part of a fourth wave of global feminism (Satgar and Ntlokotse 2023). This fourth wave is breaking with liberal feminism and neoliberal feminism, arguing that liberal/neoliberal feminism is imbricated in the hierarchies of power and oppression created by globalising capitalism. Merely having more women in boardrooms is happening at the expense of subaltern women – precarious working class, peasants and indigenous women – who bear the brunt of inequality-based exclusion. Moreover, liberal/neoliberal feminism has been implicated in the making of a crisis-ridden marketising neoliberal capitalism, including its polycrisis. In this context, social reproduction analysis offers a crucial way to understand the contemporary crisis but also provides a way forward for struggles.

Nancy Fraser's (2017) innovative theoretical work on social reproduction theory is important for our approach, but with a few divergences. Fraser's starting pointing recognises that unwaged care labour is both material and affective and without it society cannot be reproduced: there can be no culture, economy or political organisation without care labour. Thus, the crisis of care is part of a larger crisis of social reproduction of society and the general crisis of capitalism. While it is directly imbricated in the general crisis, the crisis of social reproduction has to be grasped together with the other structural contradictions in capitalism: nature, public power and imperial expansion. Fraser brings this analysis together in a compelling framing in *Cannibal Capitalism* (2022). Theoretically, the social reproductive contradiction of financialised capitalism exists because social reproduction is necessary for capitalist accumulation, but endless accumulation threatens to undermine the reproductive processes and capacities that capital and society need. This contradiction sits at the interconnection between production and reproduction; it is not 'intra-production' and neither is it 'intra-domestic'. As the logic of capitalism destabilises social reproduction, it also undermines long-term accumulation. Every capitalist society harbours a deep-seated systemic tendency towards a crisis of social reproduction. The background condition of social reproduction, together with nature, capital-controlled politics and imperial expansion are crucial for capitalism to exist. This also means capitalism cannot be understood in a narrow economistic way but has to be understood in a broader sense as it relates also to its 'non-economic' background conditions, a point made above in relation to reductionist approaches to capitalist crisis.

Fraser provides a concrete and rich historicisation of waged labour (production) and unwaged care labour (reproduction, in its expanded sense and not exclusively in the family) regimes spanning nineteenth-century liberal competitive capitalism, post-World War II state-managed capitalism and, more recently, financialised capitalism. She explores the social reproduction contradiction (both in the centres and in the peripheries), its crisis tendencies and ruling-class responses to the making of the gender order. In this historical tracing, Fraser pinpoints how the realm of social reproduction was constituted and gender relations institutionalised: factory legislation and a bourgeois imaginary of domesticity shaped the liberal production-reproduction regime; public investments in social goods, mass consumption and a compromise between marketisation and social protection shaped the gender order of state-managed capitalism; and low wage employment, corporate and state divestment from social welfare and privatised reproductive care (buttressing the mobility of professional middle-class women), and debt marked the financialised capitalist gender order. It is in this context that there has been an upsurge of boundary struggles, intertwined with class struggles, but related to production/social reproduction. Moreover, she argues, a triad of forces – marketisation, social protection and emancipation – are contending in these boundary struggles. Ultimately, she hopes social protection and emancipation triumph and determine how the boundaries between production/reproduction and capitalism/society are set.

Building on Fraser's approach to social reproduction, there are four points of divergence in our conception of socio-ecological reproduction. First, Fraser's approach is based on an analytical separation of nature from societal contradictions of capitalism. While useful analytically as it spotlights how capitalism relates to nature, it elides the relationality of the human-nature relationship. For our purposes, integrating human-nature relations, socio-ecological reproduction, is central to understanding transformative alternatives. Interestingly, Marx saw humans and nature as interconnected in his conception of the human as socio-ecological beings (Satgar 2023). This derives from the ecological premises underpinning Marx's thought: (i) humans are dependent on nature and this is a starting point for historical materialist analysis; (ii) human beings are part of nature; (iii) nature is a source of wealth together with labour; and (iv) human impacts on and the limits of nature are of concern.[6]

Second, the social metabolism of capitalism requires the exploitation of women and care labour in the realm of social reproduction but simultaneously implicates natural relations at two levels. At the level of production, capitalism requires energy and resources for its social metabolic processes (Pinealt 2023). This means extraction

and exploitation of natural relations is integral and simultane-
ous to the exploitation of labour. Conversely, as the realm of social
reproduction is exploited, it also impacts the natural basis of social
reproduction: water, food and human capacity to work, for instance.
In other words, natural relations are also exploited as part of the
structural oppression of women and the exploitation of labour.

Third, social reproduction regimes are not separate from other
forms of exploitation, oppression and appropriation. Therefore,
they need to incorporate the exploitation of labour, the oppression
of women, the exploitation of natural relations and eco-imperialism.
Thus, in this framing, Fraser's background conditions are twofold:
social (reproduction, public power and imperialism) and ecological
(nature). This maps onto the social commons and the natural
commons as integral to the background conditions of capitalism. As
highlighted above, the separation between social and ecological is
an artificial separation because humans are socio-ecological beings
and the social metabolism of capitalism exploits simultaneously
nature and labour in the realm of production and nature, and care
in the realm of social reproduction. Thus, the concept of socio-
ecological reproduction captures this interrelated web of life at
both the social and ecological levels. This means regimes of socio-
ecological reproduction are more appropriate to locate the polycrisis
– which is a polycrisis of socio-ecological reproduction – and to
understand interconnections of these crises tendencies. Capitalism's
annihilations of its background conditions is also an annihilation
of the natural and social commons. The planetary polycrisis of
capitalism is a crisis of the commons, its last great dispossession.
At the same time, the agentic dimension of such regimes implicate
class, gender, race and ecological relations. Through this framework
we focus on the emancipatory forces reshaping regimes of
socio-ecological reproduction, that is, forces of transformative
socio-ecological reproduction seeking to create emancipatory
lifeworlds. Like Barca (2020), we believe this emphasis breaks with
productivist modes of thinking that emphasise the primacy of 'forces
of production' as the driver of social change, but it also goes further
to show how transformative forces of socio-ecological reproduction

are engaged in political projects at different scales grounded in the commons.

Fourth, Fraser frames resistance around boundary struggles with marketisation in contradiction with social protection and emancipation, but does not explicate emancipatory forces nor the necessary politics to achieve emancipation. We elaborate on emancipatory politics as transformative politics and demonstrate how such a transformative praxis defines a new contemporary left politics centred on transformative forces of socio-ecological reproduction. The latter does not privilege the working class as the historical agent of change but recognises that the working class, together with other groups imbricated in the planetary polycrisis of socio-ecological reproduction, shapes and determines the remit of boundary struggles.

Our empirical chapters highlight the commoning practices of worker cooperatives and solidarity economy-based cooperative systems and provide concrete insights into how boundary struggles are being waged to overcome capital's attempts to destroy the background conditions. Our empirical cases demonstrate that there are other ways to organise socio-ecological reproduction that do not lead to the destruction of lifeworlds. They are not perfect nor do they have every aspect of emancipation figured out, but certainly they show how institutionalised commoning of creative human capacities can reproduce human and all life with greater care.

THE LAST GREAT DISPOSSESSION OF THE COMMONS AND HISTORICAL TRANSFORMATIVE FORCES OF SOCIO-ECOLOGICAL REPRODUCTION

At stake today is how we overcome the last great dispossession of the natural and social commons so that commoning returns to its rightful place in sustaining life (Brand et al. 2021; Rockström et al. 2009). The concept of the commons refers to three distinct and interrelated things: (i) a natural and social commonwealth of life-enabling socio-ecological systems (that is, water, land, biodiversity, creative human labour, renewable energy, cultural heritage, public infrastructure, public goods, knowledge and the earth system);

(ii) governed together ethically and democratically by a community of commoners; and (iii) ensuring that the common good and the web of life are reproduced and that such systems thrive. Thus, the commons as a mode of production seeks the general good through organising human labour, natural relations and socio-ecological reproduction.

Commons has always been part of human history. Prior to capitalism the commons enabled the reproduction of life in early commons societies, in slave societies, in feudalism and it continues to provide the ecological and material substratum for the reproduction of capitalism. Marx (1976) described the enclosure of the commons both in the heartlands and peripheries of capitalism when attempting to understand how primitive accumulation provided the enabling conditions for the development of capitalism. While he observed enclosures in the heartlands in which peasantries were separated from the means of production and thus compelled to sell their labour power and become wage earners, he also recognised how colonialism unleashed brute force in the colonial peripheries through slavery, racism and the appropriation of land. The process of primitive accumulation produced racialised colonial subjectivities, wage labour and private property regimes. Karl Polanyi (2001) also observed the creation of enclosures in the heartlands transmogrified land, and labour into fictitious commodities. Rosa Luxemburg (2003) observed how colonial and imperial expansion into the peripheries is premised on the destruction of the 'natural economy'. These insights confirm a pattern of dispossession of the commons. At the same time, there have also been important forms of resistance through historical transformative forces of socio-ecological reproduction to defend the commons from proto capitalism to the present. These have been life preserving and reproducing struggles.

The commons provided the basis for the commons' mode of production for about 200,000 years. In slave societies, such as the Roman Empire, *res communis* was recognised as a special category of natural relations. Transformative forces of socio-ecological reproduction have risen to defend the commons through feudal society's

Charter of the Forest, run-away slave communities in the Americas, cooperatives (consumer and worker) in the nineteenth century, maintaining indigenous land sovereignty and even in capitalism and colonialism despite the enclosures.[7] These struggles have been waged by indigenous peoples, slaves, working classes, grassroots women, small-scale fishers, environmentalists, climate justice activists and many more. Many of these histories of resistance have been erased, occluded or denied. Capitalism's counter-response has tried to delegitimise such struggles by framing them as 'primitive' and halting the march of progress. However, these struggles continue to echo into the present and provide a basis for contemporary forces that are resisting the last great dispossession of the commons. To understand the importance of commons systems as a transformative alternative we have to turn to its ontological importance and its actual pattern of existence. It is this theoretical and ideological shift that situates the primacy of transformative forces of socio-ecological reproduction in this book.

A TRANSFORMATIVE ALTERNATIVE:
THE LIFE-CENTRIC ONTOLOGY OF THE COMMONS

Despite the dispossession of the commons underway, it has not disappeared. Marketisation and commodification of our lifeworlds have not been able to wipe out the commons. While neoliberal reason and its economists privilege the market-state dyad, their dogmatic ontology occludes the commons. Yet, across the planet people rely on forests, oceans, rivers, ecosystems, public infrastructure, seed sharing, land sharing, knowledge systems, cyber platforms, cooperation, cultural practices, cooperatives and solidarity practices to meet needs. Underpinning the reality of the commons is a fundamentally different ontology, that is, another way of being and conceiving reality. In metaphysical thinking in philosophy, ontology can be highly technical and abstract. Simply, ontology is like a binocular, a tool to figure out a pathway, scan a horizon or provide a clear picture of reality. Adjustments to the binoculars that give sharpness, depth and magnification are the tools of ontology; in other words, the presuppositions, assumptions and beliefs that we hold about reality. Ontology also reveals relations between and among objects. What follows is an attempt to highlight key ontological aspects of a relational and life-centric commons that anchors the transformative praxis of forces of socio-ecological reproduction.

Contrary to the coloniality of neoliberal reason and its Euro-American supremacist conception of our lifeworld, the ontology of the commons is life-centric in the sense of being consistent with evolution and accession of life. The natural commons (land, water, biodiversity, renewable energy, creative labour and the earth system) and social commons (public goods and infrastructure, cultural practices and heritage, and knowledge) are deeply imbricated in socio-ecological relations. It is profoundly relational, which breaks with duality and binary-centred thinking of western thought, such as state/market, public/private, nature/society and so on. Furthermore, it places humans as social relational beings deeply embedded within the web of life as opposed to the western thinking that reifies humans' 'true nature' as atomised, competitive, economically rational and as possessive individuals. The western version of the human does not exist in the real world, despite enormous efforts to socially construct it (for example, through education, reward systems, economic incentives and classification struggles). Critical economic thought confirms that it is a fallacy as do decolonial conceptions of the self that are grounded in extant cultures of the colonised.[8] In short, we are socio-ecological beings who are part of a rich, complex and fragile web of life; we live in and are part of systems. This is one of the fundamental insights of the life-centric ontology of the commons.

History matters as process and is constitutive of commons relations. As mentioned earlier, the commons existed for about 200,000 years: from hunter–gatherers to agrarian communities, slave societies and feudalism. Over history, some became class societies while others did not. These different modes of socio-ecological reproduction based on the commons saw varying relations between the commons and human society. For example, alongside nomadic hunter–gatherers, settled agricultural societies and their surpluses provided social arrangements for organising commons/human society relations. The political hierarchies, divisions of labour and spatial interconnections that provided order also ensured that the commons were organised as a basis for provisioning. In this regard, use rights, communal sharing arrangements, cultural ceremonies, gifting, bartering and trading, for instance, all played a part in organising relationships based on the commons. The spread of capitalism, including the colonial encounter that unleashed an ecocidal logic, imposed a dualism of human society versus nature with devastating consequences. Neoliberal reason continues this dualism and gives licence to pursuing the last great dispossession of the commons. By contrast, the commons challenges the universal claims of neoliberal reason and does not see life-making reduced to one civilisational standard and linear history. Rather the commons affirms diversity, cultural richness and poly epistemologies of life-making.

To be clear, the commons is neither a blueprint nor does it spontaneously appear in society. People choose to enact the commons based on commoning practices, which requires thinking and acting like commoners. The commons ontology is about commoning praxis to reproduce the web of life, grounded in an ethics of care and democratic arrangements. The labour at the heart of the commons is ethical care labour. In this regard, there are variegated local commons based on particular histories, ecosystem dynamics, culture, geography and political traditions. Varied local conditions give the commons diverse peer governance arrangements, provisioning practices and, ultimately, its constitutive character. For instance, seed saving or forest sharing arrangements will differ based on ecosystem endowments, local knowledge, cultural practices and seasonal patterns. Moreover, worker cooperatives will common time, creative labour, finance, collective capacity (knowledge, power and culture) and natural relations through its own conscious choices and internal mechanisms. It is this rich variation rooted in lived experiences of place that brings a universal aspect to life-making and situates the commons centrally within planetary transformative forces of socio-ecological reproduction.

MARKET	COMMONS
STATE	SOCIETY

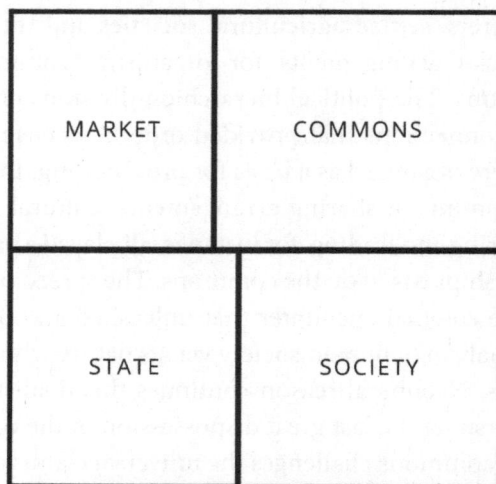

Figure 1.1   Commons-centred quadratic
relations.

Finally, the commons is not a residual third sector of resources: state/market/commons. Bauwens (cited in Bollier 2014, 145) conceptualises the commons based on this triadic perspective, but fails to see that it neglects a place for societal relations or society. Given the historical processes and relational dynamics of the commons, we prefer a quadratic understanding of the commons: state/market/society/commons. While we place it alongside the other three dimensions, in reality, the commons systems are central and foundational to our lifeworld. In counterfactual terms, if you take away biodiversity, kill all life in the oceans, deplete water systems and destroy the vitality of soils, current forms of human and non-human life are impossible. In other words, the commons have a primacy and foundational importance for the state, market and society. Unlike much of the literature on the commons (for example, Bollier 2014; De Angelis 2019), our framework does not see the commons simply as a resource to be used. Indeed, a resource-centred approach treats the commons with instrumental reason that further entrenches an Anthropocentric and supremacist approach to the commons as an object of exploitative extraction. In addition, it occludes the systems nature of the commons reducing it to discrete resources. For instance, a river is not simply one body of flowing water but is part of the water cycle and ecosystem of a region and the planet. Commoning to share in the river is also about its broader relationality to ensure governance of the water cycle and ecosystem. Such complex systems add up to institutional dynamics that could find permutations within the state/market/society/commons framework. But the transformative challenge is recognising that the state/market/society spheres have contradictory relations with the commons. Hence, part of transformative politics of socio-ecological reproduction requires bringing the commons and a commoning logic into these other institutional spaces. Markets can be socialised, states can be locked into public commons partnerships and societies can practise commoning as the basis to meet everyday needs. Many commoners seek to do this through expanding regimes of socio-ecological reproduction from below. In the transition to commoning at different scales, including the planetary, we have to keep our sights homed on the quadratic view and how the commons and its deep democracy commoning practices can be given their rightful place as the dominant logic of ordering planetary life. Doing so provides a different strategic locus for transformative forces of socio-ecological reproduction. We elaborate on this in the next chapter on transformative politics and planetary care and in the empirical chapters focusing on transformative worker cooperatives and solidarity economy-based cooperative systems, as part of the commons and commoning.

THE COMMONS PATTERN IN THE CONTEMPORARY WORLD AND TRANSFORMATIVE FORCES OF SOCIO-ECOLOGICAL REPRODUCTION

In the development literature the term 'best practice' is often used to describe specific examples or case studies considered to be important for social change. As a concept, best practice suggests a formula or recipe for change. Such practices can be transposed into any context and replicated. Contemporary capitalism with its emphasis on neoliberal standards as the basis for a globalised economy also works with best practice approaches to diffusion. However, despite the overbearing reach of global capitalism, Euro-American domination, and its dominant logic, will never be complete; it engenders contestation, spreads through uneven geographies of accumulation on a global scale and excludes several domains of socio-ecological life from its accumulation circuits. In other words, it is not monolithic or omnipresent, despite its planetary presence.

Despite the planetary crisis of socio-ecological reproduction caused by capitalism, transformative forces of socio-ecological reproduction continue to nurture, augment and accentuate the commons pattern from below. Such a commons pattern cannot be encapsulated within best practice thinking, neither can it be modelled into cause and effect frameworks, such as Elinor Ostrom's (2015 [1990]) approach of Institutional Analysis and Development (IAD) and its rigid model thinking. Helfrich (2015, 29) clarifies this as follows: 'the dynamics of a commons cannot be captured by an input/output calculus; there is more going on than causality'. Hence commons thinkers such as Helfrich and others in the Commons Strategy Group prefer to draw on pattern theory to capture the subjective dynamics of commoning practices and processes. For Helfrich (2015, 30):

Patterns have the potential to capture the principles and inner dynamics of self-organisation, helping to make them more easily reproducible and able to bring about a more profound social-ecological transformation. Patterns theory does not insist upon strict causal relationships; instead, it helps identify the subjective, contingent complexities of any commons. Here, patterns can be seen as structures within which things crystallize so that commoning can develop in as many different spheres and on as many levels as possible.

From this perspective various studies of the commons pattern affirm its vibrancy and growth in relation to worker cooperatives, solidarity economy-based cooperative systems, food sovereignty, enduring ancient commons (particularly in relation to forests and irrigation systems), neighbourhood commons (such as water, farmland and renewable energy systems), biocultural commons (local specific food crops and permaculture, for instance), arts and culture (such as museums, libraries, archives, food festivals celebrating food as culture and more), collaborative technology commons (for example, open design, open hardware, commons for research and design, knowledge sharing), exchange and credit commons (for example, credit unions, cooperative banks, local currencies), support tools for commoning (such as crowd funding, disaster support, mapping shared wealth, licenses for commoning), spaces for co-learning (for example, open technology labs, media labs, media cooperatives) and omni-commons (involving multiple commoning institutional forms and practices on a societal scale).

There is no exhaustive inventory of the commons. The commons emerges as and when it is needed (Bollier 2014, 11). It has both very particularistic aspects and more general characteristics as part of the commons pattern. Its socio-ecological relationships, peer governance practices and provisioning approaches to meet need are extremely diverse and variegated. In Chapters 4–6, we explore some of these commons practices in relation to worker cooperatives and solidarity economy-based cooperative systems. They offer very specific and concrete examples of the transformative forces of socio-ecological reproduction that bring such commoning practices into existence to ensure that human and natural relations thrive.

CONCLUSION

The planetary polycrisis of socio-ecological reproduction arrived in the mid-2000s and continues to intensify. Capitalism's onward march continues to raise the stakes with planetary consequences for all forms of life. To confront this we need a unitary understanding of the total crisis that highlights its destructive regime of socio-ecological reproduction and how it is engendering crisis tendencies in its background conditions, including the natural and social commons. This fourth great crisis of capitalism is not prospective, as the WEF would like to believe, but is underway. With earth and capitalist relations intertwined, the last great dispossession of the commons expresses itself within the everyday, systemic, neoliberal class project, imperial and earth system levels. We are living a planetary polycrisis. Such crisis tendencies threaten to wipe out human life and certainly most of non-human life. Ruling classes are incapable of resolving this planetary polycrisis and, instead, are shifting allegiances to authoritarianism, including neo-fascism. Try as they may, ruling classes are not capable of handling the earth's response to the capitalist harms inflicted. Rather, securing life and making a new world requires counterhegemonic resistance from transformative forces of socio-ecological reproduction that centres defending, renewing and advancing the commons. Placing the commons at the centre of our lives means embracing its life-centric relationality, its historicity, ethical care labour and its primacy in our lifeworld. These horizons of hope and transformative resistance, of the commons pattern, are explored in the rest of the book.

2
The Rise of Transformative Politics and Planetary Care from Below

Despite declarations about the 'end of history' and 'capitalist realism', market-centric utopia has not eclipsed left politics. Old left projects that shaped the twentieth century have been defeated, but a new transformative left has been rising through three cycles of global resistance, with a fourth underway, coming out of the Covid-19 pandemic. These cycles of resistance have been responding to the planetary polycrisis of socio-ecological reproduction. In this ferment and renewal of the left imagination, a conscious self-reflexivity has come to the fore with a trenchant critique of the twentieth-century left. While the collapse of the Soviet Union unleashed a plethora of critique and renewal, the cycles of resistance have gone further to question the state-centric imaginary of the twentieth-century left, its de-democratising rationality, its anti-ecological (productivist) mould and its limited regard for care labour. This chapter commences with a brief overview of the problems that emerged in the dominant left imaginary in the twentieth century and what the new global left committed to transformative politics is leaving behind. At the same time, the new global left is centring the transformative forces of socio-ecological reproduction and the life-centric ontology of the commons – ultimately, planetary care from below.

In this chapter, we situate the horizons of transformative politics within the global cycles of counterhegemonic resistance. In these struggles, emancipatory, tacit and experiential knowledge grounds transformative praxis and is generative in enabling responses to the neoliberal onslaught on life-making and the fourth great crisis of capitalism. Systemic alternatives are central to this new emancipatory utopian imaginary to confront the root causes of the crisis, but not all resistance forces have been moving in a transformative direction. These challenges are highlighted in the chapter; we also further unpack the shift in global left political subjectivity, imaginary and politics. While capitalism destroys our lifeworlds, transformative politics defends, renews and rebuilds our lifeworlds through (i) centring transformative praxis as opposed to reform or revolution; (ii) practising emancipatory utopia as method of world making; (iii) advancing an ethics of care and experimenting with new political instruments; (iv) embracing poly epistemologies of transformative praxis; and (v) experimenting with constitutive forms of political power, which in some cases go further as political projects to advance democratic systemic reforms. In short, this is the politics of planetary care from below that constitutes an engaged transformative politics.

Transformative politics takes left subjectivity and praxis to new political ground and furnishes forces of socio-ecological reproduction with a mode of politics to situate the life-centric ontology of the commons and planetary care. The chapter concludes by exploring how transformative politics advances systems change through deep just transitions to exit the polycrisis, and at different scalar levels, while recognising the interconnection with earth relations. Worker cooperatives, commons and deep democracy are centrally situated in such transitions so that their transformative politics inspires and informs the acceleration of deep just transitions.

THE OLD LEFT AND CRISES OF TWENTIETH-CENTURY STATE-CENTRIC SOCIALISM

Socialism developed out of struggles and was always variegated. In the nineteenth century, workers imagined socialism as an alternative to the exploitation and oppressions of capitalism. Marx took this in his own direction and championed a 'scientific socialism' against other forms of socialism and anarchism. By the twentieth century, the socialist left was defined by three political projects: social democracy, Soviet socialism (and its copies) and revolutionary nationalism (Amin 1994).[1] A strong state centrism was expressed in each of these projects, which meant politics began and ended with the state. In this approach, if state-centred politics failed, everything failed.

The planetary polycrisis we face today cannot be based on state-centred politics. While still recognising that the state has a pivotal and strategic role to play, it requires deep democracy shaping its forms, functions and capacities. State control and state-centred politics unleashed a de-democratising rationality such that mass agency was eviscerated, neutralised or rendered propagandistic. Ruling classes fixated on 'development' and 'catch-up modernisation' and, as a result, reproduced a colonial understanding of progress and social change. The 'forces of production' were unleashed with devastating ecological consequences such that twentieth-century forms of socialism were no different from capitalist rationality. Ultimately, nature and the planet were treated as an object of conquest. Care labour also went through uneven processes of gender transformation. To get a better sense of state-centred politics, we explore these problems further below.

The twentieth century gave rise to three traditions of state-centred politics: social democracy in western Europe, Soviet socialism and revolutionary nationalism in the peripheries. We discuss each in turn. In Europe in the late nineteenth century, the emergence of mass-based worker parties and trade unions spawned social democracy as a form of evolutionary and managed capitalism based on class compromise. The Cold War and geopolitical considerations gave greater impetus to institutionalising worker movement demands and ensuring a relatively stable social contract as a political basis of the welfare state together with mass Fordist production and consumption. Public goods from public transport systems, social housing (including rental controls), public health systems and even free education narrowed inequalities and ensured capital was tamed by an embedded logic based on taxation and redistribution. However, state centrism of a technocratic kind mixed with a market economy also placed limits on democratising logics. The main channel for social discontent became electoral competition. The stabilisation of post-World War II social democracy meant workers traded militancy for state provisioning, but social democracy failed to confront the crises of capitalism in the twentieth century. In fact, the productivist and expansionary logics of capitalism were so deeply embedded that it did everything to ensure the imperial mode of living of its citizens was maintained at the expense of the peripheries (Brand and Wissen 2021). It thus embraced jingoistic and exclusionary nationalism, while its extraction of resources through unequal ecological exchange from the peripheries and its high carbon footprints and resource-intensive ways of living contributed to the logic of accumulation through ecocide on a planetary scale.

The first workers' revolution in 1917 produced the Russian Revolution, which eventually consolidated in the mould of a one-party state, a one-sided worker–peasant alliance, which favoured the workers, central planning and a coercive bureaucracy. Dissent was not tolerated in politics or in the everyday lives of people, and coercion was constantly calibrated to deal with 'internal threats'. Among a plethora of attempts to police the realm of freedom a few stand out, such as the killing of sailors in Kronstadt, Stalin's show trials of the 1930s, liquidation of peasantries, the Gulag and Russian invasions of Poland and Czechoslovakia to crush dissent. All of this revealed the deeply authoritarian nature of internal Soviet life. As in social democracy, important public goods were provided to the population and industrialisation was pursued at immense ecological costs. The Chernobyl nuclear disaster, pollution in freshwater lakes and the end of conservation practices under Stalin fed into the productivist mould of catch-up socialist modernisation. The Cold War skewed the Soviet economy as it pursued geostrategic symmetry. The irrationality of this brought the world to the brink of nuclear annihilation. Various revolutionary breakthroughs mimicked the Soviet model, with a few variations. For instance, the Chinese worker–peasant alliance was grounded in an attempt to ensure balanced urban and rural development, and it used a cheap labour accumulation process to find its place in the global division of labour. This not only skewed its internal and poverty wage economy but ensured it was deeply globalised and dependent on western markets. The

Chinese state is buttressed by an extremely powerful and coercive security apparatus. China is one of the leading champions of cheap labour deep globalisation, with deleterious impacts on workers in all parts of the world. Its carbon emissions and pollution challenges make it a major ecological disaster (Li 2016).

Revolutionary nationalism was shaped and formed in the resistance to colonialism, apartheid and imperialism. In the nineteenth century, revolutionary nationalists fought Spanish colonialism in Latin America and in the twentieth century, Asia and Africa became major battle grounds for national independence. Revolutionary nationalism embodied scientific socialism (Vietnam, Mozambique and Angola), anticapitalism (South Africa) and indigenous variants of socialism (Nehruvian socialism and African socialisms). The state-centric imaginary loomed large in all these struggles. Yet the advances and breakthroughs made produced monopolies on state power and thin postcolonial democracies. Party machine politics at the nexus of state power and class formation dominated and still dominates political life (for example, in Vietnam, Mozambique and Angola). Africa moved from colonialism and apartheid to neocolonialism and US neoliberal domination. In this context, a defeated Africa produced a post-Cold War scramble for Africa's energy endowments, mineral resources and land. Transnationalising and criminal ruling classes embraced Afro-neoliberal accumulation and deep globalisation (Southall 2013). South Africa is an excellent example of a deeply globalised economy with a corrupt and criminalised market democracy, underpinned by deep inequality and eroding state capacity. Revolutionary nationalism either in its socialist guise or as defeated variants of neoliberalism worked with a conquest of nature rationality. Extractivist economies through 'green revolution' agricultural practices, resource extraction, widespread pollution and waste dumping are its legacy.

As this brief history shows, the conception of politics within twentieth-century left politics and socialist projects were state-centric, de-democratising and anti-ecological, but these were not their only weaknesses. While three waves of feminism impacted these political projects, reproduction regimes varied and women's emancipation was extremely uneven within and across these three political traditions. Welfare state provisioning provided a socialising aspect to care labour but has been retreating as precaritisation and privatisation encroach on social welfare systems (Bakker and Gill 2003). Women were brought into the labour market and labour process to different degrees in these political projects, rather than socialising and de-gendering care labour. Ultimately, social democracy, Soviet socialism and revolutionary nationalism did not achieve their feminist aspiration. South Africa, for example, has laudable feminist goals in legislation and enshrined in the Constitution, but continues to be in the grip of femicide with endemic violence against women and children.

In addition, these socialist projects lost their way. Social democracy became such an effective and pragmatic manager of capitalism, it turned its back on the working class and was eventually coopted by the neoliberal turn. Soviet socialism was eaten up by its own internal contradictions and Cold War rivalries. Revolutionary nationalism succumbed to debt and surrendered to the global power structure. Central to all these experiences were state centrism, de-democratisation, anti-ecological practices and limited care labour commitments. These were not projects that enabled transformative forces of socio-ecological reproduction to prevail as state-centric rationality overpowered or suppressed these impulses and possible paths. Cooperatives and grassroots village democracy, for instance, were instrumentalised for top-down agrarian collectivisation or pushed into the background of the welfare state bureaucracy (Williams 2014). With state-centric politics, the centrifugal force controlling societies meant that if the state failed or degenerated, then these societies did not advance transformation. The twentieth-century left and its socialist projects provide a rich historical inheritance from which to learn critical lessons for the twenty-first century. This synoptic reflection merely highlights some of the key issues that have informed the making of the twenty-first century global left.

CYCLES OF COUNTERHEGEMONIC TRANSFORMATIVE RESISTANCE AND THE MAKINGS OF AN EMANCIPATORY UTOPIAN IMAGINARY

Most readings of Antonio Gramsci tend to pose the binary of hegemony/counterhegemony in an atemporal way. The struggle happens unchanged over a period of time. However, in actual struggles, hegemony/counterhegemony are never static, there are ebbs and flows, and cyclical dynamics. For instance, forms of counterhegemonic transformative resistance advance, retreat and are even defeated until breakthroughs occur in terms of political projects for societies. In some instances, there is a constant process of self-reflexivity and collective learning to build capacities. Such projects institutionalise constituted forms of class and popular power from below to redesign socio-ecological systems and provide a new basis for socio-ecological reproduction. Prefiguration, policies, laws and the making of systemic alternatives, as part of deep just transitions, are all central to transformative politics. In short, an emancipatory utopian imaginary is constantly seeking a better condition of existence. Its dreams, desires and yearnings are not mere demands but horizons for new regimes of socio-ecological reproduction, a transformed society that cares for social and earth relations. After the end of twentieth-century socialism, struggles and resistance did not end, but continue, with profound implications for left subjectivity and imaginaries (see, for example, Lang, König and Regelmann 2018).

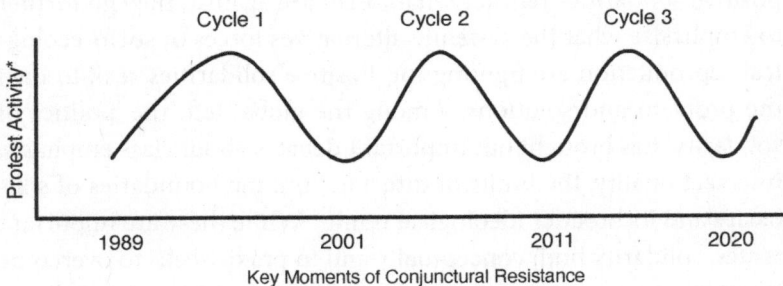

Figure 2.1 Conjunctural cycles of counterhegemonic resistance.

During the conjuncture of neoliberal restructuring (1980 to present) and the fourth great crisis of capitalism, new forms of counterhegemonic transformative resistance came to the fore. Three cycles of resistance mark this conjuncture with a fourth underway, coming out of the Covid-19 pandemic (see Figure 2.1). Given the societal scale of restructuring engendered by neoliberalism, several contradictions feature within financialised social reproduction: commodification, oppression, exploitation, extractivism, global corporate power, the continuity of fossil fuels and the hollowing out of sovereignties. These contradictions go to the heart of the planetary polycrisis of socio-ecological reproduction. Confronting these contradictions means confronting the challenge of planetary care. For instance, stopping the destruction of rainforests, preventing water privatisation, ending pollution in the oceans, blocking more coal, oil and gas extraction or just keeping local libraries open are all struggles to defend the social and natural commons and, ultimately, to ensure planetary care.

In the twentieth century, the material grounding of solidarity was advanced by powerful labour movements in the global north and south. After neoliberalism, labour was significantly weakened and, hence, the current cycles of resistance have been inventive in renewing a new politics of solidarity. In practice, contemporary struggles express both positive and negative solidarities as part of transformative politics. Negative solidarities emphasise what resisting forces are against but can even hand over the struggle to the state or the powerful to solve the problem. Conversely, while positive solidarities register what forces are against, they go further to emphasise what the systemic alternatives forces of socio-ecological reproduction are fighting for. Positive solidarities seek to own the problem and solutions. Among the global left, the 'politics of solidarity' has brought out important debates about class emphasis, intersectionality, the limits of direct action, the boundaries of solidarity and its broader ideological remit.[2] While these are important issues, solidarity both conceptually and in praxis seeks to overcome the atomistic, possessive and greedy subject of neoliberal capitalism. It is a counter to a fragmenting and polarising world. Positive soli-

Table 2.1 Counterhegemonic resistance and alternatives.

Form of resistance	Forces of socio-ecological reproduction	Alternatives
Anti-commodification	Movements, communities, activist groups, policy NGOs, indigenous peoples, cooperative movements and solidarity economy networks	Public goods, defence of the commons and people's land
Anti-oppression	Communities, movements, activist groups, policy NGOs, public intellectuals, trade unions	Anti-discrimination, solidarity, affirming rights, recognising unpaid labour, gender consciousness, economic inclusion, worker cooperatives
Anti-exploitation	Trade unions, worker committees, activist groups, policy NGOs, solidarity economy networks	Descent work, insourcing, worker rights, worker takeover of factories in Argentina, Brazil and Venezuela
Anti-extractivism	Communities, networks, indigenous peoples, movements, activist groups, policy NGOs, cooperatives	No to mining, defend the commons, phase out fossil fuels, 'keep the coal and fossil fuel in the ground', climate justice, divestment, polluter pays, regenerative agriculture, food sovereignty, indigenous restoration
Confronting global power	Movements, networks, activist groups, policy NGOs, public intellectuals	Reform of multilateral institutions, scrap debt of poor countries, address climate debt, development not free trade
Advancing deep just transitions through systemic alternatives	Indigenous peoples, community organisations, networks, movements, trade unions, policy NGOS, parties, cooperatives	Food sovereignty, solidarity economy, worker cooperatives, climate jobs, universal basic income, socially owned renewable energy, clean energy public transport systems, rights of nature
Counterhegemonic deglobalisation/delinking	Governments, parties, alliances, movements, policy NGOs, communities, public intellectuals	Reclaim sovereignty, alternative accumulation models, new regional blocs, new socio-ecological regimes of reproduction and deep democracy

darity has also been about giving substance to the claims of 'another world is possible' and 'systems change not climate change'; in other words, there are alternatives and answers to the contradictions of financialised social reproduction and the planetary polycrisis that we can fight for, build and advance from below. Table 2.1 provides an overview of the forms of resistance, forces of socio-ecological reproduction and alternatives that have been championed.

In the ferment of four cycles of counterhegemonic transformative resistance, several experiments emerged as the agential basis to elaborate transformative politics. We discuss each cycle in detail.

Cycle 1: 1989–2001

The first cycle of resistance began with the 'Caracazo' in Venezuela in 1989, which opposed the imposition of an International Monetary Fund (IMF)-led structural adjustment programme, particularly the imposed increases in the price of gasoline and transport (Robertson 2014). Hundreds were killed in the week of mass protests, and it was in this context that Hugo Chavez emerged as a coup leader. A few years later, the rise of the Zapatistas in Mexico in 1994 fighting against the North American Free Trade Agreement, and their declaration of war against the Mexican state, heralded the emergence of a movement that was willing to consider armed struggle defensively to protect land and cultural heritage, and to ensure indigenous control of local resources (Collier and Quaratiello 2005). The Zapatistas went on to also use civil resistance tactics creatively to defend the commons. In 1996, in Kerala, India, the left party in power decentralised 40 per cent of the provincial state budget as part of the People's Campaign for Democratic Decentralisation and laid the basis for a participatory form of local governance (Parayil 2000). In the same year, indigenous movements in Ecuador openly challenged and created a crisis for the neoliberal state. In South Africa in 1998, the Treatment Action Campaign succeeded in securing HIV treatment to prevent mother-to-child transmission and secured a legal victory to compel the South African state to decommodify HIV-AIDS drugs and produce generics. This was a challenge to global pharmaceutical corporations and defending a politics of care. The rise of transnational activism made its mark in 1999, when Seattle became the theatre of mass street protests against the newly formed World Trade Organization (WTO) and its liberalising approach to global trade (Mertes 2004). In the same year, 'water wars' began in Bolivia against a transnational and privatised control, which had dramatic consequences for the realignment of forces in Bolivia, particularly the indigenous movement. In 2001, Argentina's economy collapsed after two decades of intense neoliberalisation, mass street politics brought down several governments while workers took over stressed or abandoned factories, neighbourhood assemblies emerged and new movements of the unemployed shaped pathways for systemic alternatives (Starr 2005). The resistance in Cycle 1 is primarily characterised by defensive national struggles from below against neoliberal states and transnational corporations. In the next cycle, we see the rise of left leaders in government and attempts to bring the disparate struggles into global forums of solidarity, sharing ideas and movement building.

Cycle 2: 2001–2011

The formation of the World Social Forum in 2001 gave a major boost to transnational activism (Fisher and Ponniah 2003). It provided a space for solidarity of national and transnational social movements and advanced an emancipatory utopian imagination that strengthened various systemic alternatives to neoliberal globalisation and affirmed an alter globalisation practice in various national contexts. At the same time, various left and centre-left governments were elected into power in different countries in Latin America (Brazil, Venezuela, Bolivia and Uruguay, for instance), which inaugurated what has been termed the 'pink tide' (Sader 2011). These governments were not united in their approach to resisting neoliberalism but certainly wanted to affirm national and regional development priorities. For Venezuela's government, being in state power was about a break with neoliberalism and the advance of a twenty-first century socialism. Several worker cooperatives and commune prefigurative experiments emerged in the 'Bolivarian process' in Venezuela. For Brazil's Workers' Party (Partido dos Trabalhadores,

PT), being in power was about a 'neo-developmentalism' that included more redistributive reforms, active industrial policy and limited land reform while maintaining a globalised posture. Having the PT in power opened space for movements and, in 2003, based on the momentum developed by the solidarity economy network in Brazil, the Brazilian Forum for Solidarity Economy was established (discussed in Chapter 6). Together with the Secretariat for the Solidarity Economy in government, Brazil began trailblazing a new way forward for self-managed and democratic enterprises to achieve a structural space of their own in the Brazilian economy (cooperatives and worker cooperatives were central to this).

Another crucial systemic alternative championed by La Via Campesina gained further momentum with the adoption of the Nyeleni Declaration of 2007 by 500 delegates from 80 countries who committed to advancing food sovereignty. The Nyeleni Declaration represents an alternative to food security and corporate control of food systems. In 2009, protests against the financial crisis in Iceland intensified, also referred to as the 'pots and pans revolution', which led to the largest protests in Icelandic history, the fall of a right-wing government and eventually to a new constitution. Given the deepening crisis of multilateral climate change negotiations, including Obama hijacking the process in Copenhagen and shifting more countries to a pledge and review approach, Bolivia hosted the World People's Conference on Climate Change and the Rights of Mother Earth in April 2010, which catalysed the climate justice movement, affirmed the patriarchal nature of climate injustice and provided a platform for various systemic alternatives to be championed. Bolivia attempted to lock industrialised countries into a climate-debt framework to legally compel them to bring down their emissions, while affirming the rights of mother earth for all living creatures. In 2010, several movements came to the fore in the uprisings in Arab and North African countries (Hanieh 2013). Cycle 2 was characterised by attempts to find solidarities at a global level and directly take on political and corporate power by providing alternative ways of living, producing, consuming and being. Cycle 3 sees a rise in protests against oppressive systems, increasing poverty and inequality, dysfunctional states and the callousness of political and economic ruling classes.

Cycle 3: 2011–2019

The year 2011 witnessed a massive upsurge of mass resistance against authoritarian and neoliberal regimes in the Arab world, referred to by some as the 'Arab Spring'. Assemblies in Tahrir Square in Egypt had a knock-on effect globally (Mason 2012). In Spain, the Indignados (also known as the anti-austerity movement) grew out of various youth and social networks and occupied squares in Spain (Della Porta 2015). They challenged the high unemployment rates and precariousness among youth in a crisis-ridden Spanish economy. This struggle also spawned a left party, PODEMOS, which contributed to the end of two-party control in the Spanish political system. In India, an anti-corruption movement rose using non-violent tactics, such as fasting, and demanded reforms to give citizens more power to hold government officials accountable. Systemic corruption in India needed to be confronted with greater transparency, accountability and citizens' power. The civil resistance of this movement rolled on for months into 2012. Coming out of this movement was the formation of the Common Person's Party. In September 2011, the Occupy Wall Street movement took off in Zuccotti Park and spread in cities across the United States (Chomsky 2012). Zuccotti Park occupation garnered symbolic power against the power of finance on Wall Street. After the Zucotti Park Assembly was shut down by authorities in early November, #Occupy gained expression in local struggles against foreclosure and student debt, and it continued to challenge banks and corporations. The meme 'we are the 99 per cent versus the 1 per cent' was globalised and drew attention to the deep inequalities in the USA and globally.

In South Africa, the climate justice movement gathered in the People's Space and on the streets alongside the 17th session of the United Nations (UN) Conference of the Parties (COP17, November 2011), making a compelling case for system change. The crisis of multilateral negotiations, the commitment to false solutions and the lack of systemic alternatives were confirmed at COP17. Climate justice forces increasingly looked to national spaces to advance deep just transitions. In the USA, continued state violence against African Americans and systemic racism gave rise to the #BlackLivesMatter (BLM) network in 2013, which is largely considered the new civil rights movement in the USA. Powerful student protests rocked South Africa between 2015 and 2016 with demands for decolonisation, decommodification and insourcing of cleaning and grounds staff at some universities. The ambitions of the Dakota Access Pipeline project to move fossil fuels across various communities evoked massive grassroots resistance. The Standing Rock Sioux community established an encampment in April 2016 as a point of convergence of resistance, attracting thousands of supporters. Standing Rock has become an iconic struggle of indigenous peoples against ecocidal fossil capital in different parts of the Americas. In South Korea, the 2016–2017 Candlelight Protests demanded the impeachment of President Park Geun-Hye, but also incorporated myriad other demands. They brought a broad spectrum of organisations and millions of civic-minded people to the streets, inaugurating a new era of mass protests celebrated on social media for the festival-like atmosphere. The Candlelight Protests emerged on the back of dangerous 'high-altitude occupations' waged by workers who climbed enormously high cranes at shipyards and factories to draw attention to myriad assaults on workers' rights and the increasingly precarious and irregular employment conditions. While the Candlelight Protests succeeded in getting the president impeached, they did not address the deeper structural issues of neoliberal capitalism (Chun 2022). On 23 June 2016, a slim majority of British citizens chose to leave the European Union, which came to be known as Brexit. It is generally understood as a deeply nationalist response to a failed project of neoliberal regionalisation. However, in the complex cauldron of the politics of the United Kingdom (UK), the British Labour Party went through a grassroots driven resurgence led by left leader Jeremy Corbyn. Across the Atlantic, Bernie Sanders continued to build a 'new deal' style movement within US society. These attempts at renewing social democracy and positioning it to the left were short lived but inspiring.

Cycle 4: 2020 and Beyond

The Covid-19 pandemic was unprecedented for current generations. It disrupted failing socio-ecological reproduction regimes and forced ruling classes to feign concern for the crisis of care (Dowling 2021). Solidarities from below pushed for responsiveness and rose to the challenge to deal with the shortcomings of private health care systems, precarity and hunger. In many societies, the state and private sector came short and solidarities held societies together. Many voices rose calling for universal basic income transfers to be instituted (Satgar 2022b); global solidarities converged against vaccine apartheid and the need for patent rights exemptions to the WTO intellectual property rights regime so that countries in the global south could vaccinate their populations. Electrifying the Covid-19 moment was the murder of George Floyd by a police officer on 25 May 2020. Once again, this murder foregrounded the entrenched systemic and institutional racism in the USA and the racist and militaristic practices of policing. Millions took to the streets in subsequent months demanding racial justice, #BlackLivesMatter, and drew attention to the racial fault line at the heart of American society. Since September 2020, India's farmers have resisted fiercely and occupied the outskirts of the capital city Delhi for months to register their vehement opposition to the imposition of agrarian reforms that favour corporate capital. Food system struggles continued on the streets outside and in parallel events to the UN food summit in September 2021. Calls for food sovereignty, indigenous knowledge, regenerative agriculture and the end to deeply globalised food systems have framed the transformative narrative. Climate justice struggles have continued during the period with the world's first Climate Justice Charter handed to South Africa's parliament for adoption on 16 October 2020. On the streets outside the Glasgow COP (November 2021), thousands demanded more than the rapid phase out of coal but of all fossil fuels, greater commitment to loss and damage funds, and climate debt to be paid to the global south.

While these cycles of resistance have been crucial for renewing a new global left, not all forces rising have been committed to transformative forces of socio-ecological reproduction. The neoliberal polarisations of society have also impacted and limited the mass resistance of transformative politics. For four decades, the marketising of societies has remade state–civil society relations. States have been transformed into market actors managing the risk to capital. Sovereignty has been hollowed out as inordinate power has been given to corporations to prevail over state, society, economy and the commons. In this context, two forms of mass politics have also featured in the cycles of resistance. The first is the declassed, heterogenous and everyday person. Social media, celebrities and symbolic crowd gatherings constitute political subjectivity; we are the 'multitude' (Hardt and Negri 2005). Tactics range from crowd marches and occupying public spaces to catchy celebrity narratives. Such a form of politics meets the impervious state, multilateral and non-state actors (such as the WEF) and has not shifted the underlying class power that entrenches neoliberalism and the sovereignty of capital. The World Social Forum was crucial in inciting resistance after 2001, Occupy Wall Street and then later #Feesmustfall, #FridaysforFuture and Extinction Rebellion. These have been important struggles, providing a symbolic point of reference in everyday common sense, but have not been able to institutionalise a new mass and strategic transformative politics. This stands in contrast to twentieth-century mass movements that built institutionalised forms of strategic power and resistance. Ultimately, these are forms of resistance with potential for counterhegemony but are not capable of advancing counterhegemonic transformative resistance beyond the symbolic. Their conception of the political is limited.

Close to but different from militant crowd politics has been the professionalised social movement, and non-governmental organisation (NGO)-centred politics, that carries donor-driven mandates, resources and intervention capacity (Satgar 2024, 32). This is the second form of politics that contests mass consciousness. The politics of these social forces has dangerously allowed the state to retreat so that they can come in through food security, social economy and corporate social responsibility. Billionaire philanthropy and foreign donor architectures generally assist in producing a neoliberal civil society that is fixated on amelioration. Tactics range from legal challenges to lobbying and technical 'policy' and, ultimately, these forms of contention fit in with market-centred rationality. Deeper systemic solutions are not on the agenda and neither is there a questioning of the limits of market democracy. Inadvertently, they normalise and routinise high-stakes contradictions in the name of defending market democracy. Disconnected elites are made to seem like they are acting in the public interest, and performative politicians reinforce this narrow 'problem solving' approach in the mainstream of society, while inequality and suffering continues. Both militant crowd politics and neoliberal civil society stand in the way of transformative politics and are not capable of meeting the challenge of the planetary polycrisis of socio-ecological reproduction.

MOVING BEYOND REFORM VERSUS REVOLUTION THROUGH TRANSFORMATIVE PRAXIS

In the cycles of resistance that have emerged over four decades, a new conception of the political has come to the fore which breaks with the twentieth-century approaches of reform versus revolution. The limits of these modes of politics when in power, including crowd and neoliberal civil society, were highlighted above. Transformative politics differs from reform and revolution on ontological grounds, its conception of the power paradigm, strategic orientation and agency. In other words, its praxis is fundamentally different from the twentieth-century approaches. Rather than seeking to manage or pull down capitalism, the political imaginary and agency of transformative politics seeks to erode, tame and exit capitalism simultaneously. At the heart of this is ensuring life-making and overcoming the destruction of the conditions necessary for socio-ecological reproduction. This means defending, renewing and transforming the background conditions of capitalist accumulation through transformative politics. Commodifying logics need to be supplanted with socialising logics that foreground the commons pattern as the basis for planetary care. This will become clearer as transformative praxis is distinguished from reform and revolution (see Table 2.2).

Table 2.2 Types of political praxis: reform, revolution and transformative.

Key distinguishing features	Reform	Revolution	Transformative
Ontology	Capitalism as gradual progress	Capitalist war and general crisis	Planetary poly crisis of socio-ecological reproduction/the last great dispossession of the commons
Power paradigm	Party-centric with vertical and technocratic state power over trade unions and society	Party-centric with vertical and coercive party-state power over class alliances	Anti-party movements and social forces constitutive of forms of power from below
Strategic orientation	Pragmatic management of capitalism	Smash capitalist state to set up dictatorship of the proletariat	Advance democratic systemic reforms to erode, tame and exit capitalism
Agency	Working class, middle class and fractions of globalising monopoly capital voting for reforms	Vanguard party, workers and peasants instrumentalised for revolution and to advance objectives of coercive state bureaucracy	Transformative forces of socio-ecological reproduction such as workers, peasants, indigenous peoples, grassroots women, the permanently unemployed and the precarious middle-class building capacities, resisting and making democratic systemic reforms from below, grounded in an ethics of care

Ontologically reformist politics understands capitalist reality as centred on gradual progress. It is a system that must be managed to limit its negative side effects while allowing its accumulation, competitive and resource-intensive logics to lead the gradual change of societies. In other words, capitalism is inherently progressive. Revolutionary politics differs from reformist politics ontologically as it recognises that capitalism is prone to crises and its crisis tendencies and expansionary logics tend towards general systemic crises and inter-imperial war. The chaos, violence and social fragility of such moments provide the conditions for revolutionary advance and rupture. Transformative praxis differs ontologically in that it recognises the planetary polycrisis dynamics of capitalism that annihilate the background conditions of capitalism, namely reproduction, nature, public power and through intensive extraction from peripheries. It seeks to turn the contradictions of capitalism against it and overcome the dispossession of our commons. As a result, the commonwealth (water, land, biodiversity, creative labour, renewable energy, the earth system, knowledge, public infrastructure and goods, and cultural heritage) of life-enabling systems is central to this ontology and its transformative politics to overcome the polycrisis of socio-ecological reproduction.

The power paradigm of both reform and revolution politics centred the state as the embodiment of power. Secure the state through electoral means or insurrection and then such power can be used from above to bring about social change. The vertical rationalities of state-centric power have been demonstrated historically to disable society. State centrism and de-democratisation in twentieth-century socialist projects have been disastrous. Transformative praxis, by contrast, works with a constitutive and relational notion of power. Power is made in workplaces, homes, communities and various spatial locales as transformative alternatives are constituted from below. In theoretical terms, this involves systemic, movement, direct, discursive, state democratising and planetary solidarity coefficients of power making from below. It is only through power making from below that the annihilation of the background conditions of capitalism can be stopped and transformed. Ultimately, the state is subsumed, democratised and transformed by these relations and 'power from below' logic. This is further developed below when clarifying the strategic notion of democratic systemic reforms.

The strategic orientation of reform politics is towards harnessing political legitimacy for pragmatic reforms that do not disrupt the inner logic of capitalism. Even in moments of crisis, such politics fails to use the weaknesses of capitalism against it but rather seeks to manage change. Revolutionary politics seeks a rupture with capitalism; its orientation is towards establishing a coercive political order through a 'dictatorship of the proletariat'.

Transformative praxis through building power from below seeks to translate this into democratic systemic reforms that can erode, tame and exit capitalism.[3] It does not seek to manage capitalism nor achieve a big bang rupture. This is a contingent strategic orientation based on the aggregation of societal power which seeks to shift relations of power democratically and within societal limits. Deep democracy unleashes systemic transformation and the momentum for change is anchored and driven by conscious agency with, against and beyond the state.[4] Our case studies in this book give concrete insight into what this means for building socio-ecological regimes of reproduction and advancing planetary care from below (see Chapters 4–6).

The agential locus in reform politics seeks to bring together the common interests of various social forces, such as working classes, middle classes and fractions of globalising monopoly capital, while revolutionary politics has centred the working class as the universal agent of history. In some parts of the periphery, worker–peasant alliances have been countenanced as well. Transformative praxis unites, aggregates and builds with all subaltern forces as well as progressive middle classes facing the planetary polycrisis of socio-ecological reproduction and who have the potential to advance transformative alternatives. Such forces include the working class, peasants, indigenous peoples, grassroots women, the permanently unemployed and precarious middle classes. It builds capacities from below for large-scale transformations, grounding transformative praxis in an ethics of care of human and more-than-human life forms. This is an agency alive to means, ends and consequences. Moreover, it understands limits and responsibilities. In short, it is ethically grounded to advance planetary care from below.

As mentioned, the emerging new global left has been learning from the reform and revolution strategic rationalities that produced state centrism, de-democratisation, limited feminist commitments and anti-ecology in the twentieth century. The new global left is certainly not wanting to repeat those mistakes. In this regard, the strategic politics of the twentieth-century left and its limits have been questioned. The old left binary of reform versus revolution is rejected, even ignored, as part of renewing a new transformative praxis to realise world making by the subaltern through counter-hegemony that is led by transformative forces of socio-ecological reproduction. However, there is more at work within transformative politics and the new global left politics, which is explored further.

TRANSFORMATIVE FORCES OF SOCIO-ECOLOGICAL REPRODUCTION AND EMANCIPATORY UTOPIA AS METHOD OF WORLD MAKING

Utopia and its other, dystopia, have taken on different forms: novels, movies, architecture, garden making and so on (Claeys and Sargent 1999). These forms, however, are narrow forms of utopia/dystopia. The desire to have a different lifeworld free from suffering has given rise to a collective utopian praxis. Marx and Engels had a difficult relationship with utopian thinking and in general had an aversion to blueprinting alternatives in the mid-nineteenth century. Their critiques of utopian socialists were very much about trying to find a distinctive place for their version of 'scientific socialism' and sometimes struck a sectarian tone. It also appeared that they rejected cooperatives, but this was not the case particularly as Marx himself went beyond state centrism that was writ large in *The Communist Manifesto*.[5] Nonetheless, they were correct in highlighting the underlying materialist processes of capitalist history, even as the basis to advance prefiguration. Since then, many Marxists and concrete struggles have demonstrated the importance of utopian thinking as integral to struggles and historical world making from below. For instance, Ernst Bloch, a Marxist philosopher, understood utopia as expressing complex temporalities in its concreteness and as a basis to resist the privatisation of hope (Thompson and Žižek 2014). As Acaroglu (2021, 120) argues for Bloch: 'Hope, in contrast, is postured towards the future, and draws its impetus from the Not-Yet. It sits uneasily at the present, reactivating the past and anticipating the future. It is thus an interlocutor between the present, and the futures in the process of becoming.' In Wright's (2010, 6) *Envisioning Real Utopias*, he shows that we need 'ideals that are grounded in the real potentials of humanity, utopian destinations that have accessible waystations, utopian designs of institutions that can inform our practical tasks of navigating a world of imperfect conditions for social change'. Ultimately, utopian thought has been a battle ground for overcoming suppressed ways of being and, in itself, is not a guarantee of a different future. In this regard, it must find its place in actual struggles as a concrete method of emancipatory world making and as integral to transformative politics.

In the South African context, Marxist philosopher Rick Turner recognised that utopia as emancipatory method of world making entailed collective imagining in struggle, it required historicising oppression to understand its social construction and it required values, consciousness and institution building to come together. Building on Turner, in contemporary South Africa emancipatory utopia as a method of world making has been tested in solidarity economy, food sovereignty and climate justice spaces (Satgar 2024). More generally, in the current cycles of resistance and through the influence of the World Social Forum, the idea of 'Another World is Possible' and the assertions of climate justice forces wanting 'systems change, not climate change' has ensured emancipatory utopia as method of world making has also travelled into struggles of transformative forces of socio-ecological production resisting neoliberalisation but that also seeks exits from the polycrisis. Such forces dream of worlds in which socio-ecological reproduction works differently to address suffering, oppression and exploitation. This means overcoming mentalities of oppression: boss/worker, company/peasant, state/citizen, colonial state/indigenous people and constituting agential forms of democratised power.[6] Such shifts from oppressed to emancipatory consciousness are facilitated by desiring, dreaming and articulating transformative systemic alternatives as part of transformative subjectivity. Thus, emancipatory utopia as method of world making is integral to transformative politics and provides new pathways for building an alternative society in the present that secures a new basis for commoning and planetary care.

New political projects, new horizons and new praxis-centred politics ground the social dreaming of these forces. Consciousness shifts from the immediate to the whole, from the particular to the general, from single issues to a larger political project. This happens even without conscious recognition by these forces or awareness of how political subjectivity is unfolding. In many instances, this is an organic process in which social dreaming is a use value of transformative resistance. Learning from solidarity economy cooperative systems, commoning and worker cooperatives, emancipatory utopia as world making entails several conscious and sometimes unconscious deliberative steps. In the academic space, this is recognised as utopia as method for the imaginary reconstitution of society (Levitas 2009). Grounded in transformative thought and politics of movements, emancipatory utopia as method of world making seeks to construct new socio-ecological regimes of reproduction to survive the worsening capitalist polycrisis and to ensure that the web of life thrives.

ETHICS OF CARE AND THE POLITICAL FORM

Cooperative forms, solidarity economy systems and, generally, forces of socio-ecological reproduction are grounded in an ethics of care. Genuine cooperatives have ethical values inscribed in their institutional arrangements and everyday practices. Waste pickers in the solidarity economy in Brazil care about the communities they operate in and want them to be safe and clean.[7] Commoning practices more generally are about the web of life and recognising limits. This was very apparent with coffee cooperatives in Tanzania and Ethiopia, for instance. In both these cases, coffee was not a cash crop based on super exploitation of humans and non-humans. Instead, these cooperatives wanted ethical and fair trade recognition and practices (Williams 2013).[8] The labour process and process of production in nature was important for them.

More generally, in global left politics today, from community transition towns and indigenous ecology to climate justice politics, there is a serious commitment to care labour and an ethics of care. This is planetary care in action. Transformative praxis is conscious of its ethical choices, its ethics of care, compared to the twentieth-century left. Care labour at the heart of emancipatory feminist thinking is grounded in an awareness of sex, birth, childrearing and other care practices all produce a species, a society and regime of socio-ecological reproduction (Satgar and Ntlokotse 2023). Without it, we do not exist. Beyond the structural realities of social reproduction, there is a conscious ethical choice at work here. A good example in this regard is nursing whereby nurses (both men and women) want to bring patients comfort and ensure harms are overcome. In the worker cooperatives that we studied, the gender division of labour was such that flexible working time arrangements gave worker–owners more time for self-care and development.[9] For eco-feminists, our ethics of care extends to the more-than-human realm as well (Plumwood 2002). The soils, seeds, rivers, plants, trees, insects, animals, oceans and even the earth system require a conscious ethics of preventing harm. While we co-exist with nature, we are not superior to nature and have to ensure an ethics of care that meets the needs of humans without destroying the ecological basis of life. Intrinsically, nature is valued as a life-giving system.

This is beyond liberal rights-based discourses of the single individual or homo economicus of the rational and utility maximising subject of neoliberalisation. Ethics of care is about recognising individual and collective limits and responsibilities. It is about being eco-humans within a larger web of life and sharing a planetary condition. Gibson-Graham et al. (2013, xviii) appreciate that our times call for 'ethical action' and such ethical action means:

surviving together well and equitably;
distributing surplus to enrich social and environmental health;

encountering others in ways that support their wellbeing as well
as ours;

consuming sustainably;

caring for – maintaining, replenishing, and growing – our
natural and cultural commons; and

investing our wealth in future generations so that they can live
well.

However, such an ethics of care also calls into question how political forms are constituted. Panitch and Gindin (2017) recognise
that twentieth-century working class political forms are in crisis
and that we need new political forms. Wainwright (2017) takes this
further to look closer at the contemporary cycles of resistance and
the new left political forms that have emerged. Her case studies
have explored the Brazilian Workers' Party, Syrizia in Greece and
the Corbyn campaign in the UK. She discerns in all these examples
potential for a new articulation between political forms and mass
movements. While these examples did not yield a new political form
that broke with 'power from above', they did hold the promise of it.
The key is to continue inventing and learning from such experiences. In the global south, Marta Harnecker has also made the case
for new political forms given the crisis of the old left party forms.
Her starting point for a new political form is: 'unite your members
around a community of values and a concrete program' (Harnecker
2007, 100-101). This brings us back to the ethical basis of transformative politics. Such ethics of care already exist in the life worlds
of transformative forces of socio-ecological reproduction, the conscious bearers of transformative politics. The challenge is to invent
political forms that coordinate such forces, embody their ethics
of care and affirm its collective praxis as part of a larger political
project. This also means the constitutive forms of power central to
transformative politics, state and mass-driven power, are not only
essential but also have to be straddled by political instruments to
enable power as 'transformative capacity from below'. This is a point
we return to below when engaging the strategic concept of democratic systemic reforms.

POLY EPISTEMOLOGIES OF TRANSFORMATIVE POLITICS

Wainwright's (2017, 1-37) critical engagement with neoliberalism recognises in Hayek that there is a powerful insight about knowledge that transformative forces of socio-ecological reproduction can draw on. This relates to practical knowledge that social forces develop which is not codified or even valued, but is the tacit knowledge imbricated in praxis. It is the how to act, do and make aspects of knowledge. This aspect and division of knowledge in struggle is important but it does not go far enough to understand the epistemological richness emerging from contemporary cycles of resistance. The poly epistemologies of transformative praxis are crucial for contemporary transformative politics and also assist in distinguishing it from twentieth-century left state-centric, anti-ecological (productivist), de-democratising and limited emancipatory feminist commitments. Moreover, these forms of knowledge depart from neoliberal reason and its epistemological crisis by furnishing a crucial anchoring for transformative praxis and politics that seek to build a transformed regime of socio-ecological reproduction from below. In other words, they are central to how political subjectivity develops from awareness of victimhood and suffering to the need for positive solidarities and for full-blown transformation of the system. From the research of worker cooperatives, solidarity economy-based cooperative systems and commoning that informs this book, crucial moments of self-formation of transformative forces of socio-ecological reproduction and knowledge generation have been observed as part of the larger cycles of resistance.

First is the recognition of suffering in the realm of the everyday, through oppression, exploitation, living the polycrisis of socio-ecological reproduction, ecocide or dispossession, which engenders the need for solidarity centred power. The experience of these realities precedes thought and is lived, actual and material. Common sense and phenomenological knowledge (experiential) are embodied in these subjectivities as these realities engulf lifeworlds. Put differently, this is knowledge that informs the raw militancy and rage of struggle. It frames a harm, an injustice and even a fear of loss.

It is the affective moment of subjective identity. Most importantly, these realities are the roots of the metaphoric tree of emancipatory knowledge required to engage in transformative socio-ecological reproduction (see Figure 2.2). Instances of this include workers having worked for decades in a factory suddenly facing retrenchment;[10] indigenous peoples wanting land justice and protecting the natural commons; waste pickers realising that without collective power they cannot bargain a space in corporate-controlled value chains. There are litanies of faultiness and flashpoints during the cycles of resistance that have prompted a common sense and experiential awakening of political subjectivity.

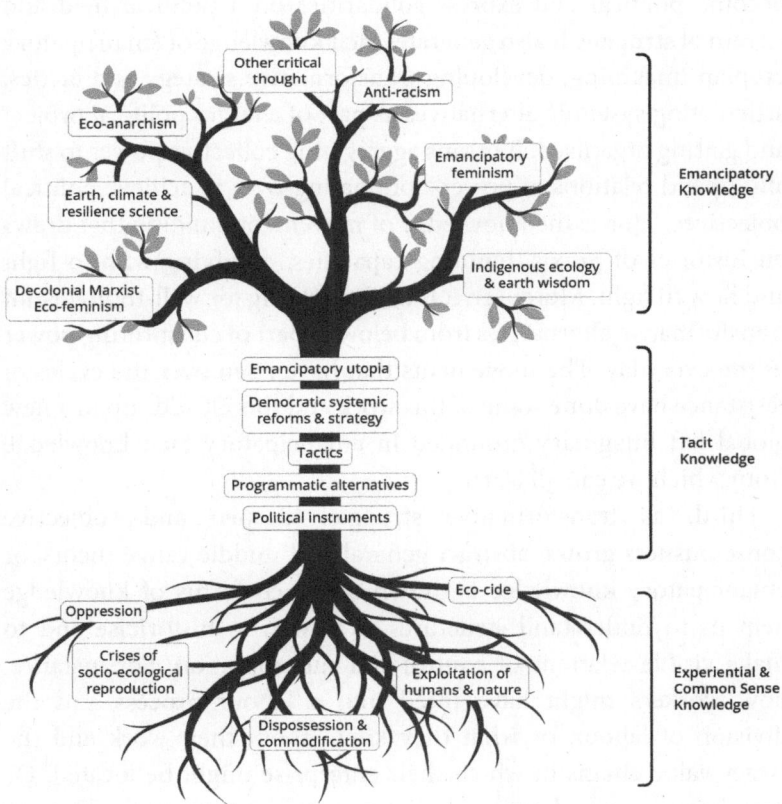

Figure 2.2   The tree of emancipatory/transformative praxis and poly epistemologies.

Second is clarifying how to overcome the specific contradictions of suffering and organise subjective power. This starts with imagining a factory without a boss, the reclamation of common land or healing the rupture in the earth system through food sovereignty commons systems or organising as a women's grassroots collective to have more voice and power. Or, as we observed in our fieldwork, institutionalising transformative praxis through worker cooperatives and solidarity economy-based cooperative systems. While we did not visit Jackson Mississippi, their inspiring example of solidarity economy building captures explicitly the importance of tacit knowledge.[11] Such a moment is a process of figuring out how to become political and express solidarities on a political field and terrain of struggle. It also generates tacit knowledge of emancipatory utopian imagining, developing transformative strategy and tactics, articulating systemic alternatives as part of a larger political project and getting organised. It means aggregating collective power to shift and upend relations of power-dominating-over to achieve political objectives. This is the knowledge of movement building that draws on histories of praxis, building capacities, clarifying who to fight and how to fight. Moreover, it is about fighting for well-thought-out transformative alternatives from below as part of constituting power in the everyday. The movements that have risen over the cycles of resistance have done some of this work and this all adds up to a new global left imaginary grounded in emancipatory tacit knowledge from which we can all learn.[12]

Third, as transformative struggles deepen and subjective consciousness grows, abstract general and middle range theory or emancipatory knowledge is drawn on. Such forms of knowledge help us to understand structures of power, to historicise and to make visible relations of control and subordination. For instance, how workers might have fitted into a labour process and the division of labour, or what they knew about their work and the larger value chains in which their enterprise might be located. Or how has a person been excluded because of race, caste, class or gender from performing certain jobs. Or the histories of violence and dispossession suffered by indigenous peoples. Moreover, emancipatory knowledge explains, structurally locates the subject of history and further explicates the potentials of self-agency. Such emancipatory knowledge resides on the branches of the tree of emancipatory/transformative praxis but also strengthens the trunk of the tree and everyday consciousness in resistance. Today there are various anticapitalisms coming to the fore that appreciate the importance of planetary care from below. Different branches of emancipatory thought on the tree of emancipatory/transformative praxis illustrate this: decolonial eco-feminist Marxism, emancipatory feminism, critical thought, indigenous knowledge, earth science and eco-anarchism, for instance (see Figure 2.2).[13] Worker cooperatives, new commoning arrangements, solidarity economies and more bring this to the fore. They ground this in an understanding of risks, challenges and solidarities that provide emancipatory utopia with a materiality that is far from fictive imagining.

CONSTITUTIVE POLITICAL POWER AND DEMOCRATIC SYSTEMIC REFORMS

Emancipatory utopia as method, ethics of care (for planetary life and to build caring movements and political instruments) and the poly epistemologies of transformative praxis are integral to transformative politics. Transformative politics shifts oppressed consciousness to emancipatory consciousness towards a recognition of political subjectivity in which self-power is understood as the basis to confront the power that prevails over one's self and lifeworld. Wainwright (2017, 100; 2018, 13) characterises top-down power as 'power over' or 'power-as-domination'. However, the remaking of political subjectivity does not stop with an awareness of one's own power and the sinews of power from above. From here it can go in several directions when confronting 'power-as-domination', including in the direction of protest (such as symbolic action and lobbying) or it can be generative. Williams (2008, 10) argues that generative politics is central to transformative politics as it moves beyond the limits of narrow protest politics and is counterhegemonic in its expression of alternative forms of social organisation.

Both Wainwright and Williams point us in the direction of power from below. Wainwright characterises power from below as 'power-as-transformative capacity'. In this, the politics of knowledge, particularly tacit knowledge, is crucial for new leadership that encourages bottom-up transformation by forces of socio-ecological reproduction. However, there is another side to 'power-as-transformative capacity' that advances systemic alternatives and regimes of socio-ecological reproduction from below. In this regard, transformative politics has also rethought power. The twentieth-century conception of power began and ended with the state. Contemporary anarchism has swung the stick to the other extreme with total rejection of state power. Holloway's (2002) *Change the World Without Taking Power* is a case in point. Rejecting the state is not helpful; it dogmatically closes the potentials of power as constitutive. Transformative political subjectivity works with a new paradigm of power as made, built and expressed through different resources. Drawing on labour studies, scholarship transformative politics recognises the following forms of constitutive power: systemic, movement, direct, discursive, democratising the state and planetary solidarity.[14]

Systemic power builds new systems to meet need. A cooperative banking system is an example of controlling capital and using it to build new production and consumption systems. The Mondragón worker cooperative complex is a good example in this regard. Another example is food sovereignty pathway building that exits corporate-controlled value chains. Commoning water, oceans or forests also provide systemic power for democratic agency. Movement power aggregates capacities through members' care labour, financial contributions, research, the tacit knowledge commons and the growth of member densities. For example, the cooperatives in this book display movement power as they work together. This gives a rootedness in the class structure and more generally in society. Direct power includes campaigns, street protests and symbolic actions. In the cycles of resistance, numerous examples stand out from #FeesMustFall to #BlackLivesMatter to #FridaysForFuture. Discursive power is about contesting dominant narratives and ways of understanding through one's own research, media engagements, collective intellectual interventions and symbolic representations. The recovered factory movement in Argentina developed its own documentation centres, media networks and also made movies about its struggles, which it shared widely.

Democratising state power emerges through contesting the state from below and being in the state such that power-as-domination becomes power-as-accountability. Syrizia in Greece, supported by solidarity networks, failed to achieve this and continued in the power-as-domination mould. In Chapter 6 we show how Mondragón and Kerala both contest and engage the state to be power-as-accountability. In addition, the policy and regulatory frameworks of the state bring societal power into the state–civil society nexus to embed it, and to change its character, form and functioning. Some of the case studies in this book show this. Finally, planetary solidarity is about building a transformative bloc of forces of socio-ecological reproduction of people, workers, movements and vulnerable governments. Such forces articulate the capacities, ideas and institutional basis to end the last great dispossession of the commons and secure planetary care. Since the World Social Forum, various forces have been building planetary solidarities through climate justice, resistance to rising fascism and have been providing a more strategic coordination of global struggles. There is still a lot to do to institutionalise such solidarities. Cooperatives in Argentina, Venezuela, Mondragón, Kerala, Trentino and Brazil have built interesting solidarity relationships but have not translated this into a convergence with other mass movements, such as the climate justice movement or La Via Campesina, despite the potentials being there.

However, such power and its capacities are about making and driving democratic systemic reforms from community to workplace, sectoral level and even in the state. This is a strategic approach to translate the prefigurative, localised and variegated scales of transformation into large-scale societal change. Democracy is the anchor to enable the transformative historical subject to become, to act consciously and be a world-making agent. It is also why capital today wants to hollow out democracy; it is against deep democracy but for shallow market democracy in which the sovereignty of capital prevails. In opposition, transformative forces of socio-ecological reproduction champion deep democracy – participatory, direct, representative, processual and rights based. Deep democracy ensures that transformative forces of socio-ecological reproduction and society own the dangerous contradictions or problems of the planetary polycrisis but also the solutions; transformation is in the hands of society and not ruling classes. Building, regenerating and redesigning socio-ecological systems starts from below, embedded in deep democratising rationalities, such that root causes of the polycrisis are tackled. The dangerous contradictions that come to the fore from the planetary polycrisis, such as the climate crisis, biodiversity loss, hunger, financialised inequality and degenerate market democracies, are tackled head-on through democratic systemic reforms. Driven from below, by constitutive forms of power (systemic, movement, direct, discursive, state democratising and planetary solidarity), such democratic systemic reforms can be weak, strong or transformative, depending on the strength of transformative forces of socio-ecological reproduction and the extent to which they harnessed their power to galvanise, champion and lock in such reforms as part of counterhegemonic practice from below.

TRANSFORMATIVE FORCES OF SOCIO-ECOLOGICAL REPRODUCTION, SYSTEMS CHANGE AND PLANETARY CARE

Our precarious web of life grew out of the natural commons and developed synergistically. Today, social and natural relations are coeval in the larger planetary history of our lifeworld. Our homes, communities and workplaces all exist in ecosystems, the biosphere and, more generally, the earth system. As capital has transformed the natural and social commons into commodities, it has intertwined social relations and earth relations more tightly such that these systems are being pushed beyond their natural cycles, limits and capacities. Commons life-enabling systems, as part of capitalism's background conditions and socio-ecological reproduction regime, are in crisis. Capitalism as a parasitic system is killing the planetary conditions that sustain life and is causing the planetary polycrisis of socio-ecological reproduction.

With capital destroying the planetary conditions that sustain life, the challenge for transformative forces of socio-ecological reproduction are the opposite: reproducing our lives in the everyday in ways that do not create crisis and destroy the planet; such forces express planetary care labour. Grounded in transformative politics (transformative praxis, emancipatory utopia, ethics of care, poly epistemologies and constitutive power relations), such forces are attempting to bring about systems change to ensure we end the capitalism–nature binary; conquest and domination of earth relations is supplanted with planetary care. This is a serious struggle and determining of whether our species and more-than-human life have a future. The positive side to all of this is that transformative politics exists, and planetary care has been underway for a long time with current cycles of counterhegemonic resistance merely foregrounding this. However, for us to learn from this and bring this more centrally into the mainstream of planetary and societal transformative process we have to deal with two challenges.

First, we must overcome the entrenched class power of global monopoly capital. Many believe it is impossible to win against capital given that it has rigged everything in its favour. This argument sometimes goes further to suggest that smashing capitalism is the only way forward. This book offers a sharp counterpoint. Besides the politics of smashing capitalism unleashing more chaos and violence, it also does not appreciate the limits of contemporary capitalism. Capital today cannot solve the planetary polycrisis it is causing. In fact, it is an asymmetrical power relationship with earth and the latter will prevail. This will not come as a big bang collapse of capitalism but instead is imbricated in complex temporal, scalar level and geographic unevenness as capitalist systems fail, unravel or reach their limits. If we just think about the climate polycrisis dimension: the earth's response to the harms inflicted is to unleash climate extremes that are increasing risk to capital, engendering more uncertainty and even increasing the prospect of insolvency of governments as climate costs start to escalate.[15] Capitalist modes of rule are reaching their limits, as insurance companies withdraw from 'high-risk markets', the tragic loss of homes and lives increases with more climate extremes and the migration of millions of stateless refugees intensifies. The planet's erosion of capitalism is underway, which is pushing our societies to embrace the climate emergency. At the same time, the planet is inviting us to reclaim the commons and commoning on different scales, as a new basis to care and reproduce life before it is too late.

Second, to ensure a transformative response to the planet, the just transition championed by climate justice forces at different scales has to be taken to a new strategic level, such that the climate emergency erodes capitalism, tames capital and finds exits from capitalism (Cock 2018; Satgar 2018). Climate justice forces have to be centrally involved with transformative forces of socio-ecological reproduction, such that the just transition has to become a deep just transition that recentres the commons and commoning. As mentioned, the earth is already eroding capitalism. This has to be complimented by erosion efforts of transformative forces of socio-ecological reproduction. Eroding capitalism recognises that alternatives are built in *and* alongside capitalism, consciously evolving commons, market, state and societal relations along alternative principles. Here, too, the power of capitalist class relations is a constant threat; the more successful these transformative alternatives are, the more likely they are to engender a backlash. Thus, part of the struggle to build alternatives is also to weaken capitalist class relations through their values, principles and transformative politics. Solidarity economy-based cooperative systems aggregate various forms of power (systemic, movement, direct, discursive, state democratising and planetary solidarity) that could potentially challenge capitalism's social power. The case studies we foreground in Chapters 4–6 demonstrate this. However, their transformative possibility also depends on a larger transformative politics that includes rallying a wider array of transformative forces of socio-ecological reproduction – other movements, class forces, political organisations and widespread support from society.

The taming of capitalism is already on the political agenda, either through active political calls for such or through possibilities that accelerate the deep just transition out of the planetary crisis. This is evident, for instance, in greater calls for banning dangerous pesticides, industrial-scale fishing and certain plastics. The phasing out of fossil fuels including divestment, while slower than needed, is also a push in this direction. Affirming public commons infrastructure, such as clean energy public transport systems, libraries, public health care and commons cultural heritage, is also about placing limits on capitalist accumulation. Redirecting pension funds into democratic systemic reforms is another. Passing cooperative laws including cooperative banking further diversifies the financial system and tames finance capital. The need for the democratic planning of food and water systems and increasingly a push for public–commons partnerships would also squeeze capital. Ultimately, advancing democratising state power from below, as part of taming capitalism, requires the state to adopt and re-enforce people- and worker-driven democratic systemic reforms that regulate and overcome the pernicious externalities generated in capitalism.

Exiting capitalism is about people choosing to opt out of capitalist relations. Within the context of the uneven geographies of capitalism, many local spaces outside of capitalism have inadvertently escaped the domination of capitalism, providing communities space to survive through the natural commons (water, land, biodiversity, creative labour, energy and the earth system) and social commons (cultural heritage and knowledge systems, for instance). For example, Xolobeni community has been at the forefront of commoning struggles against the enclosure of their communally owned pristine land along the 'wild coast' in the Eastern Cape, South Africa.[16] In a life-and-death struggle against the state and a powerful international mining company who want to mine titanium and other minerals from their rich soil, for 20 years Xolobeni has used indigenous knowledge and practices to defend the commons, and has so far won legal battles all the way to the Constitutional Court.

While pockets exist outside of capitalist relations, it is increasingly difficult to survive in these spaces. Capitalism's expansionist logic incessantly looks for new areas to ex/appropriate and subsume what remains of the commons. This is part of a last great dispossession. For example, while researching cooperatives in Tanzania, we had the privilege of spending time with a Maasai chief who was at the frontline in the struggle to defend their grazing rights to the commons. For the Maasai, cattle are central to their cosmology and for centuries, perhaps millennia, they have roamed freely across the grasslands of the Ngorogoro and Serengeti plains. Despite having constitutionally guaranteed communal land rights for grazing their cattle, they have increasingly been pushed off communal and pastoral land to make way for cultivated, capitalist farms and national game parks enjoyed by international tourists. When we met the chief, they were defending their rights to graze in the Ngorogoro Conservation Area. Sadly, in January 2024 the Tanzanian government announced that it would begin to evict the Maasai pastoralist from the Ngorogoro area, effectively enclosing the life-enabling commons upon which the Maasai depend for their existence (Oakland Institute 2024). In this context, struggles to defend the commons are at the frontline of trying to maintain life-making conditions outside capitalist relations. In other words, socio-ecological reproduction outside of capitalism by indigenous peoples, peasants, subsistence fishers and grassroots communities is coming under serious threat by intensifying commodification. Recentring the commons and commoning, in the mainstream and as part of the deep just transition, will give these forces the opportunity to defend and renew what they have as part of continuing planetary care (see Table 2.3).

Essentially, eroding, taming and exiting capitalism potentially complement one another; all envision transcending capitalism in the long term. We argue that worker cooperatives and solidarity economy-based cooperative systems – often working with commoning logics of care labour, time, finance, natural relations and collective capacity – attempt to erode and exit capitalism. They also generate compulsion in the state to tame capitalism and potentially provide a basis on which to transition beyond and deepen planetary care. A necessary condition in this regard is grounding such systemic alternatives in transformative politics. Many of the case studies we

Table 2.3 Transformative politics, worker cooperatives and solidarity economy systems.

Worker cooperative and solidarity economy system	Duration of transformative praxis	Emancipatory utopia as method of world making	Ethics of care	Poly epistemologies	Constitutive forms of power
ULCCS (Kerala)	1924 onwards practising transformative praxis	Imagining an alternative to caste exclusion	Institutionalised	Anti-caste, tacit knowledge and everyday experience of suffering	All forms
Uniforja (Brazil)	2000 onwards practising transformative praxis	Imagining an alternative to enterprise decline	Institutionalised	Worker self-management, tacit knowledge and everyday experience	All forms except democratising state power from below
Chilavert (Argentina)	Occupation in 2002, expropriation in 2004. From occupation practising transformative praxis	Imagining an alternative to enterprise decline	Institutionalised	Worker self-management, tacit knowledge and everyday experience	All forms
Cecosesola (Venezuela)	1967 onwards practising transformative praxis	Imagining an alternative to rural marginalisation	Institutionalised	Liberation theology and eco-anarchism, tacit knowledge and everyday experience	All forms except democratising state power from below
Heiveld (South Africa)	2000 onwards practising transformative praxis	Imagining an alternative to centuries of colonial dispossession	Institutionalised	Anti-racism, tacit knowledge and everyday experience	All forms except democratising state power from below
Trentino (Italy)	1895 onwards practising transformative praxis	Imagining an alternative to late nineteenth-century capitalist crisis and exclusion	Institutionalised	Progressive social reform Catholicism, tacit knowledge and everyday experience	All forms
Mondragón (Spain)	1956 onwards practising transformative praxis	Imagining an alternative to World War II devastation and exclusion	Institutionalised	Progressive social reform Catholicism, tacit knowledge and everyday experience	All forms

foreground in Chapters 4–6 exhibit characteristics of transformative politics, each with its own specificities. These case studies help us to learn and they inform us how to accelerate the deep just transition, to centre commoning and planetary care. The chapters give us deeper insights into how transformative worker cooperatives and solidarity economy-based cooperative systems are an alternative to the annihilation of capitalism. Such institutional forms are at the forefront of taking up the planets invite to mainstream the commons and engage in planetary care as they reproduce life in the everyday. Before we get to the empirical cases, in the next chapter we provide a context on cooperatives and solidarity economy more generally.

CONCLUSION

The worker cooperative and solidarity economy-based cooperative systems in this book provide a compass – possible pathways – towards transformative futures-making in the present. They express living practices of emancipatory utopian ideas of reconstituting socio-ecological reproduction from the lived experiences of cooperatives. They help us conceptualise empirical experiments that exist simultaneously inside and alongside capitalism. By operating on anti-capitalist principles of production (that is, collective ownership, democratic decision making, capital in the service of labour, one member one vote) and ethical values, but still existing within capitalist markets, many cooperatives are prefiguratively developing anti-capitalist pathways through quadratic relations (commons/state/market/society) that centre the commons and its commoning logic. While these emancipatory alternatives and transformative politics have perdured for over a century, they have largely been on the margins of capitalism. Today's worsening planetary poly crisis of socio-ecological reproduction and the unravelling of US hegemony has opened new spaces, forced a rethink of old notions and practices, emboldened new ideas and created a context of anything is possible, including democratic, ecological and feminist anti-capitalist alternatives. It is in these moments that the possibilities for various scalar level transformations, through the deep just transition, can be inspired by transformative pre-figuration rooted in consistent transformative praxis. In the next chapter, we explore the transformative potentials of worker cooperatives and solidarity economy based cooperative systems. We highlight how such forms are different from mainstream cooperatives that operate as typical capitalist enterprises.

3

Cooperatives and Transformative Change

Palaeontologists tell us that modern humans have inhabited the earth for approximately 200,000 years, with early humans evolving around 300,000 years ago. Roaming the earth in small family groups – leaving little evidence of their presence – and working together was the recipe for success. It was only with the emergence of writing in Mesopotamia around 3400 BCE that we have scattered historical records of human activity. We see evidence corroborating this in the texts from ancient religions and indigenous traditions of Africa, the Americas, Asia and the Pacific islands, and communities of Gauls and Celts in Europe, all of whom lived in groups and shared in the available commonwealth. For much of human history, we lived collectively with one another, communally sharing natural systems that ensured commoning relations with the natural world. This is not to say that these were easy times; there were also harsh conditions, disease, wars, feuds among groups, climate events such as droughts and floods, and various episodic disasters. Rather the point we are making is that communal groups living within natural boundaries characterised much of human existence. Even the major empires of ancient history, such as the Egyptian, Ottoman and Roman empires, the Qing Dynasty and the Abbasid Caliphate, could not eliminate the collaborative ways of living of their subjects.

Given this long history, the changes in the last few centuries are especially curious as they go against the grain of much of human history. The enlightenment's valorisation of human rationality married to industrial capitalism paved the way for human activity to alter the conditions on earth and remake social relations in fundamental ways. The enlightenment introduced new ontologies that

turned nature into a commodity to be conquered and turned possessive individualism and greed into 'innate' human characteristics
to be celebrated (discussed in Chapter 1). The mining and burning
of fossil fuels went from a driver of capitalist development to its
gravedigger. Capitalism's promotion of competition rather than
solidarity, individual ambition and reward rather than collective
and commons public goods, and the private ownership of nearly
all things has fundamentally broken with the past and actively
destroys collaborative ways of being and the commons. Today, large
swaths of humanity are alienated from one another and the natural
world. While these developments are wreaking havoc, we see rising
threats of fascism in Europe, the US, India and Russia, climate disasters from mega-floods and super storms to multi-year droughts
destroying lives, and the fraying of social bonds and solidarities.
The noise of disaster is so overwhelming; many people feel hopeless
and despair about the future. While these destructive tendencies are
engulfing much of the world, there are also countertendencies of
people coming together to (re)find modes of living and being, new
ways of relating to each other and natural relations, new approaches
to forging economies and organising socio-ecological relations that
often draw lessons from history's ancient traditions.

While the experiments are many, in this book we focus on worker
cooperatives and solidarity economy-based cooperative systems
in forging transformative politics. We show how experiences in
economic democracy can translate into transformative politics by
overcoming the institutional divisions inherent in capitalism. We
integrate the crisis of the natural commons (water, land, biodiversity, creative labour, renewable energy and earth system) and social
commons (public infrastructure and goods, cultural heritage and
knowledge) into the institutional divisions that make up capitalism's background conditions to understand the planetary polycrisis
of socio-ecological reproduction. While capitalism is annihilat-
ing its background conditions of reproduction and bringing about
the last great dispossession of the commons, transformative
socio-ecological practices are trying to prevent harm to human and
more-than-human life. Through everyday experiments in trans-

formative alternatives, we show how the planetary crisis is being addressed. How we run factories, foundries, farms, manage finance, build infrastructure, publish and organise our economies can all be done with care labour for planetary life. We show that when worker cooperatives and solidarity economy-based cooperative systems are internally democratic, articulate anti-capitalist and ethical values, pursue commoning practices and influence and change their broader environments, they begin to become transformative forces of socio-ecological reproduction. They live transformation through transformative praxis.

Together with a transformative subjectivity, transforming to self-management at the point of production and embedding the economy in socio-ecological relations, these cooperatives build emancipatory regimes of socio-ecological reproduction. Labour is not just emancipated from the capital–labour relation but is also care labour for all planetary life. Harnessing various forms of power through their cooperative practices places the cooperatives at the intersection of economic, social and political change. In other words, these transformative alternatives challenge capitalism both in the economic realm – democratising production and ownership – and in the broader conditions on which the economy rests. By achieving self-management and embedding economic activity within the wider socio-ecological relations, they articulate a transformative politics. In Fraser's framing, they engage in both *class struggle* and *boundary struggles* (Fraser and Jaeggi 2018; Fraser 2022). It is this twin challenge that makes solidarity economy-based cooperative systems and worker cooperatives anti-capitalist and potentially world making.

The book draws on research from over 368 interviews and engagements with 146 worker cooperatives and solidarity economy-based cooperative systems in 15 countries. Through extensive and rich empirical material, we show how ordinary people in varied spaces and places are pioneering novel socio-ecological relations anchored in democratically run economies. To be clear, none of these experiments are a blueprint, nor do they see themselves as such, but rather they offer a series of experimentations, becomings and attempts to re-order economic, ecological and social relations – a compass to help navigate our turbulent times – so that all on planet earth, humans and non-humans alike, can survive and thrive. In this chapter, we provide an overview of cooperatives and their role in the economy and society. We also discuss the importance of ethical values and principles and what makes them potentially transformative in practice.

MODERN COOPERATIVES: AN OVERVIEW

Working and living collectively has been part of human history from the beginning. In many ways, modern cooperatives simply took this practice of collective living to the industrial workplace when, in February 1819, English tobacco workers took over production after an 11-day strike (Lorenzo 2013, 68). The takeover of the tobacco factory demonstrated that workers in modern production could organise production themselves.[1] The idea of the modern cooperative came out of these experiences of worker control and, because of their transformative potential, became etched into the left imagination (Ness and Azzellini 2011). Whether they are seen as defensive struggles in the battle against capitalism's pernicious effects as Marx, Engels and Lenin saw them, or utopian experiments creating alternative economic and social relations as Robert Owen and the Rochdale Pioneers understood them,[2] or as prefigurative moments (working in strategic relation with the state and other organisations) that laid the basis for a future egalitarian society based on a democratic logic of social organisation as Kerala and Chavez's experiments in Venezuela envisioned,[3] cooperatives provide the potential for anti-capitalist social relations based on solidarity, reciprocity, democratic decision making and collective ownership (Engels 1953; Lenin 1966; Lorenzo 2013; Marx 1996; Satgar 2014; Thompson 1830).

Since these early experiments, worker-controlled workplaces and producer, consumer and financial cooperatives have spread across the globe, grown in size and diversity, and established themselves in key sectors in many countries (Williams 2007; Williams and

Satgar 2019). Cooperatives today occupy a plethora of places on a spectrum from transformative alternatives, as envisioned by the early cooperators, to ameliorative entities that help placate the pernicious edge of capitalism and efficient business models that focus exclusively on member benefits. The global cooperative movement tallies over one billion people in 300 million consumer, producer and financial cooperatives globally, that is, twelve per cent of the world's population (ICA 2024). In some countries, there is considerable concentration of cooperative membership. For example, in 2015, 40 per cent of the Canadian population were in at least one cooperative and in the French-speaking province of Quebec the number was as high as 70 per cent. In Malaysia, cooperatives had nearly seven million members, representing 27 per cent of the population, and in Paraguay 18 per cent of the population (783,000 people) were members of cooperatives (Kaleido Scoops 2015). Italy has one of the highest cooperative memberships in Europe with eleven million members in 70,000 cooperatives and 1.1 million workers, earning approximately seven per cent of the national GDP (Emmolo 2019, 2). Looking at membership alone, however, paints an incomplete picture.

One of the most comprehensive surveys of cooperatives is the UN Department for Economic and Social Affairs' 2014 global census of cooperatives. While there are 300 million cooperatives, with a membership base of one billion,[4] a substantial proportion of these memberships are multiple memberships (UN 2014). For example, France has 66 million people, but 147 million cooperative members, which is over double the size of the national population. Therefore, membership numbers must be viewed cautiously. Employment and other social indicators paint a fuller picture of the ameliorative (and potentially transformative) social welfare role that cooperatives play within capitalism as millions of people in the global north and south derive their livelihoods and incomes from cooperatives.

In 2021, cooperatives provided jobs or work opportunities to 280 million people across the globe, which is 10 per cent of the world's wage-earning population (ICA 2024). This is an increase from the 2014 figures where 2.5 million cooperatives employed 250 million people (including 10.8 million worker members and 223.7 million producer members and their employees) (UN 2014, 1-2). In G20 countries, 234 million people (that is, 11.65 per cent of the total population) gained their livelihoods from cooperatives in 2014 (Roelants, Hyungsik and Terrasi 2014, 30). China registered the highest number with 21 per cent of the population working in cooperatives followed by approximately ten per cent of the populations in South Korea, Italy, India and Turkey. Europe registers 7.6 per cent of the working population in cooperatives whereas in the UK and US only 1.3 per cent of their working populations are in cooperatives (Roelants, Hyungsik and Terrasi 2014, 30-31). To further illustrate the role of cooperatives in livelihoods in various countries, in France 21,000 cooperatives provide over one million jobs to 3.5 per cent of the working population, while in Colombia cooperatives provide 3.65 per cent of all jobs in the country (137,888 through employment and 559,118 as worker–owners) and in Kenya 63 per cent of the population gain most of their incomes from cooperatives.

While the employment numbers begin to give a fuller picture of the role cooperatives play, the UN's Cooperative Economy Index further nuances this picture by looking at the 'most cooperative economies in the world' and measuring three different categories in relation to a country's population and GDP to provide a more textured picture. The ratio looks at membership penetration and employment by cooperatives relative to the population, and annual turnover of cooperatives relative to the GDP of the country. The index shows that 'two-thirds of the countries listed in the top ten most cooperative economies also make up eight of the top twelve spots on the Social Progress Index (SPI). The SPI has 54 measures and includes items like basic human needs, opportunity and access to knowledge' (UN 2014, 3-4).[5] The SPI was developed by the Social Progress Imperative to measure social indicators for a sense of the social well-being of countries. What their numbers show is that there is a high level of correlation between cooperative economies and social progress (UN 2014). Thus, even ameliorative cooperatives working within capitalism provide social inclusion to millions of people and have positive knock-on effects in their societies that could lay the basis for more transformative change.

While we recognise the significant role cooperatives play in ameliorating capitalism, for our purposes we home our attention on worker cooperatives and solidarity economy-based cooperative systems with explicitly transformative agendas. We chose those that consciously identified as anti-capitalist and that harbour transformative visions and practices. The fact that these cooperatives operate within capitalism does not mean that they are capitalist-oriented enterprises but rather reflects the fact that they must operate within the prevailing economic conditions of our times. Our discussion regarding cooperatives operating in and through the interstitial spaces of capitalism to erode, tame and exit capitalism is instructive here. Operating within the global capitalist system does not preclude the cooperatives from pursuing anti-capitalist generative practices. Rather, what is important is whether the cooperative sees itself as an efficient business model within capitalism or a more radical form of economic activity grounded in transformative aspirations and praxis. Before we discuss the transformative possibility of cooperatives, we briefly discuss cooperatives that see themselves as efficient business models within capitalism. This discussion highlights that operating within capitalism perhaps places limits on cooperatives, but it does not determine where the cooperative lies on the continuum. Rather, cooperatives are fundamentally shaped by their vision, principles, goals and practices that are either transformative or capitalist oriented.

Cooperatives as an Efficient Business Model

The fact that cooperatives lie on a continuum from efficient business models to ameliorative entities and more transformative alternatives has led to various fault lines among the global left. One of the debates coursing through the global cooperative movement is whether cooperatives represent an anti-capitalist alternative or an efficient business model within capitalism (Satgar and Williams 2011a).[6] The reason the debate has such traction is twofold: (1) cooperatives represent both strands and (2) even those that are anti-capitalist still exist within capitalism (Etxagibel, Cheney and Udaondo 2012). There are two primary clusters of views on the core vision and mandate of cooperatives. The first sees cooperatives as an efficient business model within capitalism. The other maintains that cooperatives are based on alternative values, principles and vision that challenge capitalism even if they must operate within capitalism in order to survive. Cooperatives as efficient businesses limit their vision to representing member needs and, at most, soften the negative social effects of market economies in which states have retreated from their social welfare role. The social economy idea captures this role such that cooperatives try to make capitalism more inclusive and less pernicious, and they try to make the most profit for their members.[7] This contrasts with cooperatives holding a transformative vision that seeks to change the fundamental relations of power in a given economy, society and natural relations (Ranis 2016). In short, one seeks limited social inclusion and business success, and the other social, economic and ecological transformation. It is useful to think of them as located at the opposite ends of a continuum, with the one end representing working within capitalism and the other working to transcend it.

One of the best examples of the business model is the mainstream German cooperative movement headed by the Deutscher Genossenschafts Raiffeisen Verband (DGRV) which has 18 million members[8] and is strongest in the banking and agricultural sectors.[9] The DGRV cooperatives do not see themselves as social enterprises with an alternative vision or mandate, but rather as an efficient organisational form representing their members' interests in the competitive and globalised market economy. For the DGRV, democratic decision making is not a value in its own right but rather increases efficiency and allows the cooperatives to compete more effectively in the global economy. The primary role of the DGRV is to represent members' interests by assisting members with access to markets. It is clear that it is not attempting to create an alternative system or challenge capitalism. For example, the DGRV argues against any special status or particular assistance from government, which goes against the majority of cooperatives in Europe who lobby the European Union (EU) for special recognition for cooperatives. It is not against lobbying for farmers, only against special status for cooperatives as it maintains that as a business model they do not require special recognition. Indeed, it is one of the most powerful lobby groups for agricultural subsidies, including for green technologies, for its farmers. Its position on farmer subsidies is driven by its commitment to its members even though subsidies undermine farmers in the global south. Its approach to solidarity takes the form of supporting cooperative development in various countries in the global south, but it has little commitment to social justice that extends beyond its members. For the DGRV, its social contribution comes through taxes (its members pay billions of euros annually). For our purposes, cooperatives such as the DGRV are not transformative and lie at the opposite end of the continuum as they are driven by narrow member interests of profits.

A good example of ameliorative cooperatives is the USA's 82-year-old National Rural Electric Cooperative Association (NRECA), which provides electricity to 56 per cent of the US electric landscape across 48 states, including 42 million people.[10] Electricity cooperatives began in 1942 to provide electrification to rural America; utility companies were not interested in rural areas as they were not profitable. What is interesting about NRECA is that the majority of their regions are counties with persistent poverty and one in four of their households are low income with a household annual income below US$35,000. In total, they provide power to 22 million businesses, homes (53 per cent of their electricity services households), schools and farms through 832 distribution cooperatives and 64 generation and transmission cooperatives. Because electric cooperatives belong to the communities they serve and are therefore locally rooted, they are very attuned to the importance of keeping electricity affordable but at the same time meeting member expectations to reduce emissions. In this regard, NRECA reduced its reliance on coal from 41 per cent in 2016 to 30 per cent in 2022, increased its use of natural gas from 26 per cent to 32 per cent and renewable energy (mostly wind and solar) from 17 per cent to 22 per cent while nuclear remained constant at 15 per cent in the same period. Electricity cooperatives have increased their renewable capacity from 8.2 gigawatts to nearly 15.8 gigawatts and in 2023, they added 1.3 gigawatts renewable capacity with their wind and solar farms producing enough energy to service 3.5 million homes. In total, it reduced sulphur dioxide emissions by 83 per cent, nitrogen oxide emissions by 68 per cent and carbon dioxide emissions by 14 per cent between 2005 and 2022. Clearly the electricity cooperatives play an ameliorative role in providing electricity to regions that were historically excluded as well as in adopting renewable energy transitions.

These approaches to cooperatives are implicitly supported by the International Cooperative Alliance's (ICA) global 300 ranking, which measures cooperatives' contribution to capitalist economies. According to their World Cooperative Monitor 2023 Report (ICA and EURICSE 2023, 13–16), cooperatives increasingly play a vital role in the global economy with the world's 300 largest cooperatives collective annual turnover registering at US$2,409.41 billion (for 2021), including 105 agricultural cooperatives, 96 insurance cooperatives and 57 wholesale and retail cooperatives (ICA and EURICSE 2023). The majority in the top 300 are producer cooperatives (130 in total) from the agriculture and retail sectors, followed by 80 mutuals and 72 consumer cooperatives. Only five worker cooperatives made it into the top 300 ranking based on their economic activity. These metrics also show geographical concentration. Of the top 300 by turnover, 275 are located in the global north with 166 in Europe, 80 in the USA and Canada, 21 in Japan, five in New Zealand and three in Australia. The leading cooperatives with annual turnovers of over US$49 billion are all in the global north (France, Japan, Germany and South Korea).

While these figures are impressive, they only speak to the role of economically large cooperatives in the global capitalist economy. The focus on quantitative indicators of turnover, revenue and number of members and jobs elides the actual practices, values and characteristics of the cooperatives.

COOPERATIVES AS TRANSFORMATIVE ALTERNATIVES

Focusing on worker cooperatives and solidarity economy-based cooperative systems homes our attention to the central role of refashioning the ways in which we produce, consume and exchange goods and services in building emancipatory alternatives. After a few centuries of capitalism, and four decades of neoliberal capitalism, our relations to nearly all spheres of life are mediated through the market. Economic activity with profit-maximising accumulation and possessive individualism are the centrifugal forces driving the system (Brown 2015).

By contrast, worker cooperatives reconfigure the point of production and refashion the socio-ecological relations of economic activity. Because they are owned and managed by the workers, they change the way workers relate to one another, the production process and the goods and services they produce, as well as the economy's relationship to socio-ecological conditions. Rather than workers, society and nature being at the service of economic activity, they re-embed economic activity to serve social, ecological and economic needs of the workers, communities, ecosystems and society, recognising the importance of working within natural boundaries. This upends the constitutive divisions of capitalism, which promotes the separation of economic activity from social reproduction, the separation of humans from the natural world, the separation of economics from politics and competitive relations based on territorial expansion and appropriation (Fraser and Jaeggi 2018). Worker cooperatives and solidarity economy-based cooperative systems, thus, play an important part in a larger process of interdependent transformations, including economic democracy (for example, cooperatives), promoting social justice and human well-being, working within ecological boundaries and ecological interconnections, developing deep forms of democracy (institutional, processual, rights, direct/indirect), valuing varied knowledges (experiential, tacit and emancipatory), and harnessing solidaristic inter- and intra-national relations.[11] Through embedding economic activity, worker cooperatives and solidarity economy-based cooperative systems begin to develop new ways of operating that promote these transformations. How do they do this?

Worker Cooperatives: Transformative Possibility

At their core, worker cooperatives are guided by ethical principles of solidarity, justice, ecological sensitivity and democracy. Worker cooperatives democratise economic activity at the factory, farm, community or enterprise by engaging in democratic decision making within the cooperative from the labour process to big strategic decisions. The most basic characteristic of a worker cooperative is the transformation of work at the point of production. Worker cooperatives have historically been defined by a few key features: (1) meet member needs; (2) direct democracy at the workplace in which worker–owners democratically make decisions based on one member one vote; (3) workers collectively own the means of production, whether a factory, farm, bakery or any other type of enterprise[12]; and (4) workers collectively decide how surplus is distributed and how losses are managed. In addition to these basic features, worker cooperatives align with the International Cooperative Alliance's seven guiding principles: voluntary and open membership, democratic member control, member economic participation, autonomy and independence from outside influence, continuous education, training and information for members, cooperation among cooperatives, and concern for their communities (ICA 1996).

The *sine qua non* for cooperatives seeking anti-capitalist transformative alternatives is deliberative and democratic decision making and collective self-management and ownership. Yet, democracy can mean many things to different social forces. The degree to which democratic decision making is internalised in an organisation and the quality of the democratic processes has profound bearing on the quality of the democracy. Drawing on Pateman's (1970) distinction between different degrees of participation (pseudo, partial and real), we argue that meaningful participation requires that members have the capacity to deliberate over a range of decisions, regular access to information and transparent leadership. They must also have the power to make decisions that are then implemented (Etxagibel, Cheney and Udaondo 2012, 86). This focus on meaningful participation does not negate the necessity for delegation of some decision making for practical functioning of a cooperative. For some cooperatives, horizontal decision making that involves all members happens daily, while for other cooperatives horizontal decision making that involves all members on a daily basis is impossible given their size or geographical spread, which leads them to opt for more decentralised or delegated systems of decision making. The point is that decisions are made by workers themselves, which relates to how self-management is institutionalised.

Self-management has grown out of two centuries of history in advancing worker control (Bayat 1991). We see this from early attempts of workers taking over failing factories in the nineteenth century to the Russian Revolution and various attempts by workers to shape social democracy from below, and even in the global south in the context of anti-colonial and socialist struggles. Many of these attempts were short lived in the twentieth century as state-centric and de-democratising rationalities came to the fore in socialist imaginaries. Moreover, while the theoretical understanding of self-management placed workers at the forefront of building a new socialist society from below, it was very productivist and did not appreciate care labour.[13] Workers would take over enterprises, ownership and control, and merely ensure the labour process affirmed worker-controlled work and even subordinated the role of technology in the division of labour (Bayat 1991, 177–203). In current cycles of resistance, self-management has been recast while recognising emancipated work and working conditions is crucial, based on worker–owner self-determination. In the twenty-first century this is referred to as *autogestion* for a 'new cooperativism' and the 'labour commons' (Vieta 2016). However, self-management has to have an ecological basis. In other words, self-management has to also be about the commons and, ultimately, the web of life (Caffentzis 2016; Kioupkkiolis and Karyotis 2015; Collier and Quaratiello 2005). This means self-management has to incorporate commoning time, creative labour, finance, collective capacity (knowledge, power and culture) and natural relations (water, land, biodiversity, renewable energy and earth system relations). In this book, we take this further to highlight how self-management is also about care labour for worker–owners and their wider socio-ecological relations, in other words, self-management for planetary care.

Determining the conditions of work through collective deliberation about production, distribution, sharing of profits and losses fundamentally transforms a worker's role from a powerless employee in a capitalist company to an empowered worker–owner in a collaborative and self-managed enterprise (Satgar and Williams 2011a). Thus, the transformative potential of worker cooperatives is embedded in the democratic processes and self-managed worker control of production, distribution and consumption but, ultimately, in commons relations. They place care labour at the centre of the enterprise, rather than in the service of it, and this transforms the boundary between production and socio-ecological reproduction. It is the transformation at the point of production that makes worker cooperatives potentially prefigurative anti-capitalist institutions as worker cooperatives embed economic activity in socio-ecological relations. Class and transformative struggle for worker cooperatives is in part waged through building social and economic power among worker–owners.

The cooperatives we researched move beyond the enterprise level to build new socio-ecological relations. To do this, they integrate socio-ecological relations in the production process through prioritising worker needs and human well-being, connecting with and embedding themselves in local communities and working within the boundaries of the natural commons.

To illustrate, the Cheese Board Collective in Berkeley, California is an excellent example of these defining characteristics of a worker cooperative.[14] The Cheese Board sells an impressive range of cheeses (local and international), freshly baked breads and pastries, locally roasted coffee and a daily gourmet pizza. It is a beloved institution in the community with a vibrant atmosphere in the cheese shop of regulars and newcomers alike, and long queues of eager patrons waiting for pizza (local jazz musicians play in the pizza shop, which adds to the atmosphere). Formed in 1971 amid the vibrancy of the political movements of the 1960s and 1970s, the Cheese Board Collective imbibes human-centred values reflected in its internal relationships as well as its engagement with the local community. In an era in which young people were experimenting with democratic forms of organising life, the Cheese Board Collective formed as a worker-owned collective that prioritised the interconnections among themselves, a shared ethics of care-based work, solidarity with other cooperatives and commitment to high standards in the service of their community. Through deliberation and debate, decisions – including decisions about the labour process, products sold, pricing, benefits, and remuneration – are made collectively in a myriad of meetings that happen daily, monthly and annually. In addition, it is committed to building a broader network of cooperatives by providing training and sharing experiences with other cooperatives in the area on a weekly basis. For over 50 years, the Cheese Board has not lost its commitment to democratic decision making, which the worker–owners maintain has allowed them to invest in themselves and the collective while providing customers with excellent service. It is an excellent example of a worker-owned and worker-managed enterprise but also it has nurtured relations with and rooted itself in the local community and among other cooperatives in the area.

The uniqueness of worker cooperatives comes into sharp relief when we compare them to consumer cooperatives where members are consumers of goods and services, and reward incentives are through their consumption activities. Consumer members do not work in the organisation and the decisions they make do not affect their own role in the production process or the labour process in general. Unlike a worker cooperative that democratises the labour process, a consumer cooperative focuses decisions on procurement and consumption. For example, REI sporting goods – a US-based national cooperative selling high-quality outdoor equipment and clothing – has millions of consumer members who can participate in the annual general meeting and who receive annual dividends in the form of store credits based on the amount of money spent in the year. The employees of REI are not worker–owners, but rather members based on their consumption. While consumer cooperatives provide benefits to their consumer members, they are not transformative in the way that worker-owned cooperatives are when they democratise social relations at the point of production. Some consumer cooperatives might do this as well, but it is not inherent to their structure as it is for worker cooperatives.

There are variations on this model with some more radical consumer cooperatives such as the Park Slope Food Coop in Brooklyn, New York, which requires all members to volunteer a certain number of hours a month in order to maintain membership. Park Slope Food Coop only sells to cooperative members and all members of a household must belong to the cooperative. In this way Park Slope Food Coop has tried to ensure a greater degree of member involvement than most consumer cooperatives. Other consumer cooperatives, such as the Community Food Cooperative in Bozeman, Montana, have a long history of rootedness in the local community that blends social justice and economic success with local procurement and local consumption. For the Community Food Cooperative, members are consumers, but a high level of rootedness has ensured that members remain active in the larger emancipatory vision of the cooperative. Similarly, Williamson (Willy) Street Grocery Cooperative in Madison, Wisconsin is a consumer cooperative that prioritises the needs of the local community through local, organic, natural, sustainable, humane and fairly traded products. The rootedness of Willy Street Cooperative has helped maintain its values of economic, social and environmental justice with employee interests integral to the cooperative's values. Rainbow Grocery Cooperative in San Francisco is one of the few grocery store cooperatives that we know of that is a worker cooperative where the members are the workers, not the consumers.[15] Interestingly, all four cooperatives started in the 1970s, are deeply rooted in their local communities, procure local foods, promote healthy food choices, maintain values of economic, social and environmental justice and each of the various models is enormously successful without losing its commitments to emancipatory workplaces, social justice and environmental concerns.[16]

While consumer cooperatives are potentially an important part of a transformative politics (especially like the grocery stores above that are consciously rooted in transformative alternative practices), in this book we primarily focus on worker cooperatives as they challenge capitalism through ownership and democratic decision making, break down capitalist boundaries with social reproduction, nature, public power, and interenterprise and international solidarity relations and, thus, provide counterhegemonic prefigurative examples. In the next section, we explore the importance of the values, principles, origins and wider environment in understanding cooperatives.

Origin Stories, Values, and Principles Shape the Cooperative

To unravel the different trajectories of cooperatives from business models to transformative alternatives, we found that the origins of the cooperative play an important role in defining its trajectory. Modern cooperatives primarily emerge through two pathways: (1) cooperatives 'invent' themselves through member-initiated bottom-up processes; and (2) cooperatives are 'invited' to form through government initiated top-down processes (Isaac and Williams 2017). These two different approaches to the formation of the cooperative have far-reaching implications in terms of characteristics and the broader conditions under which cooperatives operate. The founding moment also shapes the vision and principles of the cooperative.

Member-initiated cooperatives often emerge through defensive struggles against capitalism's pernicious effects (for example, poverty, joblessness, precarity), such as in Brazil, Argentina and Mondragón and in attempts to create egalitarian societies in many UK and US worker cooperatives and communes worldwide[17] (Altuna Gabilondo, Loyola Idiakez and Pagalday Tricio 2013; Azkarraga et al. 2012; Esteves 2014; Owen 1991, 1993; Restakis 2010; Ruggeri 2013; Webster et al. 2011). People coming together to form cooperatives encodes the cooperatives with principles and values but also shapes the individuals who participate in them. Forming a cooperative requires a great deal of commitment and sacrifice from the founding members, often involving fierce struggles with the private sector, government institutions and the generally hostile market environment. The practices that individuals and the collective glean from the process of formation leave an indelible mark on the cooperative for many years to come. We saw this in many of the worker cooperatives we studied. For example, in the Mondragón cooperatives and ULCCS, we regularly heard stories harking back to their founding years and the importance of the values that come out of that period (Azkarraga et al. 2012, 83–84; Isaac and Williams 2017). Their founding stories are intensely etched into their identity, and they instil a strong sense of purpose among members, serving as a benchmark against which members evaluate their practices and decisions. We also found that the process of struggle and the conscious articulation of transformative alternatives translated into deeply rooted democratic practices within the cooperatives and among the members. Member-initiated cooperatives instil a deep sense of their cooperative identity, enduring member commitment and experience in practising democracy, collective deliberation and self-management. The cooperatives we studied were member-initiated cooperatives.

Linked to the founding period is a strong sense of values and principles that originate from members dreaming about a different world and having the courage to start a cooperative. Indeed, emancipatory experiments require a form of utopian social dreaming that valorises the use value of all things and sutures together the necessary elements for human and nature's well-being. In Chapters 1 and 2, we discuss the ontology required for such transformative practices. Collectively imagining emancipatory ways of existing at the frontlines of the everyday is even more relevant today as we navigate the systemic polycrisis. In other words, envisioning a world based on different principles, values, ideas and practices is essential for cooperatives. While the ICA's seven guiding principles are important, they are not enough.

Transformative alternatives also require values that are anti-capitalist and that promote human solidarity, planetary care, people over profits, community well-being and the embedding of economic activity in communities. These principles ultimately embed economic activity within socio-ecological relations and democratise power relations within economic enterprises. They harbour the possibility of dismantling the boundary between economic activity and socio-ecological relations. The principles also promote cooperation and solidarity among enterprises, rather than competition. Thus, cooperatives change economic activity within the enterprises as well as potentially beyond the enterprises. Having a strong anti-capitalist vision dreams a society beyond capitalism. While the vision is not reflected in reality, as all the cooperatives have to work under the conditions of capitalism, it is important in guiding their long-term goals and practices. It provides a bedrock on which cooperatives can anchor their activities that work against the grain of capitalist relations.

To move beyond the cooperative enterprise and build solidarity relationships requires building institutional spaces. For example, the US Federation of Worker Cooperatives (USFWC) has built an impressive support infrastructure that has helped turn worker cooperatives and regional worker cooperative associations into a powerful movement.[18] Started in 2004 to create a national sector-specific membership-based organisation to help 'build a thriving ecosystem for worker-owned and controlled businesses and their cooperative leaders to power movements for racial justice and economic democracy'.[19] By 2024, the federation included over 400 organisational members and represents over 1,000 worker cooperatives with 10,000 worker–owners across the US. The federation provides a range of support from consulting and technical advice to facilitating inter-cooperative relations and advocacy work. Realising they need a dedicated entity for research, education, training, and organising work, they created the Democracy at Work Institute, which was first an educational project and eventually scaled up to become an independent entity in 2013. Through 'research, education and relationship-building' the Democracy at Work

Institute focuses on marginalised communities and developing worker cooperatives across the country. The Institute sees itself as a donor funded 'movement-based think-and-do tank' that keeps worker cooperatives on the cutting edge of transformation. Building such organisations is vital for cooperatives and the possibilities of transformative change. All the cooperatives we studied were member initiated and had strongly engrained anti-capitalist values and principles that continue to influence the cooperatives.

By contrast, state-initiated cooperatives are often formed to help the state meet people's needs (and quell potential resistance to the state). While there are a few examples of state-initiated cooperative movements that seek to create alternatives to capitalism, for example, Kerala's initiatives around women's groups or Venezuela under Chavez (Azzellini 2013; Pineiro Harnecker 2013a, 2013b; Williams 2020, 2017), the majority of examples of state-initiated cooperatives are seen as stepping stones into capitalist entrepreneurial activities (for example, South Africa; Satgar and Williams 2011a) or arms of the state to be controlled (for example, Tanzania). In both cases, the state forms cooperatives to address social and economic needs, but ultimately treats cooperatives as means to an end (such as reducing poverty, providing jobs, delivering services) rather than ends in themselves (such as a democratic economic space and transform-ative alternative). Thus, cooperatives are instrumentalised to meet government targets. For example, in post-apartheid South Africa, the number of cooperatives jumped from 1,300 in 1994 to 31,898 in 2010 and 48,000 in 2016 as a result of massive state support for starting up cooperatives. Wanting to show quantitative growth, government support emphasised legal registration and fast-track incubation through financial incentives, which did not result in genuine empowerment based on cooperative principles and values. Rather, government support resulted in cooperatives becoming steppingstones to small and medium-sized capitalist businesses for poor people and skills development for entry into capitalist firms (Satgar and Williams 2011a, 2011c). The emphasis on numbers hid the fact that many of the cooperatives did not function according to cooperative principles and that a significant number only existed on paper with an 88 per cent failure rate (DTI 2009). The top-down and heavy-handed manner in which the post-apartheid state financially invested in cooperatives led to perversities, such as a lack of a racially integrated cooperative movement, and created patronage networks with the state (Williams 2013).

This approach is buttressed by global institutions such as the World Bank and International Labour Organization (ILO), which promote business-oriented cooperatives and the 'social economy'. In addition, states often control cooperatives through financial incentives, government 'support' systems and legislative frameworks. For example, state-initiated cooperative members are seen as beneficiaries', often selected by the state (either government officials or political representatives) with the criteria for selection tied to the state's goals of delivery and development rather than community-initiated goals. As a result, many state-initiated cooperatives do not see the same level of commitment from members, especially in hard times, and do not have the same legitimacy among communities.

This is not to say that states do not have an important role to play in facilitating cooperative development, especially given the fiercely competitive market conditions of the globalised economy. Rather, the type of support cooperatives need is for states to provide enabling conditions, access to alternative markets and favourable access to state tenders for public works and finance. The democratic state is not just a site of conflicting class interests but is also an 'indispensable institution to orchestrate social diversity and the harmonize [sic] common good' (Arruda 2008, 4). The democratic state has a crucial role to play. Many states, however, limit their role to regulating, controlling and instrumentalising cooperatives. Even when states try to provide conducive support, there is always the risk of dependencies that require long-term horizons, which is antithetical to the vicissitudes of politics and short-term planning horizons of most states.

For example, in the early 2000s, the Venezuelan state spent a great deal of energy and resources in trying to roll out massive cooperative programmes as part of its socialist strategy. Consequently, a large number of cooperatives popped-up through massive state programmes that created the space, training, finance and work contracts for cooperatives (Pineiro Harnecker 2012). With generous state support many cooperatives survived, but the degree to which deliberative participation and democratic decision making was maintained varies as well as the depth to which members imbibe the alternative principles. This was already visible in 2008 when we spent time with them. For a number of cooperatives, the record is mixed with many cooperatives struggling to survive without non-competitive state contracts. Despite these challenges, some cooperatives took root and demonstrated their commitment to creating socialist alternatives to capitalism through self-managed production, but many more have ceased to exist.[20]

While there are a few positive experiences of state-initiated cooperatives, in the main the state tends to use cooperatives for its own goals. The experience in Tanzania is illustrative of the controlling approach of the state, even a postcolonial socialist state. In Tanzania, cooperatives originally emerged as a response to colonial control of the local economy and were deeply rooted in local communities.[21] By the time of independence in the 1960s, Tanzanian cooperatives accounted for 82 per cent of total exports, most of which came from agriculture such as cashew, cotton, coffee and tobacco. Approximately 25 per cent of the total population (that is, over ten million people) were involved in cooperatives. The only other country in which cooperatives accounted for larger percentages of exports was Denmark. In the 1970s, the newly independent government adopted policies that controlled cooperatives and decreed compulsory membership, which led to a severe decline in the performance and vibrancy of cooperatives. Through patronage, the state used cooperatives to control communities, which eventually delinked cooperatives from their communities and devastated production. For example, coffee production dropped from 70,000 tonnes a year in the early 1970s to 15,000 tonnes a year in the 1980s and nut production dropped from 190,000 tonnes a year to 30,000 tonnes a year in the same period. In the 1980s, the government reversed its policy of state control and decreed a return to independent cooperatives (Williams 2013). While cooperatives recovered to a degree and production increased, the organic people-driven process of cooperative development did not re-emerge and the cooperative movement is a shadow of its former self with only one million people involved in cooperatives (2007 numbers). This is a 90 per cent decline from the late 1960s.

As these examples attest, the state has often played a controlling and opportunistic role in supporting cooperatives, yet it continues to be an important site of power and therefore must be taken seriously. As we see below, cooperatives engaging the state from positions of strength and autonomy begin to engender a transformative politics. In the next section, we unpack transformative practices for cooperatives.

Transformative Practices

Cooperatives are unique economic enterprises in the way they internally organise, make democratic decisions, decide on surplus and losses, improve the conditions for their members and collectively own the means of production. Truly embracing these practices is already a huge achievement for cooperatives as it requires going against the grain of capitalist business practices. While these internal characteristics are necessary and essential criteria for transformative alternatives, they remain internally oriented within the cooperative. For our purposes, we also looked at practices that went beyond the internal dynamics of the cooperative, especially those that sought to construct new socio-ecological ways of living. Unlike a politics of protest 'that aims to challenge or destroy an existing system of political and/or economic power', transformative politics innovates new forms of economic activity embedded in socio-ecological and democratic politics (Williams 2008, 9). In contrast to protest politics, transformative politics does not primarily focus on claims against the state, but rather seeks to engender new ways of living, producing and consuming that transform economic activity, socio-ecological relations and political power. Moving beyond the classical Marxist focus on state ownership as the negation of capitalism, embedding economic activity and ownership within communities and worker–owners – that is, socialising ownership – and democratising political power are vital elements of transformative politics (Wright 2006;

Wright and Burawoy 2004). Thus, cooperatives form an important part of a larger transformative politics that includes cooperative networks, social movements, community initiatives, trade unions, food sovereignty movements and progressive NGOs; they are part of forces of socio-ecological reproduction, as developed in Chapters 1 and 2. For transformative alternatives to thrive, structural conditions that allow for such changes are required. The polycrisis creates the conditions and opportunities for transformative alternatives as capitalist hegemony loses its grip on states and people (discussed in Chapter 2). Cooperatives play a potentially important role in transformative politics as they determine the nature of economic activity and can influence local politics and state policies. But how do they do this?

For our purposes, we sought cooperatives that try to develop transformative practices beyond the cooperative. As minimum criteria, transformative practices require democratic internal practices and values and principles that seek transformation beyond capitalism, as discussed above. To become transformative alternatives, however, they must also try to have a transformative effect on society more generally. Cooperatives that seek the transformation of social relations extend their practices to engage the background conditions on which economic activity depends: social reproduction and care, nature and ecological reproduction, politics and state power, relations to other movements and cooperatives, and international solidarities. Doing this requires nurturing practices that share knowledge with others, develop socio-ecological reproduction that targets cooperative members and the wider community, support other cooperatives, progressive entities and movements even in faraway places, and enhance local democratic government.

We thus look at the ways in which worker cooperatives have redrawn boundaries between the economy and social reproduction, the natural world, public power and the state, and engendered solidarities beyond the enterprise. First, worker cooperatives recognise the central life-constituting role of social reproduction and place economic activity within social reproduction rather than in command of it. We show how cooperatives have put this into practice by ensuring that human needs lie at the centre of economic activity (Chapter 4). Second, we look at the ways in which worker cooperatives relate to the natural world. Capitalism's approach to nature is one of domination and devaluation, and only sees its value in terms of economic metrics. We show how worker cooperatives find non-destructive ways of relating to nature, value its contribution to economic relations and see the importance of operating within the natural boundaries of the planet, ultimately promoting planetary care from below (Chapter 5). Third, we show the way in which solidarity economy-based cooperative systems and worker cooperatives operate on fundamentally different relationality from capitalism in relation to democracy, public power and the state, and the relations beyond the enterprise. To remake the way in which the economy operates and relates to public power and the state requires new principles, values, ideas and practices. We look at the ways in which worker cooperatives internalise democratic decision making and collective ownership into their quintessence, as well as redraw boundaries between the economy and the state and inter- and intra-national and interenterprise expansion (Chapter 6). In short, we look at how worker cooperatives as commoning institutions common time, creative labour, natural relations, collective capacity and finance to reproduce life in the everyday. They are producing a transformed and emancipatory regime of socio-ecological reproduction, distinct from capitalism. They are building emancipatory futures in the present from which we can all learn to confront the planetary polycrisis before it is too late.

Over the last few decades many worker cooperatives have developed (re)new ethos and wider practices beyond the 'shopfloor' to include communities and other solidaristic enterprises based on shared principles and values. All the solidarity economy-based cooperative systems, worker cooperatives and recovered factories we visited practise democratic decision making and collective ownership, they meet member needs and collectively decide on how profits and losses are shared, and many we visited took their efforts beyond the factory walls to pioneer linkages with other democratic entities. Building solidaristic relations with other enterprises, communities and social movements (not just cooperative movements) lays the basis for alternative economies to develop, which the cooperatives call solidarity economies.[22] Solidarity economy networks emerge when cooperatives actively seek to work with other cooperatives and democratic enterprises. For example, when cooperative grocery stores consciously procure from local and/or cooperatively owned farms and enterprises with similar values of social, economic and environmental justice, they are building solidarity economy linkages. By consciously procuring from other entities with shared values, they take an ethics of cooperation and solidarity with external actors into their production and market relations. These principles take worker cooperatives beyond their individual enterprises to create flows of mutuality, solidarity and economic exchanges with other cooperatives and democratic entities. In linking up with communities and social movements, they also take on broader issues such as environmental, social and developmental concerns, as well as the inclusion of socially excluded groups, such as migrant people and differently abled persons.

When cooperatives cascade their relationships into solidarity relations with other economic enterprises, this starts to form the basis of a solidarity economy. Underpinning the solidarity economy are shared principles of collective ownership, democratic self-management, redistribution, solidarity, reciprocity and worker and popular control of the means of production, consumption and distribution. Unlike capitalist economic relations, the solidarity economy is anchored in human-centred values, such as people over profits, solidarity over individualism and cooperation over competition. It tries to build an ethos of reciprocity, redistribution and engaged citizenship (Arruda 2006 in Esteves undated, 4–5). Solidarity economy cooperatives, for example, combine collective ownership and democratic production processes with principles of solidarity with other cooperatives and progressive entities, including international solidarity (De Sousa Santos 2006; Restakis 2010; Satgar 2014, 2019; Williams 2014). There is no set model of how this happens, but there are innovative experiments and variations rooted in local conditions.

Solidarity economies are also about the social and natural commons. This means their economics, based on care labour, is very different from an extractive, exploitative, wasteful and destructive capitalist economy. In many ways solidarity economies are post-growth and work within social and natural limits, given rationalities of commoning, self-management and care labour. Bauwens et al. (2025, 145–160) summarise the principles of commons and commoning relevant to a solidarity economy as part of the commons pattern: (i) commons economics is biophysical and recognises earth's limits; (ii) commons economics is abundance design or engineering that recognises natural abundance and favours renewability; (iii) commons economics is contributory based on what someone gives to the commons rather than what they take; (iv) commons economics recognises the commons as a central human institution; (v) commons economics is based on open collaborative systems rather than competition; (vi) commons economics requires a direct focus on the common good to benefit the 'whole system'; (vii) commons economics has a steady state temporality beyond cycles of collapse; and (viii) commons economics is relational based on communal shareholding.

Solidarity economy-based cooperative systems recognise the hegemonic role capitalism plays in intertwining our interests within capitalism through consumerism, valorising possessive individualism and competitive notions of success, promoting meritocratic educational systems that value high-paying job prospects over socially important and meaningful careers, encouraging wasteful consumption habits and creating debt-driven financial systems that incorporate homes (for example, home mortgages/bonds) and pensions, transport (for example, private cars) and living expenses (including food, clothing and other essential goods). Through integrating our interests into capitalism, it is difficult to envision a world beyond capitalism. Therefore, cooperatives and the solidarity economy understand the importance of creating alternative financial systems, leisure activities and cultural spaces, educating people in civic education, promoting and popularising 'emancipatory utopias' that practice alternatives, and empowering individuals to participate in economic decision making. It seeks to develop networks of solidarity economy enterprises that trade with one another, engage in collective action and promote anti-capitalist visions (COPAC 2010). These are aspirational norms lying at the core of the solidarity economy. While many of these are aspirational, in our fieldwork, we found many cooperatives that were deep in the process of developing solidarity economy practices.

For example, the four US-based cooperative grocery stores discussed above – Park Slope Foods in Brooklyn, Community Food Cooperative in Bozeman, Willy Street Cooperative in Madison and Rainbow Grocery in San Francisco – are not just cooperatives concerned about their members. Rather, all have consciously sought solidarity economy linkages through procurement practices, membership and solidarity with other cooperatives. They procure from cooperatively owned farms and businesses as well as local businesses with similar values of social, economic and environmental justice. They educate members about healthy food and options for better living. They use their rootedness to transform their local communities through emancipatory values of justice, fairness, tolerance and dignity. These cooperative stores appreciate that in order to change the way in which we produce, consume and distribute, we must also collectively create new ways of being and habits, new ways of organising production, new ways of engaging in economic activity and new ways of relating to one another and to the economy through solidarity among members of individual enterprises, among enterprises and initiatives and between them and the community.

Solidarity economy enterprises promote economic linkages and market relations across enterprises that are socially embedded and operate on the principle of human and ecological well-being. While there is a degree of coherence in the vision and practices that reflect a commons ontology, the solidarity economy is not a unified blueprint for an alternative society but rather a series of ongoing prefigurative economic experiments that are continuously (re)making socio-ecological relations based on democratic practices, local bottom-up processes, redistribution, solidarity, interconnections and reciprocity. Unlike the ameliorative efforts of philanthropy and social welfare, the solidarity economy promotes transformative practices that move beyond capitalism – it seeks to erode the power of capitalism and even find exits. In short, the solidarity economy is prefiguratively anti-capitalist and transformative in its creation of alternatives that place people at the centre of economic relations and social reproduction at the centre of the commons and commoning. Unlike social democracy's attempts to harness the economy through capital controls, taxation and redistribution (that is, taming capitalism by regulating the profits of economic activity), the solidarity economy focuses on economic activity itself (that is, production, consumption and distribution). By democratising economic activity, the solidarity economy seeks to embed economic activity in socio-ecological relations of reproduction. A transformative cooperative will be against the oppressions in society, exploitation of humans and nature; it will understand our dependence on natural relations, the importance of care labour and ultimately planetary care. Its transformative logic is contrary to the annihilation logic of capitalism.

The Timbuktu Collective in Andhra Pradesh in southern India provides an inspirational illustration of cooperatives working together in a collective to transform socio-ecological relations among marginalised communities in their ecologically sensitive region.[23] In its 35 years, it has evolved into a complex and vibrant collective of cooperatives and projects that promote ecological, healthy, local and rooted ways of living, working and being. The collective brings together various cooperatives – women's agricultural cooperatives, cooperatives promoting and rehabilitating the natural commons, small-scale and ecological farming practices, cooperatives providing services such as loans and finance to small-scale farmers, enterprise development through their shops selling products of the cooperatives, educational programmes for children in need and cultural programmes – into a solidarity network that works across 321 villages in the region with a net worth of US$6.9 million.[24] The hub of Timbuktu is 32 acres of agro-forested area and it has developed permaculture, sustainable living, regeneration of the environment and renewable energy. Thus, the entire Timbuktu

Collective represents an anti-capitalist transformative alternative rooted in space and place – what we call a solidarity economy-based cooperative system.

Solidarity economy-based cooperative systems and worker cooperatives' anti-capitalist practices operate on two levels: (1) within the economic sphere and (2) in the economy's relations to non-economic background conditions. In other words, they challenge class relations at the point of production and consumption *and* they reconfigure the relationship of economic activity with the non-economic socio-ecological system by prioritising human and nature-centred practices and values. To put it another way, they are engaging in an intersectional class war of position within the economy *and* socio-ecological war of position in the non-economic realms, such as social reproduction, nature and the state and public power. In this way, they are crucial examples of transformative forces attempting emancipatory futures-making in the present.

Types of Solidarity Relations: Decentralised, Synergistic and Federated

Generally, cooperatives have been understood as hierarchical movements based on the pyramid of primary, secondary and tertiary cooperatives. This has been very much part of a British and colonial legacy of cooperative movement building (Rhodes 2012). Breaking with this legacy through transformative praxis, cooperative movements have developed complex webs of solidarity, support and care. Informed by member need and constantly building capacities, such movements have become embedded in solidarity economy cooperative systems based on the natural and social commons but also bring into their orbit groups, organisations, communities and even society that may not have the form of a worker cooperative or cooperative institution but that share in the commons of ethical values, principles and care labour approach. For example, the non-profit organisation Working World's approach to financing worker cooperatives and community initiatives[25] and the Kudumbashree women's groups in Kerala that are not formalised as cooperatives but work with the values and principles of cooperatives are part of the solidarity economy-based cooperative system. From our research, worker cooperatives and solidarity economy-based cooperative systems can be categorised into three broad types based on how they extend their activities beyond the cooperative: decentralised, synergistic and federated. The decentralised system has independent cooperatives that relate to other cooperatives through myriad connections that they establish with one another, but they do not formalise the connections in a secondary structure. In the cases we focus on in this book, the best example of this is Uralungal Labour Contract Co-operative Society (ULCCS) in Kerala, but was also seen in Chilavert in Argentina and Uniforja in Brazil.[26] The synergistic system sees a layered relational approach with a central cooperative that brings together cooperatives in a dense network integrally intertwined with one another. The best example of this is Cecosesola in Venezuela, but it also characterises Heiveld in South Africa and, to a degree, Trentino in Italy. The federated model has a primary cooperative federation/group at the centre with cooperatives joining the federation but remaining largely autonomous. The best example of this approach is Mondragón, but we also see it in the Kudumbashrees and the state in Kerala and solidarity economy forums in Brazil (see Figure 3.1).

To be clear, all three approaches to relating to other cooperatives are horizontally democratic and promote inter-cooperative engagements. In all three systems, primary cooperatives maintain complete autonomy in terms of their internal cooperative practices. The three distinct approaches to relating to other cooperatives shows exciting variation and diversity, which challenges the ICA's top-down single approach. Cooperatives are finding their own ways of developing solidarity linkages based on their extant cultures, practices and conditions.

In Figure 3.1, the decentralised system is characterised by cooperatives building connections with other cooperatives, movements and progressive entities in solidarity networks. The synergistic system has a layered relational approach with a central cooperative providing the loadstone of a dense interwoven network of cooperatives. The federated system is characterised by a cooperative

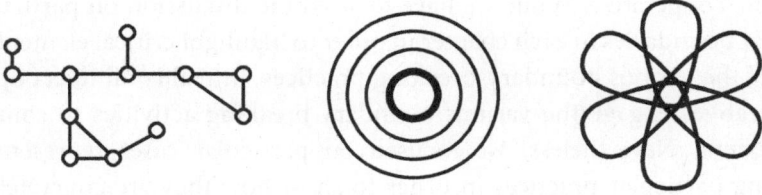

Figure 3.1 Types of cooperative networks: decentralised, synergistic and federated.

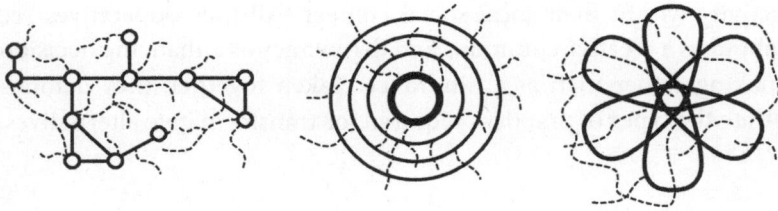

Figure 3.2 Types of cooperative networks with informal connections depicted as rhizomes.

federation/group at the centre with cooperatives joining the federation but remaining largely autonomous.

Through the imagery of rhizomes, Figure 3.2 depicts the plethora of informal relations that cooperatives develop within and across broader communities. This typology is useful in that it helps us to understand the myriad ways in which cooperatives relate to other cooperatives and progressive entities. We have used this typology as one of the axes along which we discuss the cooperatives in the empirical Chapters 4–6. The other axis is the practices that redraw boundaries between the economy and social reproduction, the natural world, public power and the state, and engendered solidarities beyond the enterprise. Thus, Chapter 4 focuses on the decentralised approach to cooperative relations and unpacks the way in which they embed social reproduction into the cooperatives. Chapter 5 looks at synergistic cooperatives and the ways in which they incorporate the natural world into the cooperatives. Chapter 6 explores cooperatives in the federated approach and how they develop relations to public power, the state and solidarities beyond the cooperative. While we have focused the discussion on particular boundaries in each chapter in order to highlight critical elements of the various boundary-breaking practices, in reality all the cooperatives engage the various boundary-breaking activities to some extent. Nevertheless, we focused on particular cases representing particular practices in order to show how they are concretely developing transformative practices. In fact, all the cooperatives we researched share the approach to a democratic workplace and collective decision making and to varying degrees embed economic activity within their local social context. All the cooperatives see labour as a creative commons and democracy as enhancing decision making rather than as a hindrance. Taken together, they demonstrate the types of practices required for transformative alternatives.

PART II

Worker Cooperatives and Solidarity Economies as Counterhegemonic Regimes of Socio-Ecological Reproduction

4

Integrating Socio-ecological Reproduction

ULCCS in Kerala, Chilavert in Argentina and Uniforja in Brazil

In this chapter, we look at the ways in which worker cooperatives have redrawn boundaries between the economy and social reproduction. As discussed in previous chapters, capitalism is not just an economic system but also depends on non-economic conditions for its existence, including human beings and raw material from nature. In this chapter, we focus on cooperatives that challenge capitalism's boundary between economic activity and the nurturing and sustenance role played by social reproduction. We focus on cooperatives that operate with a decentralised typology, as discussed in Chapter 3. Social reproduction refers to the unwaged care work that nurtures and shapes human beings, but also the work of caring within families, building bonds within communities and creating cultures that establish shared meanings and uphold social relations. It is the activity that forms 'human subjects, sustaining them as embodied natural beings, while also constituting them as social beings, forming their habitus and the cultural ethos in which they move' (Fraser 2016, 101). Social reproduction is, thus, central to the entire socio-ecological system. Despite its centrality, capitalism positions it outside the productive work in the economy and, thus, turns the relationship upside down to appear as though social reproduction depends on production.

Capitalism's efforts to dismantle the commons through appropriation and enclosures created the conditions that waged work was necessary for survival, which reinforces the myth that social reproduction depends on capitalism's economic activity. In actuality, social reproduction continues to underpin capitalism. The social world provides the underlying conditions on which economic activity operates, but capitalism disavows these conditions, allowing it to abdicate responsibility for paying for their costs. Solidarity economy-based cooperative systems and worker cooperatives, by contrast, recognise the central life-constituting role of social reproduction and place economic activity within social reproduction rather than in command of it. Recognising that our species has long worked collectively to govern our lives, the worker cooperatives discussed here illustrate how to embed economic activity within socio-ecological relations. Similar to what Silvia Federici (2020, 1) celebrates, the worker cooperatives are finding new modes of operating through ethics, care and cooperation: 'The very sense that we are living at the edge of a volcano makes it even more crucial to realise that, in the midst of so much destruction, another world is growing, like the grass in the cracks of the urban pavement, challenging the hegemony of capital and the state and affirming our interdependence and capacity for cooperation'.

To illustrate the synergies created by recognising social reproduction as constitutive of economic activity, we have chosen three cooperatives in the decentralised typology: Uralungal Labour Contract Co-operative Society (ULCCS) in Kerala, India; Cooperativa de Trabajo Chilavert Artes Gráficas (Chilavert) in Buenos Aires, Argentina; and Uniforja, a factory on the outskirts of São Paulo, Brazil. The decentralised typology captures cooperatives who relate to other cooperatives through various forms of solidarity but remain independent from one another and do not coalesce the relations into a formal structure such as a federation. The experiences here show the plurality of approaches to counterhegemonic (anti-capitalist) social and economic relations that include construction, manufacturing and printing. They not only organise economic activity democratically but also are guided by values of social justice and human well-being, and draw on knowledge from practice. We discuss the three cooperatives by highlighting the ways in which each one has embedded economic activity within social relations and we show the ways in which they recognise the constitutive role played by communities and families in the lives of their worker–owners.

A COOPERATIVE IN THE SERVICE OF SOCIETY: ULCCS IN KERALA, INDIA

The ULCCS[1] provides an excellent illustration of a cooperative not only recognising the importance of social reproduction but also re-imagining its role in the service of sustaining and constituting both human beings and the broader communities in which it is embedded. As a hundred-year-old construction cooperative in the southern state of Kerala, India, ULCCS has vast experience in running its 2000[2] member-strong worker-owned construction cooperative that builds large public infrastructure projects such as roads, bridges and building complexes, including hospitals. The Uralungal cooperative has pioneered local-level democratic production. It epitomises many of the qualities of worker cooperatives and the solidarity economy, such as democracy, equity, solidarity, reciprocity and integrative networks. These principles are encoded in the fabric of the cooperative through its by-laws, which explicitly state that the primary objective of the cooperative is to service the interest of its members, that is, the workers in the cooperative, through secure, rewarding and well-remunerated work. Placing worker–owner well-being at the centre of the cooperative contrasts markedly to capitalist enterprises that see workers in the service of accumulation.

The centrality of workers is significant in its own right, but for ULCCS it is only part of its commitment. The cooperative takes its care role further to include the construction projects it builds for the broader community. In practice, this means it ensures the highest quality and fair price for its public infrastructure projects as it has a principle of not wasting public funds and understands the importance of public goods, such as safe bridges and good roads, for the quality of life of ordinary people. It takes pride in building commons public infrastructure and public goods for the benefit of society. In its 100 years, it has never gone over budget and almost always (two exceptions only) delivers on time. In this way, it locates the cooperative's economic activity within the social world it inhabits and consciously seeks to play a positive developmental role. By placing the cooperative at the service of society and its worker-owners, ULCCS is embedding economic activity within society and levelling the boundary that demarcates the economy from social reproduction.

To understand this deep commitment to both the worker–owners and to delivering quality public goods, we must look to its history. ULCCS was born in the turbulent times of the social renaissance and anti-colonial struggles of the early twentieth century. In the first decades of its existence, the areas in and around Uralungal[3] were in the maelstrom of the political turbulence of the 1930s and 1940s when powerful peasant and workers' movements emerged in Malabar, the region where Uralungal is located. At the same time, the nationalist movement took a radical turn and the Communist Party became a hegemonic force in Malabar. This radicalisation of Malabar in the 1930s and 1940s influenced the formative years of the cooperative by creating an ethos of democratic decision making, social justice, surplus subordinated to the social goals of the cooperative and delivering high-quality public goods to society.

These foundational values encoded the cooperative with a strong sense of purpose throughout its history. ULCCS has faced many challenges over the years, yet with every challenge the cooperative used its rich history rooted in transformative practices, democratic processes, collective decision making, tacit knowledge and alternative ethos of people before profits to creatively overcome each obstacle. By 2023, the cooperative had overseen a complex diversification process, grown its membership without losing democratic processes and gained a reputation for building some of the best public works in Kerala. Its social embeddedness registers in its 100 years of commitment to having a positive effect on its worker-owners and the wider community.

Its democratic decision making and worker control together with its social goals mark it firmly apart from capitalist enterprises. Maximising profits is the linchpin of capitalist enterprises, which they do by inflating prices and cutting costs in labour and inputs. ULCCS is liberated from this drive to maximise profits as its primary objectives are to provide secure jobs with steadily improving wages and good working conditions, as well as quality infrastructure to the people of Kerala. Given the fact that much of its work (such as roads and public buildings) is for public consumption, it consciously sees its role as embedding its activity as a service to the communities for which it builds. The fact that its own worker–owners also consume these same public services provides extra incentive for it to deliver fair cost and high-quality infrastructure.[4] This is not to ignore the fact that for the cooperative to survive, it must also generate surplus, but the search for profits is not what drives it.

Democracy Deepens Embeddedness, Commitment and Cooperative Production

It is worth looking in detail at ULCCS decision-making processes as it has maintained robust participatory processes despite its 10,000 workers[5] dispersed across distant worksites. For ULCCS, democratic decision making is central to its success and to the commitment of the worker–owners. Its experience challenges the typical economists' critique that democratic workplaces are less productive, efficient and competitive than typical capitalist workplaces. In fact, ULCCS shows the opposite. The cooperative recognises that workers are part of co-creating its success and therefore are central to its decision making. Therefore, democratic decision making has been deeply entrenched since its foundational years when it developed a tradition of taking difficult decisions to a general meeting of all members. For example, in its early years ULCCS tried to compete by underquoting for tenders, which required workers who were willing to work longer, harder days and often for lower wages. Whenever it faced such a situation, the board of directors placed the issue on the table at a general body meeting and let the workers decide whether they wanted to agree to the contract. If the workers did not accept the conditions of the contract, the board would not sign the contract. Thus, the need to underquote in the early years led to a tradition within the cooperative that all difficult decisions were made collectively in special general meetings. The cooperative no longer needs to underquote for its survival, but the tradition of placing decisions before the general meeting of all members remains. This is institutionalised self-management that draws on experiential and tacit knowledge of members, their collective capacity, understanding of the financial situation in the cooperative and socialised labour time. In other words, commoning practices are deeply entrenched.

The annual general meeting (AGM) is a crucial decision-making body for ULCCS. At the AGM, workers elect the board of directors and deliberate on the report covering the past year's functioning. Reflecting relations of trust in leadership, once the new board of directors is elected, the directors are given a high degree of autonomy in procuring contracts, choosing technology, allocating workers to different worksites and other routine decisions in running the cooperative. Thus, in effect, the board of directors represents the managers of the cooperative, which means that management is elected by the workers. The contrast to capitalist corporations where managers are appointed by an unelected leadership could not be starker. Given the geographical range of its construction sites – at any one time it can have well over 100 construction sites spread across the state – it would be very easy to justify centralising decision making. Instead, reflecting trust in its worker–owners, ULCCS has decentralised decision making and elaborated innovative democratic structures.

Each construction site is led by a 'site leader' who is chosen by and from the workers at the worksite. The site leader coordinates, supervises, keeps attendance, orders material and makes payments. Since the workers elect their site leaders, they are very careful to choose someone with proven managerial ability and who commands widespread respect from fellow workers. Choosing the right leaders for the day-to-day functioning of the cooperative is vital to consensual leadership and a harmonious (rather than conflictual) labour process. The construction sites are organised (including the division of labour and the procedures of the worksite) through continuous interaction among workers and site leaders. To facilitate ongoing communication, the workers have collective lunches – the cooperative provides breakfast and lunch[6] to all workers – which have become a forum for deliberation and discussion about the worksite. The collective lunches provided by the cooperative are an example of care labour internalised by the cooperative. While there is a great deal of inclusive deliberation, once a decision is made, everyone must abide by it. Disobeying site leaders' instructions, dereliction of duty, financial irregularities and deliberate lapses in performance receive disciplinary action, which is rarely needed due to the elaborate approach to inclusive worksites. Contrary to the critique levelled by mainstream economists, ULCCS demonstrates that participation leads to less shirking of responsibilities and more commitment from members, which is demonstrated in the relatively infrequent need for disciplinary action.[7] When disciplinary action is needed, it is dealt with immediately and also publicly reported at the annual general body meeting, which appears to be effective in ensuring discipline as workers do not want to lose the respect of their fellow worker–owners.

Another key to the cooperative's efficiency is the regular communication among the different levels of the cooperative. In addition to the democratic decision making at the sites, there are a number of mechanisms for collective decision making across sites and with the board. For example, all site leaders meet the board of directors every day to review the day's work. These are collective meetings that help to ensure that all sites are aware of what is going on at other sites. For logistical reasons, site leaders from distant worksites attend the meetings a couple times a week (or communicate via online technology). In addition to the daily meetings, all the site leaders, board members and technical staff meet once a week to discuss the status of the worksites. These multiple layers of meetings have proven incredibly efficient as any troubles at one site are collectively solved by all site leaders. For example, if one site is short on materials and another site has material to spare, they quickly move material across sites as needed. ULCCS maintains that their democratic and transparent management across the cooperative is highly efficient and also ensures that information about the entire cooperative is regularly shared.

In addition to the daily and weekly meetings with site leaders and board members, all worker members meet once a month to discuss new developments and raise criticisms of site leaders or decisions taken by the board of directors. In addition to these various meetings, all board members must work on a construction site at least one day a week in order to keep abreast of the construction issues and remain close to other worker–owners. This entire process from daily site meetings with workers and site leaders to the monthly general body meetings requires a great deal of commitment by workers and leaders, but the advantages are many. Indeed, engaging in participatory deliberation and holding so many meetings at the various levels – daily site meetings, daily leadership meetings, weekly review meetings, monthly general body meetings and annual general body meetings – involves a cost in terms of time and energy, but it also produces efficiencies and a sense of collective ownership, solidarity and common mission that contribute to enhancing productivity and the ethos of the cooperative. One of the many positive outcomes of regular meetings and transparent information-sharing communication is a well-informed membership.

ULCCS not only uses participatory deliberation to decide on the work process, projects and day-to-day activities, but also provides full financial disclosure at the annual general body meetings. The profit margin significantly varies from worksite to worksite[8] depending upon the type, size and location of the project as well as the rate contracted. The list of all the completed works with the statement of revenue and expenditure is presented at the annual general body meetings. Because they understand the different worksites, the workers accept that the surplus margin cannot be the same at all worksites and therefore they do not link their wages to output. Rather they understand that the overall gross surplus margin of the cooperative is what is important. The transparent and inclusive decision-making approach has created a culture in which workers understand the cooperative, including their central role and the value of their work. It also has engendered pride in the cooperative.

Embedding the Cooperative in Socio-ecological Reproduction

ULCCS recognises that the worker–owners are not lone individuals but are embedded in larger families who take responsibility for much of the care work that contributes to the workers' existence. Thus, through steadily increasing the real wages of its workers, the cooperative ensures that families' needs are catered for. For example, the real-wage earnings rose by 150 per cent between 1981–1986 and 2011–2014. A 2014 survey of ULCCS workers[9] recorded that wages for worker–owners contributed 90 per cent of income of the workers' families and for migrant workers it contributed 96 per cent of income of their families (Isaac and Williams 2017, 277; ULCCS 2014). The importance of ULCCS's wage growth comes into sharp relief when we look at global trends. For example, the Economic Policy Institute shows that there has been a pronounced divergence between productivity and workers' wages globally with productivity increasing by 2.7 times that of wages (Economic Policy Institute 2025). In the USA, workers real average wage in 2018 had a similar purchasing power to the average wage in 1978, and the wage gains that have happened have largely gone to the highest paid workers (DeSilver 2018).

In addition to wages, the various additional benefits enjoyed by the ULCCS workers also rose at a faster rate so that their share of the total emoluments increased from 27 per cent to 32 per cent between 1981–1986 and 2011–2014. The cooperative also provides a wide range of non-wage benefits such as medical aid, medical allowance, bonuses, holiday wages, welfare expenses and festival allowance. It has a special scheme for housing loans through the Kozhikode District Cooperative Bank with ULCCS acting as the guarantor for member home loans, and also offers interest-free advances on loans (Isaac and Williams 2017, 279). Taken together, the overall real benefits increased by 170 per cent. For example, in the period 2013 to 2014, the average monthly wage received by worker members was US$180 and total emoluments US$270.[10] These rewards are, by any standards, much higher than the earnings in the private sector in Kerala and India, and approximately four times above the state's poverty rate.

Comparable private contractors employ only a relatively small core team of workers who receive relatively high wages, though still lower than the wages in ULCCS, and the additional emoluments they receive are much lower. The majority of a private contractor's workforce is temporary wage workers employed by subcontractors who receive much lower wages and hardly any additional emoluments. The inequality in wages in the private sector is also much higher than in ULCCS. As a result, ULCCS has gained a reputation for not only excellent work, but also for caring for its workforce.[11] Ensuring workers earn a wage that covers the costs of their family's reproduction reflects the cooperative's commitment to workers' well-being and internalising the importance of social reproduction. One area that ULCCS has not rectified is inequality in wages among unskilled women workers, which are still lower than the male counterparts. This, in part, reflects the continuing culture of gender discrimination that is prevalent in Kerala and India (Isaac and Williams 2017, 269). ULCCS acknowledges this as a major problem and is working to improve the wages of women workers.

In other ways, ULCCS has shown impressive sensitivity to the care needs of its workers. Internalising care work into the cooperative is seen in ULCCS's meal programme that provides breakfast and lunch to everyone in the cooperative, and the catering team are also members of the cooperative. For those living at worksites far from their homes, the cooperative provides all meals at a nominal rate of US$0.30 (25 rupees), which contributes to the purchasing of the produce while the cooperative pays for all other costs. In addition, the cooperative provides free accommodation for all its workers at worksites that are far from their homes and pays a stipend for the workers to travel home once a week. Incorporating daily meals, accommodation and transport into the cooperative's responsibilities reflects a shift in the care responsibility whereby the nutrition and physical well-being of workers is part of the cooperative's concern. Providing meals to all worksites is an enormous undertaking, which the cooperative has incorporated into its core activities and thus internalised as an element of care labour. There are a number of other measures demonstrating its attention to care beyond its own members. For example, ULCCS has also built homes for elderly people who need homes and provides bursaries for tertiary education for the children of worker–owners and the community. In these ostensibly small acts, ULCCS further dismantles the boundary between economic activity and social reproduction.

The food programme also gave it pause to think about how it can change its relationship to nature. Recognising the deleterious ecological effects construction has on local ecologies through its extraction of rock and sand, the cooperative decided to buy land for its quarries, which are re-greened with food plantations to feed its workers. By replanting the land where it extracts resources for the construction process with fruit-bearing trees and vegetables used to feed its members, it not only recognises the importance of social reproduction of workers, but also the importance of taking care of and rehabilitating nature. Through this ecological and innovative move, ULCCS created a closed loop system in which it re-greens the land it uses and feeds its workforce through the food grown. In this way, it brings socio-ecological reproduction centrally into the cooperative.

The cooperative's care role was further demonstrated during Covid-19. When India went into lockdown due to Covid-19, ULCCS had over 4,000 migrant workers in Kerala. In stark contrast to the rest of India where migrant workers were left to fend for themselves, some of whom walked thousands of kilometres home, ULCCS provided safe transport for all its migrant workers back to their homes, often thousands of kilometres away. Those who chose to remain in Kerala were assured food and support. Reflecting its strong relations to local government bodies (discussed in Chapter 6), the cooperative also assisted the state by providing transport of food and supplies to communities through its trucks and drivers. It established a strong volunteer corps to support local communities throughout the pandemic. The speed and ease with which it shifted into these supportive activities reflects its connections to communities and its ethics of care.

Internal Innovation on Membership

Because of the secure employment and relatively better labour conditions that ULCCS guarantees, the demand for membership was historically very high, which allowed the cooperative to have a strict recruitment system. An aspirant member would have to work in a quarry site for two to three years, becoming a skilled stone crusher and imbuing a sense of discipline. During this probation period the cooperative would assess the aspirant member's temperament and commitment to work and to the cooperative. This strict membership system changed with the growth and success of the cooperative that required a greater need for temporary workers from the 1970s. With increased mechanisation and the growing distances in which they worked, ULCCS's labour demands were evolving and the importance of non-member workers increased. At the same time, their traditional recruitment source – local workers – began to dry up as the children of worker–owners became more educated. The new generation of educated youth increasingly withdrew from construction work,[12] an unintended consequence of the progressive and successful state government programmes to increase access to education and the cooperative's scholarship support for the children of members and the community. As a result, ULCCS was compelled to employ migrant workers from north India (Chaudhary 2005).

Given its principles, the growing number of employed workers (i.e. non-members) was an embarrassment to the cooperative, which responded by actively encouraging employed workers to become members. However, many migrant workers were reluctant to become members as they did not plan to remain in Kerala and therefore were not interested in membership, which required paying a membership fee to the cooperative. The cooperative developed an innovative solution: a new class of membership, 'C Class', was created to provide membership to non-member workers.[13] After one year, a non-member worker could request C Class membership. The value of a C Class share was US$0.06[14] until 2007, when it was raised to US$0.30. Such a 'nominal member' was entitled to receive all fringe benefits of 'A Class' members such as a bonus, leave with wages, medical allowances, provident funds, employment state insurance, gratuity and holiday wages. They were not, however, entitled to receive a dividend nor to participate in general body meetings where long-term strategic decisions are made. This creative approach to different membership types again demonstrates ULCCS's attempt to listen to the needs and interests of its workers, this time non-Keralite migrant workers, without jeopardising its values of and commitment to cooperative principles. This example of inclusive solidarity has nurtured a culture of tolerance and inclusion in the cooperative as well.

While there are four categories of membership, the A and C Class members constitute the worker members and make up the total membership of the cooperative. The various membership categories are part of the cooperative's approach to raising finance for the cooperative. It is worth discussing the membership and corresponding share values in detail as it provides a view into its complex structure and self-reliance. The combined share value in 2018–2019 of A Class members and C Class members was US$2.45 million (205 million rupees).[15] The B and D Class members were innovative ways to increase share capital without jeopardising the cooperative principles, as these members do not have voting rights. The increase in share capital contribution over the years was due to a number of creative initiatives by the board of directors. For example, all members had to take at least one A Class share worth US$ 0.30 (25 rupees; later 100 rupees, which is US$1.20). By 2018–2019, the majority of members (2,344 or 81 per cent) held one share with 543 members choosing to have more than one share. In 1954, compulsory thrift of one anna per rupee (6.25 per cent) was introduced. Whenever savings reached US$0.30 (25 rupees), it was added to share capital and if the ceiling of the number of shares one could hold had been reached the thrift was paid into a recurring deposit account. The authorised capital of the cooperative was systematically enhanced from US$150 (12,500 rupees) in 1925 to US$598 (50,000 rupees) in 1965 and further to US$119,697 (10 million rupees) in 1969. As per the revised by-law of 2008, the authorised share capital of the cooperative rose to US$11.97 million (1 billion rupees). The point is that ULCCS has very successfully used a complex membership system with various categories of membership with corresponding share value to raise significant finance for the cooperative, which has ensured it has financial independence from capitalist finance houses. Control over finance and its own finance common pool has been crucial. The fact that all members contribute to the financial stability of the cooperative also creates a culture in which all membership types are valued and it ensures that members themselves are committed to the cooperative (Isaac and Williams 2017, 122-132).

The success of ULCCS has gained it a great deal of respect and attention from other cooperators in Kerala and the country. For example, in 1999 ULCCS jointly hosted a two-day workshop with the local municipality, Onchiyam panchayat, to popularise worker cooperatives and share experiences. As a result of such efforts, ULCCS inspired many worker cooperatives in the state. For example, ULCCS has close ties with the Udayapuram Labour Contract Cooperative Society (LCCS) in the northern town of Kasargod. ULCCS regularly provides technical and logistical advice but has also extended short-term loans to LCCS (Isaac and Williams 2017, 179-181). Such acts of solidarity are not unique for ULCCS, which actively seeks relationships with other cooperatives even in faraway places. For example, ULCCS reached out to other cooperative networks internationally, such as Mondragón, to share experiences and learn from one another.

The efforts of ULCCS to internalise its role in providing for the interests of workers and community embeds the cooperative within socio-ecological relations, as opposed to capitalism's disavowal of them. Rather than acting as though it is outside of society, ULCCS is deeply embedded in its workers' lives, the local communities and Kerala as a whole. In this way it has internalised social reproductive activity into the *raison d'être* of the cooperative. We now turn to a cooperative recovered printing press halfway across the world that has also integrated social reproduction.

HUMANISING WORK AND BUILDING SOLIDARITY: THE ARGENTINE RECOVERED FACTORY MOVEMENT

We have thus far discussed the way in which a worker cooperative internalised social reproduction and embedded economic activity within social relations. We now look more explicitly at the way in which the Argentine recovered factories infused the labour process with anti-capitalist values and practices.[16] The recovered factory movement in Argentina captured the imagination of people around the world when a critical mass of workers responded to the closure of factories by taking over their factories and refusing to put down their tools (see, for example, Magnani 2009). It is a fascinating movement both in the way in which it emerged and in the diversity of perspectives that exist within it. While sporadic cases of factory recoveries were seen throughout the 1990s in Argentina, in the period 2001–2003 it became a worker response to the economic and political crises plaguing the country. After a period of Peronist corporatism – underpinned by three pillars of social justice, economic independence and political sovereignty – in which the state mediated class conflict and the working class consolidated itself, the Argentine state implemented a series of neoliberal reforms in the 1990s that eventually led to the complete collapse of the Argentine economy in December 2001. In a period of a few weeks the middle class was reduced to poverty, unemployment skyrocketed to record levels, factories closed, banks locked their doors and froze funds, and the wealthy rushed to secure their money offshore.

The recovered factory movement emerged in this context together with an outpouring of neighbourhood assemblies, community groups and local organising in political and democratic spaces in which the middle and working classes were equally active. While many of the neighbourhood and grassroots community/ political formations withered over a couple of years as the economy recovered and the political context stabilised, the recovered factory movement had set roots that proved more durable.

By 2008, there were approximately 220 recovered factories (although the number was contested with government putting the figure at 120 and the movement at 220) and, by 2015, the official number grew to 352 registered recovered factories. One of the unintended consequences of the recovered factory movement is that it created space for worker cooperatives more generally. After 2011, there was a growth in cooperatives emerging out of self-organisation of new enterprises (as opposed to recovery of an existing factory) and by 2015, there were approximately 800 cooperative enterprises. Together with the recovered factories, there were 10,000 worker–owners and by 2022, there were over 400 recovered factories with 15,000 worker–owners.[17]

In general, factory recoveries were a response to companies closing while still owing their workers months, if not years, of backpay. The government changed the law that required companies to pay workers as their first creditors to make workers the last creditors (and banks the first). This effectively guaranteed that workers would not get the money owed to them. In response, workers started occupying factories. There were a few defining features of early worker recuperation. They were largely small and medium enterprises that responded to the economic crisis, marked by fraudulent practices of owners and predominantly concentrated in a few provinces, such as Chaco, Noreste, Pampeana and Amba. Interestingly, there were a myriad creative approaches to recovery, with the workers pioneering a variety of takeovers that included occupying buildings, using debt to buy out factories, securing legal expropriation, engaging in prolonged struggles for occupation of the factory, continuing production and protecting equipment. The approach that was emphasised largely depended on the local context, the workers' ability to gain access to the factories and support from local communities.

One of the legacies of Peronism was that the Argentine working class had a strong sense of itself as a class. The social contract it enjoyed came with a great deal of state support in terms of pension, education, healthcare and welfare. The social reproduction regime was broad in terms of welfare state support and the working class was deeply incorporated into relatively stable labour-capital relations. As a result, many workers in the recovered factories had strong identification with their companies as many had worked in the same factory for decades. This feeling of belonging also helps account for workers' willingness to take control of the factories as they felt intimately tied to the factories through a deep sense of belonging and entitlement to a rightful share in the factory. Their insistence on calling themselves the 'recovered' factory movement rather than 'takeovers' speaks to this deep sense of attachment to the factory. They were recovering the factory from errant owners and a failed economic system in an attempt to protect the factory and their jobs. This deep connection to their factories also placed workers in a strong position to recover production as they knew how the factories worked and could easily maintain the production process. Indeed, many challenges they faced had nothing to do with the actual production process, but rather the biggest challenges linked to gaining state sanction for the expropriation and securing access to markets. The conditions varied with some recovered factories maintaining the same clients, while others had to find new clients. For example, the printing and graphics recovered factory, Chilavert, cultivated all new clients. They wanted to break with the previous reliance on a couple of large clients and sought many small clients (discussed below), while others, such as a balloon factory, sought to keep some of its old clients.[18] Regardless of which approach, securing clients has been an ongoing struggle for many of the recovered factories.

The first wave of recovered factories grew out of a response to the economic meltdown, while the continued growth in the number of recovered factories occurred amid a sustained period of economic growth. For many recovered factories, this demonstrates their viability beyond crisis moments and suggests that they consolidated their position as an alternative way to organise production within the Argentine economy. The growth of cooperatives in general in this period suggests that workers were looking for ways to strengthen worker control and ownership at the point of production. With 1,200 recovered factories and cooperatives and over 15,000 worker–owners, the potential for solidarity economy linkages grew immensely. Indeed, part of the success of the movement has been the dense web of relations across cooperatives and the innovative communication among them. However, nurturing a network did not come easily because many of the recovered factories tended to be inward looking and focused on their internal and immediate struggles, often neglecting to build crucial networks. Some in the movement realised this inward focus could destroy the movement. As a result, they started to give special attention to information sharing and fostering linkages across recovered factories. For example, Zanon, a recovered tile factory, was very open to sharing its experiences, did a great deal of solidarity work and popularised horizontal labour relations. Popularising and sharing experiences reflects conscious effort to provide inspiration and support to other enterprises. The importance of information sharing and dissemination is exemplified in Lavaca, a collective of journalists who provide internet-based news, made several documentary films, gave media coverage to the factory recoveries, people's assemblies, mass protests and public events, and popularised the experiences across society. Lavaca also covered the new forms of critical communication that emerged, such as social movements, protests, the 'Madres'[19] and so on. As a result, the Lavaca Collective played a crucial role in facilitating information dissemination, sharing experiences and exposing struggles. While there were very concerted efforts to build movements, recovered factories tended to directly link with other recovered factories and worker cooperatives in a decentralised approach.

Chilavert's Creative Approach to Humanising Work and Embedding the Cooperative

The strong worker identity coursing through the recovered factory movement finds expression in the myriad cultural and symbolic events that the movement pioneered. As the workers learnt to work in new ways that were more horizontal than hierarchical, innovating on self-management practices to common their factories, they were also forced to look beyond the factory gates to their broader communities. One of the lessons of the recovered factory movement is the importance of solidarity from the local community, including overturning the boundary between economic enterprises and the communities in which they are embedded. Given the rich history of the actual experiences of recovery and the deep solidarities that grew out of recovery, it is worth highlighting the experiences of one of the iconic struggles for recovery. Chilavert Printing Cooperative is a printing and graphic recovered factory that won definitive expropriation in 2004[20] through an intense and prolonged occupation. Similar to the Zanon tile factory, the workers of Chilavert are very politically conscious and appreciate the importance of their role in the movement, both in terms of representing a beacon of hope and in acting very concretely as the printing press for many cooperatives and the movement.[21]

Chilavert's former owner had taken large loans that he invested in personal ventures that went insolvent after the 2001 economic crisis. Despite his personal use of the loans, the enterprise was held accountable for the bankruptcy. The former owner tried to get the factory back, but he owed so much money to the banks that he did not have a legal claim. During this interim phase, the owner emptied the factory of its most valuable assets, including two expensive printing presses. In response, eight workers occupied the factory and locked themselves into the factory in order to protect the equipment and prevent the owner from stealing it. In a counter-response, the police (acting on behalf of the owner) set up a barricade outside the factory and refused to allow any deliveries into the premises or anything to leave from the factory. The police tried to block the workers from starting production by choking off all deliveries, including food for their sustenance.

The workers' family members and the local community gave solidarity by congregating in front of the factory and the next-door neighbour cut a hole in the adjoining wall to allow goods, material and food in and out through his home. Community members provided food and other goods to the workers through the neighbour's hole in the wall. The police were only allowed to block Chilavert's entrance – not the neighbour's entrance – and therefore could not stop the deliveries in and out of the neighbour's house. For the ten months of occupation, the Chilavert workers were kept alive through the support and solidarity of the local community.

The community embedded Chilavert and its workers within a collective network of social reproduction that knitted densely woven relations between Chilavert and the community into the fabric of the cooperative. During these ten months, the recovery was largely a legal battle as the workers tried to win expropriation rights, which would allow them to start production. At the end of 2002, the workers won provisional expropriation, which allowed them to start production in the factory and in 2004, they won definitive expropriation, which meant the factory was theirs. The stamina of the Chilavert workers reflects their deep identification with the factory. For example, Ernesto, like many of the others, had worked for nearly two decades in the company before the recovery.[22] Through their act of occupation they challenged capitalist property rights. Their long history in the factory entitled them to a rightful share of the factory and to protect it and their jobs from an avaricious owner. In other words, they defended their wage earning which was necessary for socio-ecological reproduction of their families by making the factory common property.

Nurturing Solidarity and Creative Commons

The support the Chilavert worker–owners received from their families, the local working-class neighbourhood and other recovered factories left an indelible mark on them. The synergies created between the Chilavert worker–owners and the neighbourhood assemblies laid the foundation for long-lasting solidarities and rootedness in their local community. Chilavert explains that this was a very special moment in the history of the factory and community. On our field visits, we were struck by the lasting deep appreciation for the community solidarity and the rootedness in the neighbourhood. There was an implicit recognition that the community had embedded Chilavert in relations of care. The workers framed the spot in the wall where the now bricked-up hole in the wall was. The solidarity and care created by the community led Chilavert to re-conceive its space as a socially rooted place for the community to congregate. During the day, the space continues to be a printing press factory, in the late afternoons and evenings it serves as a night school for adult education and over the weekends it is a cultural centre for the neighbourhood where the youth hold dances and community events. It also opens its space for local artists to display their work and, together with the local university, created a historical documentation centre housed in the factory. Rethinking the space in this way also changed the dynamics of the labour process as the working space became a playful space with art, political posters and creative works such as papier mâché hanging throughout the factory. Making the factory space available to the community deepened its social embeddedness and turned its physical space into a vibrant node in the community for education, art and history. Chilavert became a node of socio-ecological reproduction for the entire community.

The internal organisational principles are worth highlighting as Chilavert abandoned its former hierarchical systems in favour of consensus democracy through intense collective processes and self-management of its commons. The cooperative grew from eight to twelve members and maintains a strong commitment to democratic decision making through regular assemblies where they make all decisions collectively. They have regular meetings to discuss the labour process, who is doing what and whether any changes need to be made. Similar to Cecosesola (discussed in Chapter 5), organising production horizontally through consensus decision making not only proves to be efficient, but also more rewarding. Under the former owner, the workers only knew their one skilled job and were discouraged from talking to one another. As a result, they would not support one another as they were isolated from each other. If one person slowed things down, the entire process would slow down. With their horizontal approach, they work as a collective and ensure everyone is supported. With such a small workforce, collective decisions are not only crucial for the enterprise, but also for their bonds. Every member knows all the different jobs and can rotate among the different jobs when needed. They also help each other continuously. For example, if one person is struggling in a particular job others help and consequently the entire production runs smoothly. They communicate, play music, drink maté together and turn work into play.

We saw evidence of this on our visits where workers were joking and laughing with each other while they worked. We saw one member pulling another member on the delivery wagon after unloading the goods onto the truck. After work, the members continued discussing issues, ate food together and drank more maté. Redefining the world of work also affected their remuneration policy, similar to Cecosesola discussed in Chapter 5. For instance, they decided to have different criteria for wages. Thus, the first criteria was the individual's family situation (how many children and dependents) and the second criteria was the number of years in the organisation (this is to reward the longevity and seniority of members). As a result, their wage structure broke the boundary between production and socio-ecological reproduction. They socialised and embedded production into reproduction of themselves as workers and as part of families.

Chilavert also nurtures linkages to other cooperatives and is a founding member of the inter-cooperative federation, Red Grafica Cooperative. Red Grafica is an attempt to collectively gain market access and prevent cooperatives from competing with one another. Such federations are crucial as they operate in highly competitive capitalist market conditions that prioritise profits over values of solidarity, well-being and worker–ownership. Chilavert is very aware of the importance and power of solidarity among all cooperatives and actively supports and mentors recovered factories and other cooperatives. While they generously publish material for the movement, they are also profoundly aware of the need to survive and hence always balance their jobs with paying clients. In short, Chilavert is trying to create a different way of producing and a different world that is based on relations of solidarity to other enterprises and democratic organisation internally.

What is exciting about the recovered factory movement is not whether or not cooperatives and recovered factories can survive as isolated entities within a larger capitalist economy. We have plenty of examples of cooperatives surviving in such spaces (for example, the very successful cooperatives of the bay area in California). Rather, what is instructive and exciting is the ways in which they have redrawn the boundaries between the factory and community, embedding economic activity within local social relations and, ultimately, redrawing boundaries between production and socio-ecological reproduction of themselves, their families and communities. We now turn to another South American cooperative, a forging factory on the outskirts of São Paulo.

INTERNALISING SOCIO-ECOLOGICAL VALUES IN A DIRTY INDUSTRY: UNIFORJA COOPERATIVE IN BRAZIL

Moving across the border to a dirty steel-forging industry in Brazil, we see a similar commitment to creating a socially embedded cooperative enterprise with a focus on retrofitting the factory in order to reduce its deleterious impacts on the local community and the natural environment. Uniforja Cooperative on the outskirts of São Paulo is a great example of a successful recovered factory – the first of its kind in Brazil – that exemplifies the principles of worker cooperatives.[23] Uniforja is a steel-forging factory that manufactures automobile parts, heavy earth-moving equipment, ring rolling, heat treatments of steel and machine parts for different forms of energy. Steel forging and manufacturing are environmentally dirty and place a heavy burden on the environment, including high energy usage, air pollution, wastewater contaminants, hazardous and solid wastes, and noise pollution. Uniforja is located next to a residential community and the activities in the factory have a direct bearing on the community. We chose to include Uniforja since it has attempted to develop less destructive relations with nature, which also affects its immediate neighbours. It consciously thinks about how it can become less exploitative and wasteful in relation to the natural world.

The cooperative was formed in 2000 with three affiliated cooperatives – Coopertratt, Cooperlafe and Cooperfor[24] – and engineering capacity for the development and production of its own products. By 2022, Uniforja was the largest manufacturer of forged steel rings and flanges in South America. The history of Uniforja's formation is rooted in the worker recovery of a mismanaged family-owned company. After decades of a successful business with 500 employees, in the 1990s Conforja (later renamed Uniforja Cooperative) started having financial problems and by 1996 it closed under a cloud of bankruptcy. With the support of the Metalworkers Union under the leadership of Lula (later to become President of Brazil), approximately 250 of the 500 workers decided to take over the bankrupt company by buying it from the family. They decided to convert it into three primary worker cooperatives – Cooperatratt specialises in thermal treatment, Cooperlafi makes steel parts and Cooperforj makes the flanges – which they eventually combined into a secondary cooperative, Uniforja. Uniforja is responsible for the buying, financing, marketing, sales and managing, while the three primary cooperatives operate as factories responsible for the production process. As a combined cooperative, Uniforja has been highly successful in terms of its innovative model (which has been economically successful) and in improving the quality of lives for its members. This cooperative has remained relatively stable with approximately 300 worker–owners and 150 employees.[25]

Relations of Care with Nature and the Community

From its beginning, Uniforja nurtured good relations with the local community. After taking over the factory, it reached out to its neighbours in an effort to deepen its relationship with the local area. In its early interactions with local residents, it learnt that one of the persistent problems for the residents in the area was the loud thumping noise and deep vibration from the large forging machines. In response, Uniforja invested in retrofitting the forging area to decrease the noise and vibration with deep underground shock-absorbing pads and a soundproof area. The decision to do this at such an early stage of its formation is interesting as it was not yet confident of its success. Nevertheless, the worker–owners did not want the local community to suffer from their economic activity and prioritised the costly retrofitting. For local residents, the responsiveness of the new cooperative to their issues immediately marked it apart from the previous owner.

Over the years, Uniforja became increasingly aware of climate issues and the impact of steel forging on the environment. In response, it developed an ecology programme to help it become an 'ecologically sensitive' enterprise. Steel forging and thermal treatment require extremely intensive energy use, spew pollutants into the air and contaminate wastewater with hazardous waste in the forging process. These three environmental impacts – energy intensity, air pollution and wastewater contamination – account for a great deal of the steel forging industries' deleterious impacts on local communities across the world and its high ecological footprint globally. To reduce its environmental impact, Uniforja made three important and significant changes: it shifted to biodiesel for its energy, retrofitted all its furnaces to reduce emissions and installed a closed water system that recycles all the wastewater for reuse in the factory. These three changes address its most deleterious impacts on the natural world and the local community and reflect its recognition of its role in climate change as well as its attempts to mitigate its impact. The changes were expensive and were not productivity-enhancing investments. Rather they were done for the good of the environment, the local community and the workers. Uniforja's willingness to take on such an expensive retrofitting exercise reflects its commitment to changing its relations to nature. The ecological changes have also increased its linkages to other cooperatives as the biodiesel is bought from a biodiesel cooperative. Implementing such changes should not be taken for granted as they are expensive and require worker–owners to fully appreciate the cooperative's role in socio-ecological reproduction. The fact that Uniforja prioritised the expensive retrofitting demonstrates its commitment to caring for nature and people.

Decision Making, Transparency and Creative Institutional Structure

To appreciate how the forging manufacturing cooperative came to think about its relationship to the natural world, we must understand its approach to decision making and worker–owner education. Like all the worker cooperatives we researched, Uniforja maintains one member, one vote for all strategic decisions; it is self-managed. However, early in their history, the new worker–owners recognised that some jobs give some members a better understanding of the cooperative and its overall needs. For example, a person in finance or a managerial role has wider exposure to the various needs of the cooperative than a cleaner on the shopfloor. Deliberative democracy in which everyone is equally equipped to participate requires all decision makers to have knowledge and understanding of the entire enterprise. In order to ensure that all members have a holistic understanding of Uniforja, the cooperative provides extensive education to initiate members before membership is confirmed. To do this, every member spends time in the different departments, for example, financial, supplies and procurement, factory floor and engineering, in order to have in-depth knowledge of the factory and all the parts that go into making it successful.[26] In other words, incoming members are socialised into the commoning practices of the cooperative: creative labour process, collective capacity such as knowledge (experiential and tacit), finance, natural relations and time-sensitive processes. This also ensures that the discussions at the AGM are substantive, informed and facilitate timeous decision making. Uniforja insists that transparency and information sharing is crucial so that every member knows the whole factory and has the capacity to understand it. We saw similar practices in many cooperatives and recovered factories we encountered, but very few implement the process of new members shadowing all departments as we saw at Uniforja.

With an informed membership, Uniforja ensures that all strategic decisions are made democratically, while still allowing for flexibility in the day-to-day decision making in running the cooperatives. Like most cooperatives we encountered, Uniforja has a series of meetings with varying decision-making authority. Every year at the AGM, a one-year plan is developed, which is updated monthly as needed. This long-term flexible planning allows them to implement the long-term plan effectively as they do not have to call a meeting to buy a new machine, as long as it was part of the annual plan. In addition to the AGM, there is an assembly every month with all worker–owners where the performance of each of the three cooperatives is reported. This ensures that all members know how each cooperative is doing and it provides an opportunity for collective problem solving and learning. In addition to the monthly meeting with worker–owners, every three months there is a general meeting with worker–owners and employees. These meetings serve many functions: they ensure efficient communication across the three primary cooperatives, keep all members appraised of any potential problem areas, ensure the three cooperatives maintain surpluses or that losses are identified early to help correct them and create a sense of genuine participation by worker–owners. The thick structure of decision making and information sharing facilitated the cooperative's adoption of the environmental programme and supported the retrofitting required to lessen the deleterious effects on the environment and local community.

The structure of Uniforja is adapted to their needs and shows creative innovation to ensure transparency and accountability to members. The three primary cooperatives have two elected directors each and a general manager who oversees the administration. The two directors from each cooperative form the six-member board of directors of Uniforja. The AGM sets the annual budget, and the financial team must work within this budget for the year. The three cooperatives are responsible for the production process, while the financial management falls under Uniforja with a treasurer and an external auditor to ensure transparency across the membership. This transparency allows for all members to clearly see surplus and losses, which are tied to dividends. For example, the last line in the balance sheet is for member dividends; if there is no positive balance, then the members do not receive dividends. Each primary cooperative is looked at as a separate unit, which allows them to quickly assess if they are making a surplus and collectively address any issues. If, however, only one of the cooperatives did not make any surplus, but the other two made surpluses, then the members of the unit that did not make a surplus do not get a dividend. This is a different approach than ULCCS discussed above and shows the diversity of approaches by cooperatives. For Uniforja, it ringfences the three cooperatives in order to ensure the overall success of the entire cooperative.

Low Wage Ratios, External Relations and Hiring Employees

Like many of the cooperatives we visited, Uniforja has a differentiated wage structure with higher skilled jobs earning higher wages, but the maximum wage ratio of the top earner to the bottom earner cannot exceed seven times. That means that the top-earning individual member cannot make more than seven times the bottom earner. This number comes into sharp relief when compared to mainstream companies where the ratio is far higher. For example, in 2018, the USA had a wage ratio of 265, followed by India (229), the UK (201) and South Africa (180) (Dyvik 2024). In 2021, the top 300 companies in the USA had a 670-to-1 wage gap between CEOs and the median worker, while the top 49 had a wage gap of over 1,000 to 1, with Amazon's CEO, Andy Jassy, earning 6,474 times the median pay in the company (Rushe 2022).[27] For example, the median worker from the top 300 US companies earned $23,968 per year compared to the CEOs average of $10.6 million per year. Unlike capitalist firms that reward the top earners significantly more than workers, Uniforja's narrow wage structure and equally distributed end-of-year surplus dividend creates a much flatter overall wage structure for members. Flatter wage structures effectively provide a family wage to workers that covers the cost of social reproduction. In addition, Uniforja provides other direct benefits for members such as paying university fees for members' children and supporting further study of any member and employee. In fact, most cooperatives we researched did not have a flat wage structure, but the focus was on minimising wage inequality by ensuring low wage ratios between the top and bottom earners so the boundary between production and socio-ecological reproduction was overcome.

Another interesting feature of Uniforja is its relationship to the Metalworkers Union, which played a very important and supportive role in its foundation. The worker–owners as well as the employees continue to be union members, but for the worker–owners it is an act of solidarity since they are their own bosses and do not need trade union representation. To accommodate this, the Metalworkers Union changed its regulations to adapt to the cooperative model and sees its role more in terms of partnership and cooperation. Uniforja pays into a solidarity fund that supports other cooperatives and allows its factory to be used for meetings and classes of other cooperatives and groups working in the solidarity economy movement. Reflecting its commitment to embedding the factory in the local community, the cooperative supports a local church and adopted an orphanage.

While Uniforja is an impressive cooperative system, it is not without contradictions and challenges. From very early on, Uniforja cooperatives hired employees who operate under the standard labour laws and are paid industry market rates, but do not enjoy the benefits of membership, including the relatively higher salaries that worker–owners receive or participation in democratic decision making, such as electing leadership. Hiring employees rather than growing the worker–owner membership was a conscious decision of Uniforja in order to give it the flexibility to grow and reduce its workforce, given the highly competitive market environment in which it operates. In effect, it finds itself as both a cooperative and an employer, and members are both worker–owners and employers. The dual system of democratic enterprise and employer throws up numerous challenges for the cooperative but the cooperative members are very aware of this contradiction and regularly reflect on how to overcome it. This is an example of the fact that worker cooperatives, especially in manufacturing sector, have to operate within the capitalist market economy, even while they are trying to overcome capitalist market relations. Another challenge is that over time the culture of the cooperative has become more technical and administrative, and less political (Ratner 2015). The effects of this could dilute the counterhegemonic values that were crucial to its formation. Such contradictions are part of operating in the interstitial spaces of capitalism and require continuous reflection.

The challenges notwithstanding, Uniforja represents a steel factory that has pioneered a collectively owned and democratically managed enterprise while also attempting to embed its activities within a framework that recognises its relation to and dependence on natural relations. It has also been conscious about overcoming the boundary between production and socio-ecological reproduction through its internal wage and benefit structure. Uniforja is about socio-ecological reproduction through its attempt to value nature, prioritise human well-being and operate under less environmentally destructive ways.

CONCLUSION

The experiences of these three different worker cooperatives illustrates the myriad ways in which social reproduction moves from a background condition to a central feature of economic activity. Such counterhegemonic practices embedding socio-ecological reproduction within economic activity fundamentally restructure the way in which economic activity has occurred under capitalism for centuries. By bringing to the fore human well-being, these cooperatives have started recasting the way economies can operate in a way that promotes social and nature's well-being. By upending the separation of the economy from the non-economic realms and subordinating economic activity to social and natural relations as well as developing values that prioritise human well-being, community, solidarity and socio-ecological justice, the worker cooperatives discussed in this chapter illustrate the plethora of experimentations being pioneered across the world. Ultimately, they are practising planetary care from below.

5

Recalibrating Relations with Nature

Cecosesola in Venezuela, Heiveld in South Africa and Trentino in Italy

In the previous chapter, we saw the way in which worker cooperatives reconfigure relations with the social and natural world through
the examples of ULCCS, Uniforja and Chilavert. The counterhegemonic practices embedded in the cooperatives defined the
ways in which their economic activity engaged with and relied on
socio-ecological reproduction. These examples show how worker
cooperatives embed themselves in socio-ecological relations to
reproduce themselves, society and natural relations and at the same
time foster practices that help to create counterhegemonic regimes
of socio-ecological reproduction. In this chapter, we narrow our
focus to look at the background condition of natural relations, the
natural commons of land, water, biodiversity, creative labour, renewable energy and the earth system and explore the ways in which
cooperatives and solidarity economy-based cooperative systems
relate to them. For this chapter, we have chosen three very different
examples to illustrate the ways in which they have defined their relations to the natural world by embedding economic activity within
normative frameworks that recognise human dependence on and
existence within nature. As discussed in Chapters 1 and 2, placing
humans as part of nature and not separate from it requires an ontological shift from nature as something to conquer to an ontology of
humans within nature, deeply intertwined with the natural world
and giving priority to living within its systems.

The three cases in this chapter could not be more different. One is
Central Cooperativa de Servicios Sociales del Estado Lara (Cecosesola),[1] a cooperative network in the heart of Venezuela; another,

Heiveld Cooperative, a rooibos farmers' cooperative in a remote rural region of South Africa; and the third, Trentino Cooperative Movement, a dense web of cooperatives in northern Italy. We have categorised these cooperatives as part of the synergistic approach as the cooperatives covered in the chapter are a central pillar of their cooperative system and engender deep and wide relations across the cooperative network. We chose such varied examples in the synergistic approach in order to show how different cooperatives are trying to redraw relations to the natural world. They are all acutely aware that the natural world provides the necessary material resources they require but are trying to upend the destructive and exploitative relations that are hegemonic in capitalism. Demarcating nature as a realm distinct from the social world gives the appearance that nature is outside capitalism and allows capitalism to not pay the cost of exploiting and polluting nature. By acknowledging and valuing nature as integral to their own activity and human life, the worker cooperatives and solidarity economy-based cooperative systems are effectively breaking down capitalism's boundary between economic activity and the natural world. These cooperatives are engaging in planetary care from below.

Capitalism's approach to nature is one of domination and devaluation. Nature is there to extract, exploit and pollute the unlimited 'free resources' needed for production. Capitalism takes from nature's commons systems and natural resources and returns to nature the waste products of the production process. It devalues the raw forms of nature and only applies value to them once they have been extracted, manipulated, transformed and beneficiated into products sold on the market. From a commons perspective, capitalism reduces abundance to scarcity. It does not actually pay the real costs of nature's role – neither the raw nature it extracts nor the waste it dumps back into nature – and assigns value to it only once it becomes a commodity. By disavowing its value and existence within capitalism, it demarcates nature outside of production. The ontology underpinning this separation sees humans as the apex species with the capacity to transform the natural world to serve its interest and capitalism as the system that must have 'power over' natural relations. Nature is there to be taken, not seen as profoundly interwoven with our own lifeworld. At most it is 'protected' in demarcated areas of 'wild nature' so that humans can enjoy it for limited moments (Moore 2015a). The ontological shift many cooperatives are making is seeing humans as part of nature and no longer separate from it. As highlighted in the previous chapter, we engage in socio-ecological reproduction of ourselves, families, communities, societies and our planet.

In this chapter, we look at the ways in which worker cooperatives embed economic activity within nature. We show how worker cooperatives and solidarity economy-based cooperative systems are not only socially embedded but also recognise the importance of finding non-destructive ways of relating to nature. Some see it as an ontological question and position themselves with an understanding of humans and all social relations existing in nature, while others pragmatically approach the importance of protecting nature for future generations. Either way, they relate to nature by valuing its contribution to economic relations and see the importance of operating within the natural boundaries of the planet with an ethics of care.

CONSTITUTING HUMAN AND SOCIAL WELL-BEING: CECOSESOLA IN LARA PROVINCE, VENEZUELA

The Venezuelan cooperative movement Cecosesola, an association of cooperatives in Barquisimeto,[2] incorporates socio-ecological reproduction into its core values and economic activities with an emphasis on food production, distribution, consumption, financial services and health care. Of the 146 cooperatives we visited, Cecosesola perhaps went the furthest in erasing boundaries between socio-ecological reproduction and their economic activity through centring individual and collective well-being at the heart of the cooperative's *raison d'état*.[3] Central to this has been developing alternative values and norms, such as commoning, solidarity, human well-being, caring, gender equality and community well-being. Cecosesola sees its values consciously challenging hegemonic values of capitalism, such as possessive individualism, competition, patriarchy, self-interest and supremacy of economic activity. The alternative values shape social relations in the cooperatives, corroborating the idea that emancipatory alternatives are vested in counterhegemonic value systems that upend hegemonic values perpetuated by capitalism. Through its alternative value system, Cecosesola places its economic activity, which includes the internal organisation of the network, within human and community well-being. It is deeply committed to creating a socially embedded cooperative enterprise with deep roots in the region.

Placing Cecosesola within its larger context of Venezuela brings out its uniqueness both in terms of its values and its socially oriented economic activities. With 18 per cent of global reserves,[4] petroleum dominates the country's economy and accounts for 95 per cent of its exports, ranking it the eighth-largest petroleum producer in the Organization of the Petroleum Exporting Countries (OPEC). After oil, the manufacturing sector plays an important role in the economy, largely focusing on cement, steel and aluminium. With its emphasis on dirty industries in manufacturing and fossil fuels, Venezuela is a large carbon emitter, having registered 6.15 tonnes per capita in 2012, which put it on par with the USA.[5] Agriculture accounts for only 4.7 per cent of its GDP and about 7 per cent of labour in the country, and most of the country is not food secure or self-reliant. Clearly, the country's economy is not geared towards the needs of the people or nature, nor is it socially embedded. The country registers high levels of poverty (approximately 91 per cent in 2022, up from 34 per cent in 2005; Statista 2023) and unemployment (approximately 35 per cent). According to the United Nations Development Programme (UNDP), inequality went from a Gini coefficient of 0.49 in 1996 to 0.39 in 2010 but then rose sharply to 0.47 by 2015. The drop in inequality in 2010 was largely due to President Chavez's social relief and redistributive programmes in the first decade of the millennium. In part due to political upheavals, the country's economy has been extremely unstable with hyperinflation, weak currency, food shortages, migration and financial crises. The middle class has edged closer and closer to poverty with

only the super-rich able to weather the multiple crises by shelter-
ing money overseas. Given this context, Cecosesola's transformative
value-centred economic activities come into sharp relief.

Founded in 1967 by idealistic young urban dwellers influenced by
the progressive values coursing through global student movements
of the 1960s, they believed cooperatives could play a transformative role in creating a better world. As a result, Cecosesola has been
value driven from its beginning. Its values are reflected in its activities, which are rooted in the common needs of people from funeral
homes to insurance, clinics, small-scale organic farming and food
processing cooperatives, and weekly organic food markets. In fact,
its economic activities directly address human needs that are vital to
quality of life. Cecosesola's structure is complex as it is a network of
about 50 cooperatives with approximately 20,000 members across
the network, and Cecosesola is also the name of the cooperative at
the centre of the network that runs the weekly markets that sell local
food and agricultural products. The individual cooperatives are
linked into an integrated network that brings together various cooperatives that provide social services and agricultural cooperatives in
the rural areas with urban-based, worker-owned consumer markets.

Over its five decades, it has grown and diversified into a substantial cooperative network that covers a range of activities. The values
are not just reflected in plethora activities that focus on social goods,
but in the non-hierarchical structure of the cooperative network;
in other words, it is self-management of commoning practices of
an entire system. All of the cooperatives within the network run
through non-hierarchical deliberative meetings that are integral
to their commitment to emancipatory education and promoting
anti-capitalist values. In fact, they designed Cecosesola to be educational in its structure and its decision-making culture as it sees its
deliberative processes as pivotal to creating transformative alternatives. They explicitly promote what Stavrides (2016, 2024) refers to
as 'emancipatory commoning' which requires building cultures of
trust, reciprocity and cooperation.

The Cecosesola cooperative has approximately 1,300 full-time
worker–owners who earn a living from their work in the coopera-

tive, which primarily focuses on the weekly markets selling healthy, organic food mostly produced by cooperatives and solidarity entities in the region. Wages within Cecosesola are about twice the government minimum wage and are based on needs of members. For example, families receive higher wages than single person households, which reflects its recognition of the role of socio-ecological reproduction in maintaining social relations and society. Over time, Cecosesola has created a commoning culture through the deliberative and self-reflexive approach of its organisational structure and deeply democratic meetings. These values have become part of the DNA of the entire network, which includes cooperatives active in a large range of activities – clinics, laboratories for blood tests, savings and loans institutions, transport, a hospital, insurance providers, farming cooperatives and cooperative markets. Many of the services they provide are often considered public goods as they are central to health and quality of life. For Cecosesola, the focus on public goods (one aspect of the social commons) reflects its commitment to not only meeting worker–owners' socio-ecological reproduction needs but also serving the wider community. As a result, early in its development, it created solidarity linkages with agricultural cooperatives that produced vegetables and fruit in the rural mountainous areas surrounding Barquisimeto to form a synergistic network.

Food Sovereignty, Natural Relations and Community Need

Food is the most intimate relationship humans have with natural relations. It is also essential for our survival. Prior to capitalism, food as commons was crucial for survival. A planet of abundance was brought under commoning arrangements from forests, prairies, oceans, rivers and mountains. Globalised agriculture systems, controlled by global monopolies, are creating scarcity through commodification. Moreover, they are destroying natural relations through several ecological rifts: soil depletion, biodiversity loss, carbon emissions, pollution of rivers and more. In this context, the food sovereignty example of Cecosesola stands out as an example of how to engage in planetary care through a localised, ecologically safe and commoning practice of food. The Cecosesola cooperative holds weekly markets from Thursday to Sunday in three locations where 500 tonnes of fruit and vegetables, sourced from agricultural cooperatives in the regions surrounding Barquisimeto, are sold to approximately 60,000 families (25 per cent of the urban population). The prices are about 30 per cent lower than those at privately operated markets. Twelve cooperative farms (made up of 200 small-scale farms of two to three hectares each) in the states of Lara and Trujillo supply the markets with fresh fruits and vegetables and freshly made bread, whole grain pasta, cereals, tomato sauce, herbs and spices, and honey. In an attempt to operate outside capitalist markets, they do not determine prices based on the market or exchange value. Rather, they look at what is necessary to produce particular vegetables (including what the producers need to live) and add up the number of kilograms produced across their entire product range as well as their costs to determine the average price per kilogram. Thus, tomatoes and potatoes, for example, are sold at the same price per kilogram. They maintain that their price per kilogram is significantly cheaper for customers and they eliminate unnecessary costs such as middlemen and seasonal fluctuations, but that this still allows them to earn what they need.

Cecosesola has drawn on several linkages for its food sovereignty system. It has nurtured relations with organic farmer cooperatives,[6] small-scale food processing cooperatives and bakery cooperatives in the rural areas outside Barquisimeto. These linkages helped to create an alternative food economy comprising products that are locally produced and consumed and therefore insulated from wider market forces. For example, during the 2003 and 2017 Venezuelan food crises, when many people across the country starved, Barquisimeto was the only region that maintained a degree of food sovereignty and prevented starvation, largely due to Cecosesola's interventions. Cecosesola's dense web of solidarity relations have been a defining feature and crucial in pursuing an anti-capitalist logic and human-centred economic activity. Recognising its impressive role in creating transformative alternatives, in September 2022, Cecosesola was a joint winner of the 'Right Livelihood Award' (what some call the alternative Nobel Prize) for 'establishing an equitable and cooperative economic model as a solid alternative to profit-based economies' (Right Livelihood 2022).

All of Cecosesola's activities relate to the needs of the community – healthy organic food, clinics and savings and loan institutions. In addition to the weekly markets, there are six health service units across the city that provide services such as laboratory blood work and more substantial services (190,000 health services are performed a year by Cecosesola). In 2009, Cecosesola opened a hospital (Centro Integral Cooperativo de Salud) where allopathic and alternative medicines are practised at considerably lower rates than private clinics to 200,000 patients annually. For example, massages and acupuncture as well as surgeries, laboratory work and X-rays are offered at the hospital. To raise the funds to build the hospital, Cecosesola used their weekly markets (they sold fruit salads as part of their fundraiser), solicited short-term, fixed interest deposits from cooperatives and individuals, and received contributions by full-time worker–owners. The credit unions facilitated this fundraising drive as well. Raising the funds through their own network and customers helped embed the hospital within the community.

Collective and Individual Development Prioritises Care Work

While its people-centred activities are a central part of its care work, what is especially relevant here is its approach to interpersonal and individual development. Cecosesola has pioneered a process-centred approach to individual, collective and organisational development based on trust and mutual cooperation. All decisions are made collectively (through an intricate process of small meetings that come together in larger meetings). The meetings are as much learning spaces as they are goal oriented. In any given year, for example, approximately 3,000 meetings are held within the cooperatives and 300 meetings between the cooperatives. Meetings are not time bound and are focused on deliberation and consensus. To ensure process-oriented decision making, all decisions are based on consensus (they never vote) with one of the primary criteria being that those who make a decision have to take responsibility for the decision and communicate it to all members. The thick network of meetings is a hallmark of Cecosesola's organisational structure that is decentralised and non-hierarchical. Over time, it has nurtured a culture of solidarity, trust, self and collective growth, and caring for and sharing with one another. As one member explained, before she joined the cooperative, she was not really aware of issues in her community or the world. Through her participation in the cooperative, she developed personally, has a much better understanding of the world and a deeper appreciation of her community, friends and family. She feels as though she belongs and is an integral part of these social relations.[7] Another interesting feature of Cecosesola is the cross-class character of its members with members coming from middle-class and working-class backgrounds. Some are professionals, while others have little formal education. This multi-class character has not led to inequality in power but rather enriches it culturally and facilitates skill sharing within and across the cooperatives. Commoning of knowledge and deep democratic culture, as part of collective capacity, is integral to the solidarity economy system.

Cecosesola sees itself as consciously addressing negative forces in society such as capitalism's possessive individualism and consumerism as well as patriarchal systems through a constant process of educating themselves and nurturing their collective bonds. They recognise that a great deal of mainstream cultures promote individualism, competition and patriarchy and therefore constantly question the effects of these on their personal lives and relationships. For example, they do not organise their work (except for the healthcare workers such as doctors) along areas of specialisation but encourage every worker–owner to voluntarily rotate among different jobs. They see this as good for the individual but also for the collective culture as it deepens wider relationships among members. Rotating duties and mutual acts of care has created an ethos of commoning work, which is diametrically opposed to the specialisation and competition promoted in capitalist workplaces. Their commitment to care is reflected in the way in which elder members of the cooperative remain involved and are not forced to retire or made to feel irrelevant due to their age. They allow elders to choose how much they want to work and always have a role for them. This is not only kind, they maintain, but also intergenerational relationships are good for everyone and enhance the culture of the cooperative. It reflects a culture of care and belonging. Cecosesola maintains that their approach is an ongoing process of development of the self through the collective. They are consciously trying to develop a new ethos and sensibilities based on commoning, respect, transparency, honesty, responsibility, trust and community through the cooperative. As they explain, they do not look for dreams that prescribe what the world should look like but look to themselves and their collective energy to co-create the future in the present.

Situating the cooperatives within social relations also spills over into their approach towards other enterprises, market relations and the broader community. The cooperatives have used their democratic systems to build networks across enterprises. Such networks of self-managed units of production, consumer associations and community controlled financial schemes have successfully placed human needs at the centre of their work. These networks have developed into solidarity economy relations in which solidarity and cooperation are central to organising economic relations (Mance 2014). In other words, rather than allowing the market to determine conditions of work and competition among enterprises, the cooperative infuses markets with values of human well-being, collaboration and solidarity. Cecosesola goes beyond isolated cooperatives or individual social enterprises that work independently from other solidarity economy enterprises to being a rich movement based on deeply engrained interconnections.

INDIGENOUS TRADITIONS OF NATURE-HUMAN RELATIONS: HEIVELD COOPERATIVE IN SOUTH AFRICA

Moving from the dense network of cooperatives in the central part of Venezuela to the organic rooibos tea farmers' cooperative, the Heiveld Cooperative Limited at the southern tip of Africa in the arid region of South Africa, shifts our focus to a fragile and unique ecosystem where the local people and natural environment are integrally intertwined. The Heiveld Cooperative vividly demonstrates the close relationship small-scale farmers have with the natural world.[8] Perhaps more than any other cooperative we researched, Heiveld's lifeblood is integrally linked to the fragile and unique local environment. Not only is it the only place in the world where rooibos grows naturally, giving it the highly prized 'wild rooibos', but also the entire production process depends on very specific climatic conditions as much of it happens through traditional practices under open skies. Southern Africa, including South Africa, are considered one of ten 'climatic hot spots' on the planet with global warming happening at twice the global average (Scholes, Engelbrecht and Vogel 2020). For Heiveld, this means that the already fragile conditions in which they work are becoming increasingly precarious in a part of the country that is expected to become hotter and drier. Many of the small-scale farmers in the cooperative are descendants of the indigenous peoples of Southern Africa (the Khoi and San), come from the area, grew up living and working on local farms and have deep local and indigenous knowledge about the region, their natural environment and the rooibos plant. For many, rooibos has been part of their lives from their earliest memories. Thus, their intimate and deep knowledge and understanding of the region's environmental conditions and flora is becoming even more salient for their survival. Indeed, knowing where the wild rooibos grows requires intimate knowledge about the region and plant life, making the local residents the guardians of the region's rooibos.

On one of our visits to the cooperative, we experienced their deep connection to their local environment. Very rarely, the Candelabra Lily (also known as Josephine Lily) blooms in this arid region if, and only if, the area received late summer rains that trigger the bulb to flower within 21 days of the rain. The event turns the dry arid area into a brilliant display of vibrant pink rounded candelabra-like flowers. There had been late summer rains the first year we visited, but a month later the flowers had not yet bloomed causing concern among local residents. There was great anticipation of the beautiful event but also worry that the flowers had not yet bloomed. We were sitting in a meeting with several cooperative members when a man ran into the office and excitedly announced that the flowers were blooming. Everyone in the room jumped up to see the spectacular display of flowers. The joy on people's faces was contagious, making us aware that we were experiencing one of nature's rare gifts. The meeting re-started a few hours later when everyone had returned. The event allowed us to experience their profound connection to the area, not hesitating to stop their meeting to enjoy the spectacle of the Candelabra Lily. The example might seem banal or insignificant, but a closer look at the moment reflects a deep connection the members had to nature.

Heiveld in Context

The achievements of Heiveld must be seen in the context of development in post-apartheid South Africa. Despite over 30 years of democracy, South Africa has become one of the most unequal societies in the world with over 50 per cent[9] of its 59.6 million inhabitants[10] living below the poverty line, a 60 per cent youth unemployment rate (Statista 2024) and nearly half the population registering as food insecure. While it scores relatively well in terms of literacy at 87 per cent, its life expectancy dropped in 2007 to 45 years of age, in part due to the HIV-AIDs pandemic, but in 2022 registered at 59 for men and 65 for women (Statistics South Africa 2017; South African Government 2021).[11] Another significant feature of the past 30 years is the country's increased contribution to climate change and global warming due to its reliance on fossil fuels, especially coal, which makes it a heavy polluter with a significantly higher ecological footprint than the rest of the continent. South Africa's per capita CO_2 emissions in 2020 were 7.62 tonnes and its per capita all greenhouse gas emissions were 9.6 tonnes in 2019.[12] In terms of cumulative emissions between 1884 and 2020, the country produced 21.16 billion tonnes of CO_2, and in 2020 its annual global share of emissions was 1.3 per cent whereas its share of global population was only 0.76 per cent (Ritchie, Roser and Rosado 2020; World Population Review 2022). During the post-apartheid period, the annual CO_2 emissions increased by 64 per cent to 502.26

million tonnes in 2020 compared to 326 million tonnes in 1991 with electricity and heating accounting for the largest portion in both periods and doubling in size to 290.29 million tonnes in 2020 from 146.55 million tonnes in 1990. Transport's share significantly grew from 30.38 million tonnes in 1990 to 58.54 million tonnes in 2020, whereas manufacturing and construction dropped from 54.53 million tonnes in 1990 to 44.76 million tonnes in 2020, and agriculture dropped from 32.37 million tonnes in 1990 to 28.88 million tonnes in 2020. Taken together, these numbers show that South Africa contributes significantly to climate change and has continued to do so over the past 30 years, but the sectors contributing have shifted overwhelmingly to electricity, heating and transport. It is in this context that the achievements of Heiveld Cooperative take on special significance.

The Heiveld Cooperative formed in 2000 in the small rustic town of Nieuwoudtville in the Cederberg Mountains of the Northern Cape province of South Africa. Lying on rugged terrain, Heiveld Cooperative produces some of the finest organic rooibos tea in the world with a market niche that reaches Europe, North America, Australia and East Asia. The farms of the Heiveld Cooperative lie scattered across the region, ranging between five and 70 kilometres outside of town on the semi-arid plateaux of the South Bokkeveld district. This part of South Africa has one of the most unique ecosystems in the world and is considered the jewel of the Cape Floral Kingdom, one of only six floral kingdoms on earth. Among its many extraordinary characteristics, the Cape Floral Kingdom is the only place in the world where rooibos grows naturally due to the area's unique climatic and soil conditions that combine to make the perfect conditions for the rare rooibos plant.

Heiveld contrasts markedly to the mainstream rooibos industry, which consists of approximately 350 large corporate farmers who produce 98 per cent of the harvest with 15,000 tonnes traded a year, amounting to a R300 million-a-year industry that employs 5,000 people. The footprint of commercial rooibos grown in uniform plantations increased from 4,000 hectares in 1991 to over 60,000 hectares by 2016, with many using chemicals and other inputs that threaten the unique biodiversity of the region. Rooibos has also attracted international attention with 141 patents registered by 2016, most of which are registered by Japanese companies, which raises serious concern about cultural and indigenous knowledge appropriation. The mainstream rooibos industry has its roots in the apartheid-era 40-year monopoly imposed by the government and continues to operate firmly within capitalist exploitative relations of production (Wynberg 2016).

Traditional and Ecological Sensitive Approaches to Rooibos Production

In contrast to the dynamics in corporate rooibos farming, Heiveld Cooperative is registered as a primary trading cooperative with 64 farmer members, all of whom are from previously disadvantaged categories.[13] The cooperative is open to all small-scale organic farmers in the region, but tightly controls the fair-trade organic farming standards of its members to ensure it maintains its high-quality tea. The five-member elected board oversees the cooperative's functioning and three employees are responsible for administration, marketing and day-to-day financial management. The structure of the cooperative is quite innovative and especially well-suited for their conditions as members are scattered across the area. The 64 members own (or rent) small-scale farms (15 farms in total), either individually or in groups (many are owned by multiple family members), and cultivate organic rooibos plants on their farms exclusively for the cooperative. While one farm might be owned collectively, all farmers are members of the cooperative. For example, one of the farms of the cooperative has eleven members. Part of the justification for individual membership rather than each farm counting as one member is that it helps empower women as each individual member receives their share of payment directly, which ensures the women have control over their own financial resources. Being sensitive to issues of gender inequality within the household, the cooperative is intervening to ensure it plays a positive gender-equalising role in the households of its members.[14]

The members are responsible for the cultivation and harvesting of the plants themselves, although the cooperative provides many forms of assistance (for example, seedlings, mentor farmers, financial support). Once the rooibos has been harvested by the farmer members, the cooperative steps into the production cycle and plays the primary role in the numerous stages that the tea must still go through before it is sent to market. The cooperative transparently records the amount of rooibos delivered by each farmer to ensure the farmers are paid correctly.

The production process draws on the age-old traditions that many of the members learnt as children. Rooibos is highly dependent on local environmental conditions. Unlike coffee beans, which are sold in their raw (washed or unwashed) form, rooibos tea is sold in its final form. Thus, the environmental conditions play a role throughout the production process. Once the rooibos has been harvested and bundled, it is brought to the tea court, where the cooperative takes over the production cycle. Once at the tea court, the rooibos must be cut, 'bruised' and allowed to 'sweat' for 12 hours before laid to dry for six to eight hours on the tea court. The hot summer sun is crucial for both the sweating and drying parts of the production cycle. The famous red colour of the rooibos tea is achieved through drying the tea in the baking hot summer sun. Indeed, climate conditions are crucial in the rooibos production cycle, which needs both cold winter nights and hot dry summer days. For example, rare summer rain will destroy the tea during the summer drying phase on the tea court. Once the tea has been dried and raked every two hours with natural wood rakes (an important indigenous technology that Heiveld maintains is crucial in the organic process), it is bagged in 50-kilogram bags and sent to the Red-T Company in Clan William for sterilisation and sifting. This is the only part of the production cycle that is outsourced. The tea is returned to Heiveld in four grades and is then ready for packaging. The tea is packaged in Cape Town at the Fair Trade Packaging Company, which is a joint-stock company owned by Heiveld, Wupperthal Cooperative (another local rooibos tea cooperative) and a progressive businessman in Cape Town. Once packaged, it is ready to ship overseas to Europe, North America, Australia and Asia.

Finding Alternative Markets

For the cooperative to function in a competitive capitalist market environment it must sell on the fair-trade market, which requires farmers adhere to the strict rules of organic farming and exclusively produce for the cooperative. Thus, all members sign a production agreement with the cooperative guaranteeing that they will only harvest rooibos tea for the cooperative. To support the farmers, the cooperative has a mentor farmer programme to assist members with farming techniques, assessing problems with plants, ensuring proper organic methods and any other forms of help needed. In 2006 Indigo, a local NGO, assisted the cooperative to map all the farms on a GPS mapping system, which assists in monitoring farms and estimating production. Moreover, it serves the additional feature of providing an easy way to link local production to global markets. International consumers can easily locate the region in which the fair-trade organic rooibos has been produced through the GPS mapping system.

The Heiveld Cooperative has consciously grown its production in relation to its capacity to access fair-trade markets. In 2006, it sold 36 tonnes of tea with a turnover of 1.5 million rand on the fair-trade market; by 2008, it raised its production to 60 tonnes of tea, of which 90 per cent sold on the fair-trade market; and by 2017, it produced between 60 and 80 tonnes, again mostly for the fair-trade market. Its production capacity is far greater but is limited by market access which is a perennial challenge faced by small-scale rooibos farmers. While some criticise the commercialisation of rooibos (see Wynberg 2017), for Heiveld the production processes have remained environmentally sensitive and embedded in the socio-ecological relations of the region. Such critiques are important in terms of the large commercial agribusiness approach to farming in general, but are not applicable to a cooperative based on small-scale farms owned by previously disadvantaged people using traditional farming methods.

The rooibos tea industry is controlled by large commercial farmers who have monopoly control over market access. A Rooibos Tea Council regulates the industry and is dominated by large commercial farmers with only one small-scale farmer represented by a member of Heiveld Cooperative. The Rooibos Tea Council is a powerful vehicle for determining standards in the industry and controlling access to the market, as well as determining the value of rooibos tea that goes through their central grading and distribution centre. The Council has prevented Heiveld Cooperative's tea from entering the local market by assigning it a low grade. When Heiveld tea is graded by an independent body, the tea receives the highest grade possible for organic rooibos tea. The Council, however, consistently lowers the grade, which ultimately means the price falls below the cost of production. It is nearly impossible to enter the South African rooibos tea market on fair terms due to this control.

With the local market difficult to penetrate, the attraction of the fair-trade market for small producers is very clear: there is often a threefold difference in price between fair trade and conventional markets. For example, in 2007 the cooperative received R22 (approximately $1.18)[15] per kilogram of tea from the fair-trade market, while the conventional market price was R8 ($0.43) per kilogram, which is nearly a threefold difference. One of the drawbacks of the fair-trade market is that it is very small, and thus the amount sold is a fraction of Heiveld's production capacity. Unlike coffee, Rooibos tea does not have a long storage life and therefore every year's harvest must be sold that year. The short lifespan of the harvested tea makes it more sensitive to climate change and extreme climate events such as severe droughts. For Heiveld the fragility of its environment is felt very immediately and directly, and therefore the farmers have had to learn quickly.

Internalising Socio-ecological Relations

After a severe three-year drought (2003–2006), Heiveld realised it had to proactively approach climate change and its impacts in order to develop an appropriate response strategy. Unlike the mainstream commercial rooibos farming, the environmental impact of Heiveld is negligible, and its activities enhance the local natural environment. In other words, it is not a cause of climate change but has to find ways to deal with the effects of climate change as it is highly dependent on a very fragile ecosystem. In response to the 2003 drought, the cooperative set up systems to review its response strategies every three months to accommodate changing weather patterns. With the help of two progressive NGOs that work on issues of climate change – Indigo and the Environmental Monitoring Group (EMG) – workshops on long-range weather forecasts, possible response options and larger effects of global warming were organised. EMG also provided education and awareness raising about environmentally sustainable farming, the importance of organic farming and organic seedling development. In addition, the cooperative developed linkages with agricultural researchers from the University of Cape Town (UCT), encouraging students to undertake relevant research on topics such as soil conditions, environmental impacts and rooibos farming methods. Tapping into scientific knowledge reinforced their experiential and traditional knowledge and has helped them to adapt to climate change in real time.

In response, the cooperative and its members invested in myriad adaptation responses, such as constructing windbreaks around the farms to limit drying, erosion and wind damage, managing run-off water to prevent soil erosion and removing water-hungry invasive plant species. In addition, the cooperative (together with agricultural researchers at the UCT) monitors members' rooibos plants to assist with advice and guidance. The members knew that wild rooibos grows more slowly, but from their experience they learnt that it is also more drought resistant. This was corroborated by farmers' experience and UCT researchers who confirmed that wild rooibos had larger roots that enabled it to withstand greater climate extremes and was more drought resistant than cultivated rooibos (Louw 2006).[16] This encouraged members to find ways to increase the growth of wild rooibos without affecting the biodiversity in the region.

In addition to adaptation methods to farming practices, they have also ensured a low ecological footprint in their production process. The surplus made through the Fair Trade Labelling Organisation premium was used to build a tea court, including installing a photovoltaic solar system for lights, water pumps and power tools. In 2015, it upgraded the solar system and added a 10,000-litre tank for rainwater harvesting. There are also two members developing organic seedlings for the cooperative, which the members buy directly from the cooperative rather than from commercial farmers. This was started in 2008 when the cooperative realised that organic seedlings was another area in which it could become self-sufficient while simultaneously ensuring high-quality organic seedlings for its members.

A few points of contrast to commercial farming are worth noting as it further illustrates the ecologically sensitive and synergistic practices of Heiveld. Unlike commercial farmers who use machines to harvest the plants by cutting most of the plant, Heiveld members hand cut only the top half of the bush. Hand cutting is much gentler on the plant, allowing the bush to grow back better. It prolongs the lifespan of each plant by a few years and requires no fuel for machines. Another contrast to commercial farmers is in the drying phase. Commercial farmers use hot blowers to quicken the drying process and reduce the amount of time the tea spends on the tea court (hence speeding up the production process). This is a more energy-intensive process. Heiveld, by contrast, allows the tea to fully dry for six to eight hours on the tea court, using the sun (a commons renewable energy source), which enhances the rich colour and flavour of the tea.

While it distinguishes itself from the large commercial farmers, the cooperative understands cooperation, rather than competition, and local knowledge sharing is an important value from which it has also benefited. For example, in their formation period, they exchanged visits with successful community-based cooperatives, which was instrumental in shaping and inspiring Heiveld members. In our interviews, members highlighted the importance of these initial exchange visits and ongoing close relations with other cooperatives. The four-day visit to a brick-making cooperative and a visit with the Wupperthal Rooibos Tea Association – made up of small-scale farmers very similar to the Heiveld farmers – inspired Heiveld farmers and made them realise that they too could pool their human, ecological and economic resources into a commons that produces organic rooibos tea collectively.

Like many other cooperatives we researched, Heiveld has deeply embedded its activities in the socio-ecological reproductive relations of its members and the broader community, which is encoded into its mission statement: 'to produce and market the finest organic rooibos tea at fair prices on behalf of our members, and thereby create a better life for small-scale farmers and other less privileged members of the community' (Oettle and Kolle 2003, 43). Like Cecosesola, Heiveld practises counterhegemonic values that are human- and nature-centred and that are synergistically connected to their local environment. One way in which this is illustrated is through valuing the contribution of all members regardless of their formal education. For example, an illiterate member with no formal education is one of the most knowledgeable rooibos farmers, born and raised on the land and who grew up cultivating rooibos plants. His contribution is invaluable, and he is often called upon for advice and guidance. Another member has a university education, and his skills are used in administration and management. Tapping into different skills not only values members' varied contributions but also creates an inclusive culture; a commoning culture. Because members are scattered across the rugged and remote region with vast distances between the farms, building a sense of community among farmers enhanced the overall sense of belonging. The sense of solidarity and commitment to uplifting the entire community was demonstrated in their various community projects which positively impacted the region.

Heiveld's constitution requires it to invest 30 per cent of its surplus in community projects that benefit the larger community by sponsoring community projects, supporting educational scholarships and upgrading the local school. It has also helped create permanent and seasonal employment for approximately 100 people. The wages the cooperative pay are guaranteed fair-trade wages, which is higher than what farmworkers normally get paid. In addition, the farmer members hire additional workers to assist with harvesting and the cooperative monitors labour relations so that farmers pay fair-trade wages. In addition to the wages, there are other benefits that assist the workers. For example, the workers are transported to the farms, given free accommodation during the week (they return home on weekends), provided with free water (there is no running water on most farms) and firewood. Job creation in a region of severe economic marginalisation is a tremendous achievement and has helped to alleviate some of the most severe forms of poverty. In addition to the jobs created in production of the rooibos, a number of additional jobs have been created in packaging and tourism. Five women's groups with three to five members each make the cotton bags and silk-screened boxes for overseas sales. In 2006 the Rooibos Heritage Route linking the farming communities of Heiveld and Wupperthal was established with women's groups providing the accommodation and catering services for the route. According to Heiveld, the Heritage Route allows tourists to 'experience the life of small-scale farmers, learn about medicinal plants and baking traditional bread, and harvest your own rooibos' (*Heiveld News*, March 2007). It is these sorts of activity that place Heiveld in a synergistic approach to cooperative relations.

The experience of Heiveld illustrates the ways in which the cooperative has integrated its connection to nature into its economic activity through a relationship of respect and working with natural relations in a non-destructive manner. Nature is not outside of its practice or worldview, but rather integrally connected to the lifeblood of the members and the cooperative and everything it does. It has successfully linked alternative forms of production at the local level with a global movement for fair-trade practices and deepened its environmentally integrated approach to growing rooibos that also expresses planetary care. In the process, it has built a community based on solidarity and is a deeply embedded cooperative in its region and the lives of those involved.

COMMONING TRADITION EVOLVES INTO A SOCIO-ECOLOGICALLY EMBEDDED COOPERATIVE NETWORK: TRENTINO, NORTHERN ITALY

Moving from the fragile and unique ecosystem that produces some of the world's best rooibos tea on the southern tip of Africa to the mountainous region of northern Italy, the autonomous province of Trentino[17] has pioneered a socio-ecological approach to economic activity. Trentino cooperatives constitute a synergistic cooperative system across society that has a long history in the region.[18] The dense network of cooperatives has maintained values of cooperation, human-centred development and well-being, and synergistically lives with nature. Indeed, the relationship to the natural world is long encoded through the region's strong history of the commons.

For nearly a millennium, the region has collaboratively managed and collectively owned common natural systems such as forests, grazing lands and water (Gretter et al. 2018, 2). The region has a long history of autonomy and self-reliance dating back at least a millennium. Through collectively managing natural systems for the common good, the cooperative has deeply entrenched practices of sharing, cooperation and living within natural systems – the remote and fragile Alpine ecosystems that require careful stewardship. Collectively owning and collaboratively managing such systems for the common interest reflects a commoning ontology in which the well-being of nature and community are integrally intertwined; it is an ontology in which humans exist in and depend on nature and must ensure that natural ecosystems are protected and maintained. Commoning is not only beneficial to communities but also has positive environmental impacts on local ecologies, as natural systems are managed based on their collective value (use value) and not their exchange value on the market. Local traditional (ecological) knowledge ensures long-term resilience and planetary care. Thus, it inherently brings an understanding to natural systems that prioritises ecological care and collective decision making based on community needs, nature's capacity, long-term vision and ensuring fair use.

Long History of the Commons Articulates through Collective Interests and Cooperatives

In Italy, the commons are anchored in customary rights embedded in community property that has been democratically managed for millennia. In Trentino, there is evidence that collective management of common systems has been practised in the region since at least the twelfth century (Gretter et al. 2018). Commoning finds resonance across Italy and was given additional force in Article 118 of the Italian Constitution, which introduced the 'principle of subsidiarity', providing for citizen initiatives (both as individuals and collectives) that are in the general interest (Senato della Repubblica 1947, Article 118). Article 118 codifies in law citizen activities that regenerate and manage collective goods based on their collective value to communities and not their value as economic resources (Gretter et al. 2018). Gretter et al. (2018, 4) argue that Article 118 provides a 'legislative platform on which to build a new model of society characterized by widespread presence of active citizens establishing an alliance with public administration in taking care of common goods'.

Thus, the Italian Constitution embeds the collaborative management of collective goods into democratic institutions of local and provincial government. Complementing this, the Italian government and the Autonomous Trentino Provincial government (cooperatives fall under the jurisdiction of provincial law) have created a layered legislative and legal framework that supports cooperative forms and civic empowerment (for example, Italian Civil Code Article 2511) and a tax system that offers myriad benefits for cooperatives[19] (OECD 2014; Borzaga and Mittone 1997; Gonzales 2010a, 2010b). The legal framework also recognises the importance of mutual purpose and the non-economic value of cooperation by explicitly highlighting the 'social function of co-operation of a mutually supportive, non-speculative nature' (Article 45).

The 'autonomous initiatives of citizens … relating to activities of general interest' (Senato della Repubblica 1947, Article 118) aligns closely with the long-held practices of Trentino and the Italian Alps more broadly. Indeed, approximately 1.5 million hectares of land in the Italian Alps is collectively owned and managed (mainly forest and grazing lands), including 60 per cent (370,000 hectares) of Trentino's 620,000 hectares. Over one-third of the land is natural parks and protected areas, and approximately 50 per cent of the area is forested and grazing land. Thus, commoning natural systems shaped the development of the area and laid the bases for cooperative forms of production, consumption and financing in the region.

With its history of autonomy and commoning, the ground was fertile for cooperatives with the first credit union forming in 1885 and the first retail cooperative in 1890, followed by the first cooperative bank in 1892.[20] By 1898, 170 cooperatives with 20,000 members had formed in the villages of Trentino and by 1914 there were 179 rural banks across Trentino (OECD 2014; Cooperazione Trentina 2006). The cooperative movement originally formed due to dire poverty in the region. The region was a crucial frontline territory between Italy and Austria–Hungary and suffered mass destruction during World War I. Thereafter, it felt a sense of neglect and discrimination from the central government due to their borderland history. After World War II, through a treaty signed by the foreign ministers of Austria and Italy, Trentino and South Tyrol became the autonomous region of Trentino Alto Adige/Südtirol under the Italian Constitution. With this history and the traditions of commoning, cooperatives resonated with the people of Trentino. Over the course of the twentieth century, cooperatives continued to grow, especially in agriculture, after World War II. The scattered and isolated villages across the mountainous areas meant that farms remained small (one to two hectares) and were highly dependent on local natural conditions. As a result, small-scale farmers formed agricultural cooperatives to bring together the privately owned small-scale farms to consolidate their activities. The agricultural cooperatives made up of small-scale farms across many villages reflects this interconnection with the natural conditions.

With its 130-year history of cooperatives in the region, Trentino has one of the highest concentrations of and the most successful cooperatives in Italy, together with Emilia Romagna. With a deep sense of collaboration and social linkages, the Trentino cooperatives are rooted in the villages and communities across the province, forming a dense network of production, agricultural, consumption, social and finance cooperatives that have transformed the local political and economic relations and embedded a socio-ecological ontology into their practices.

The Federation of Trentino Cooperatives oversees and facilitates cooperatives in the province and is home to nearly 600 cooperatives in its 223 villages with approximately 270,000 members (which is 50 per cent of the population of 540,000). There are 23,000 worker–owners in 293 cooperatives, 21,000 farmer members in 101 cooperatives, 82,000 retail members in 85 cooperatives, 108,000 members of cooperative banks and 5,400 administrators in the cooperatives and federation, who are themselves also members. The 600 cooperatives are federated into 21 secondary societies and one federation with a turnover of €2.61 billion and total net worth of €3.67 billion (FTC 2014). The strength and embeddedness of the cooperative movement strikes you at every turn. Village squares are marked by the cooperative store Famiglia Cooperative (which sources approximately 60 per cent of its products from cooperatives) and the cooperative bank Casse Rurali (which provides 60 per cent of the credit in the sector), and the surrounding areas are peppered with small-scale productive farms linked to cooperatives (OECD 2014: 33). Nearly every village has a cooperative store with 207 village cooperative shops (out of 223 villages) making it very convenient for the local people to shop in their village rather than travel distances to a large mega-store. The cooperative stores are linked into one large cooperative in which the small village stores are subsidised by the big stores. This solidarity policy within the cooperative store system keeps village stores alive as they would not survive on their own.

Cooperatives Central to Trentino's Socio-ecological Systems

The rich fabric of cooperative relations translates into socio-ecological well-being and quality of life. These three cooperative sectors – agriculture, consumer and banking – are the backbone of the rural economy and reflect a concerted effort to shape local development.

Together with the provincial government, the agricultural sector has consciously tried to make farming viable in the mountainous villages across the province and thus addressed two central issues: (1) how to generate rewards for local farmers; and (2) how to keep them in the mountainous villages. In these efforts, they used the local ecological conditions to focus on three products: wine, dairy (especially milk) and fruit (especially apples). Over 80 per cent of farmed land in Trentino is part of cooperatives. Local consumption across the province (and country) has supported the agricultural cooperatives. For example, 90 per cent of the agriculture consumed in the main town of Trento is produced by cooperatives in the region. There are 69 banks with 341 branches that provide 60 per cent of the total credit in the area. There is a central cooperative wholesaler that supplies the local cooperative shops and 38 per cent of consumer goods are sold through cooperative stores. Through the shops, eight per cent of all local agricultural produce, including wine and cheese, is sold. The rest is exported to the rest of Italy and abroad. Over 80 per cent of apples consumed in Italy are produced by the Trentino cooperatives.

The Trentino cooperative network enables myriad worker cooperatives in a range of sectors, from taxis, teaching, light manufacturing and construction to services such as eldercare and hospitality. The cooperative network has also experimented with hybrid forms such as social cooperatives that work with the local state to provide a service. The distinction between a service cooperative and a social cooperative is in whose interests they champion. For example, service cooperatives, such as teaching or taxi cooperatives, primarily focus on delivering to their members whereas social cooperatives focus on delivering a service to the community, such as eldercare and childcare. We would consider both forms worker cooperatives as the primary activity is work, and worker–owners collectively own, control and make decisions about their cooperative. Because the activity of worker cooperatives encompasses a central part of the lives and livelihoods of the members, they tend to play a much stronger role in the lives of their members. Thus, worker cooperatives produce a deeper sense of commitment and relations among members in comparison to, for example, members of a cooperative bank. With over 50 per cent of the population belonging to a cooperative, in many cases a worker cooperative, the result is a deeply embedded cooperative network in Trentino.

Agricultural Cooperatives Pioneer Socio-ecological Relations

Trentino's history of the commons and commoning is deeply reflected in its cooperative traditions today, which integrate life-enabling natural and social systems with local cultural traditions. To appreciate the role of Trentino cooperatives in socio-ecological reproduction, it is worth pausing to look more specifically at a few agricultural cooperatives. For example, the integrated and organic farming methods of Val di Gresta Fruit and Vegetable Cooperative has turned its region into the 'organic garden of Trentino'. Founded in 1969, it consists of 100 members and produces 20,000 quintals (2,000 tonnes) of produce a year of which 80 per cent is certified organic and the remaining 20 per cent is integrated cultivation that minimises inputs. It grows an impressive range of vegetables, such as radicchio, green beans, carrots, pumpkins, cabbage, potatoes, celeriac, cauliflower and onions, and also pickles products, makes compotes, syrups and sauces.

Reflecting the deeply interwoven care approach, Terre Altre Cooperative (Natural Mountain Agricultural Cooperative) was formed in 2013 to promote opportunities for 'people in a state of fragility'. Its small cooperative size made up of different membership types (three working members, five volunteer members and 19 subsidising members, including five associations) is matched by its beautiful vision of building an inclusive community 'based on human solidarity, respect and appreciation of each individual'.[21] The cooperative offers people in need organic and regenerative agricultural training that excludes herbicides, pesticides and chemical fertilisers to learn to respect the earth and its cycles, promote biodiversity, listen to the wisdom of nature and work with natural systems. It focuses on cultivating ancient varieties of grains, vegetables, fruit trees and herbs and promoting artisanal methods that have long been practised in the region. Terre Altre Cooperative believes that changing values comes through practice, education and awareness, and therefore hosts cultural activities and educational programmes to experience deep ecology. A further example of combining social and ecological reproduction into a cooperative is the Ortinbosco Le Formichine Cooperative that focuses on women in difficult situations. Inspired by the organisation Famiglia Materna, which has catered for women in need for over a century, Ortinbosco formed in 2006 on the outskirts of Rovereto village on a piece of cultivated land in a natural forest to help people in fragile situations restart their lives with new opportunities. They teach how to grow local food grounded in natural ecosystems. Implicit in the approaches of both these cooperatives is a deep appreciation of the healing power of natural relations.

Across Trentino there are cooperatives in a variety of agricultural activities, all valuing the importance of place and the natural environment, cultural heritage, organic and natural practices, and local knowledge. For example, there are dairy farms making handmade artisanal cheese based on ancient knowledge handed down through generations. Val di Fiemme-Cavalese Dairy Cooperative was founded in 1966 and has 80 dairy farmer members whose native, local breeds of livestock live on a natural diet and produce top quality milk and cheese free of preservatives and dyes. The values extend to cooperative members as they value 'loyalty, love, solidarity, and nourish collaborations everyday as in a real family'.[22] Another dairy cooperative, Gruppo Formaggi del Trentino, founded in 1993 with 17 member cooperatives and approximately 700 farmers produces one million quintals (100,000 tonnes) of milk a year. Using artisanal traditions and natural products (milk, salt and rennet) and no additives or preservatives, the cooperative produces extraordinarily flavourful local cheeses with cows exclusively fed on fresh grass, cereals and hay from local pastures. There is also Presanella Social Dairy that formed in 1976 to breed local brown cows, which had nearly 40 members at the time of our research.

The breadth of cooperative activities is staggering. The Cooperativa Castanicoltori Del Trentino Alto Adige (Trentino Alto Adige Chestnut Growers Cooperative), formed in 1994, has 70 contributing members that focus on protecting the centuries-old chestnut groves that are a collective heritage of the region by keeping the ancient cultivating practices alive and visible. Similarly, formed in 1979 and with approximately 800 members, the Sant'Orsola Cooperative focuses on cultivating small mountain patches with small fruits such as strawberries, blueberries, raspberries, blackberries and red currants. Even the trout and char traditional farms formed a cooperative in 1988, the Astro Cooperative, which includes 50 fishing farms that produce 700 tonnes of trout per year. The Alpine trout and char farms are distributed in rivers fed by glacier waters throughout the valleys and focus on following the rhythms of nature. This has secured the cooperative the prestigious 'European recognition of Protected Geographical Indication' (PGI) and the 'Friend of the sea' certification. Trentino's farming cooperatives are buttressed by a dense network of ten consumer cooperative 'families'. For example, Famiglia Cooperativa Brenta Paganella formed in 1893 and has 2,190 members. It continues to be a central reference point in the villages where it operates.

Ensuring local breeds and traditions are the basis of the farming activities, the cooperative Federazione Provinciale Allevatori (Provincial Breeders Federation) makes certain that the natural resources are preserved, the local landscape maintained and animals protected. Working exclusively with animals born and raised in Trentino and fed on local pastures and hay, the cooperative ensures local varieties remain central to their food culture. Founded in 1957, the cooperative has 1,150 breeders who have 100,000 cattle, pigs, sheep, goats and horses. The commitment to local is exemplified in their pork production – the pigs are slaughtered on the farms where they were born and raised, and the products (for example, meat curing) are processed in the cooperative's plant next to the cooperative store that sells the products. Even wine and beer are made through cooperatives and, in the case of wine, this has been the tradition for over 100 years. The grapes in the vineyards of the region are handpicked by family and friends of the farmers, socialising the harvest as a community process. The wine making is deeply rooted to territory, tradition and culture, but also engages in research and innovation in processing. The craft beer cooperative Arimanni Brewery started in 2018 and produces craft beer using ancient recipes from the region. They use local ingredients, local suppliers, mountain water and environmental packaging and processing.

A particularly interesting cooperative is Agri90 in the village of Storo in the southwestern Chiese Valley, which focuses on growing native corn varieties (made from Marano wheat, a very special local wheat) as well as fruits and vegetables with traditional farming practices of integrated farming. The cooperative formed in 1991 out of a number of older local cooperatives and has 120 members; its mill dates back to 1921 when the Storo Cooperative Family built it to service the local community. The modern mill was built in 1950 and the cooperative started retail sales in the 1980s. Today, Agri90 is famous for its Storo Yellow Flour, which is used in mountain polenta, a regional delicacy.

One of the larger cooperatives, Melinda Cooperative, was formed in 1989 and has over 4,000 producer members growing apples in the mountainous areas. The cooperative produces nearly 400,000 tonnes of applies a year that supply Italy and beyond. While it exports apples, its priority continues to be ensuring local healthy food and good local conditions, the natural environment, and care for the apple trees and farmers. In an effort to become zero waste, the cooperative collaborates with local cooperatives (and other entities) to process sauces and other products from apples that are not aesthetically unsuitable for fresh consumption.

As this selective overview of a number of agricultural cooperatives in the region demonstrates, Trentino cooperatives are deeply embedded in the socio-ecological reproduction and care economy of their region. The cooperatives are deeply interwoven with the uncontaminated nature of their local region and take great care to not contaminate it with their agricultural practices. While all the cooperatives maintain ancient traditions, they also embrace research and innovation across the sectors. Clearly there is a strong tradition of forming cooperatives for all types of activity.

The impact of the cooperative network is reflected in the fact that Trentino went from being one of the poorest to one of the wealthiest regions in Italy (and with low inequality) in large part due to this extensive cooperative network, embedded in a long history of the natural commons and commoning. For example, in 1951 Trentino was very underdeveloped and ranked 67 out of 90 Italian provinces in terms of its economic development. By 2013, Trentino ranked first in Italy in terms of quality of life (OECD 2014, 18). There is also suggestive evidence that a dense cooperative system translates into better government. For example, according to the European Quality Index (EQI), Trentino consistently ranked among the top regions in Italy in terms of quality of government in five surveys (2010, 2013, 2017, 2021, and 2024) (Charron, Lapuente and Bauhr 2022, 19). Central to its success has been creating alternative values that challenge capitalism's dominant values of competition and possessive individualism and that allowed it to develop solidarity economy relations as well as incorporating human, community and natural well-being into the fabric of the cooperative system. From its very beginning, it believed that cooperation is a universal value and insisted on tolerance and openness to all social, religious and political affiliations. The Trentino cooperatives have pioneered synergistic networks of solidarity across society and with natural relations in a non-destructive way.

CONCLUSION

By bringing to the fore human well-being and operating within natural commons boundaries, cooperatives have started recasting the way economies can operate in a way that is not destructive to the social and natural world. It requires upending the separation of the economy from the non-economic realms and subordinating economic activity to the social and natural world as well as developing values that prioritise human well-being, community and social relations, planetary care, solidarity and ecological justice. The worker cooperatives and solidarity economy-based cooperative systems discussed in this chapter provide illustrations of the myriad ways that alternative economies are being experimented with.

6

Engaging Political Power and Creating Solidarities

Mondragón in Spain, State-Civil Society
Synergies in Kerala and the Solidarity
Economy Forum in Brazil

In this chapter, we focus on attempts to embed the economy within socio-ecological relations and democratised public power at a societal level by looking at the ways in which the cooperatives have engaged political power and created webs of solidarity relations. This necessarily shifts our unit of analysis from individual cooperatives to cooperative systems, public power and the state. We chose three very different cases from the federated approach to show the synergies created between democratising political and economic power and embedding economic activity in socio-ecological relations of reproduction – ultimately creating well-being, quality of life and active citizens living within natural systems. The Mondragón cooperative system in the Basque Country of Spain represents an economy based on solidarity, well-being and community. It has raised the quality of life, enhanced local government services and expanded a cooperative economy across the region. The democratisation efforts in the state of Kerala, India offers an example of a state that has created space for cooperative and solidarity economy enterprises to flourish and, in return, to deepen democracy and facilitate the state's capacity to deliver public goods (as part of the social commons). Like Mondragón, the outcome has been increased quality of life, more accountable local government institutions, growth in cooperatives and democratic women-run microenterprises, and a vibrant citizenry. The final example comes from the Brazilian Solidarity Economy Forum, which shows a social movement that has brought together diverse economic activities into a powerful movement that ultimately pressured the government to pass enabling legislation and create a Solidarity Economy Directorate within the Labour Department.

A key argument of this chapter is that embedding economic activity in the larger socio-ecological relations begins to overcome the artificial distinction between the political and economic arenas. In other words, transformative alternatives require democratising and connecting the political and economic spheres. The separation of politics from the economy has been a central feature of capitalism, carefully orchestrated so that it appears a *sine qua non* of good governance and economic activity. In reality, the separation is a charily choreographed mirage that conceals the economy's constitutive reliance on public power and the state. Ironically, the illusion is based on *the state* passing laws, enacting legislation, developing policies and creating the conditions for the economy to operate 'independently' from the state and society. Yet, capitalism's very existence depends on public goods (including education, healthcare and transport systems), legal contracts, legislative frameworks, property relations, law and order, and public infrastructure that the state ensures. The ostensible separation serves four purposes. First, it diminishes the power of the state to discipline and control capital, tapering its capacity to govern and steer economic activity in the interest of the broader public, and focus on creating laws and conditions that serve the interest of capital. Second, it allows capitalism to disavow the state and public power, while freeriding on the services and conditions the state provides (Fraser 2022). Third, it exempts the economy from democratic decision making and collective ownership, allowing it to operate on hierarchical (even despotic) principles and ensuring the inviolability of private property. Fourth, it removes the state from engaging in economic activity. Rather than playing a constructive role in embedding economic activity within socio-ecological relations and democratised public power, the state focuses on creating conditions for corporations to thrive independent of society. In short, separating the economy from the political sphere ensures that democracy, public power and public ownership are reserved for the political realm and the state, and the economy is free from social and political responsibilities.

Similar to the social and natural reproduction that we discussed in previous chapters, separating these arenas from economic activity creates the illusion that they are outside the commodified world of capitalist relations, thereby exonerating capitalism from paying the actual costs of the 'background' on which it is built (Fraser 2022). Ironically, while public power has created the conditions for capitalism, capital is forever undermining the state through varied mechanisms such as evading taxes, pressuring governments, creating transnational bodies such as rating agencies and global financial institutions that discipline states if they do not act in the interest of capital. In the end, capitalism hollows out the state's capacity to protect people, nature and even capitalism from itself, careening capitalism into a systemic crisis that affects all aspects of society – economic, social reproduction, nature and public power.

In contrast to capitalism's approach, solidarity economy-based cooperative systems transform economic activity, redraw boundaries between the economy and the state, and develop solidarity relations among enterprises. And, when they are linked to democratic state-led initiatives that respect bottom-up power, the transformative potential increases significantly. In order to show that cooperatives do not operate on principles of imperial expansion, expropriation and conquering, we show how solidaristic relations, as opposed to capitalist cut-throat competition and global domination, is a principle on which solidarity economy-based cooperative systems operate and flourish at different scalar levels. The examples demonstrate the complementary role that worker cooperatives and solidarity economy enterprises play in socialising the economy, democratising the state and building solidarity relations. At the same time, we see how democratising public power leads the state to create enabling conditions for cooperatives to operate with strong cooperative movements that reinforce accountability of their local governments.

DEMOCRACY, POLITICAL POWER
AND EXTERNAL RELATIONS

To remake the way in which the economy operates and relates to society, public power and the state require new principles, values, ideas and practices. Relevant here are notions of radical forms of democracy that appreciate varied knowledges and a commons ontology to create caring communities, reject expropriation, exploitation and Cartesian dualism, promote solidaristic relations, whether inter- and intra-national or interenterprise, and the well-being of all life on planet earth. (Re)embedding economic activity within the broader socio-ecological relations requires democratic social relations as well as relating to public power differently and shifting from plundering territorial expansion and expropriation to human- and nature-centred systems of living within planetary and social boundaries. Thus, solidarity economy-based cooperative systems and worker cooperatives operate on a fundamentally different ontology from capitalism – one grounded in practice in relation to democracy, public power and the state, as well as relations beyond the enterprise.

Democracy is essential for any transformative politics that seeks social, ecological, economic and political justice. It is an aspirational beacon that provides essential institutions with the means to collectively organise social relations. However, democracy has also become contested as neoliberal capitalism transmogrified it into market democracy whereby corporations and the economic elite have significantly more power to shape states and state policies than citizens exercising their democratic voice. The hollowing out of democracy has given rise to neofascist and populist political leaders and parties. The bifurcated politics coursing through polities sees, on the one hand, exclusionary appeals that resonate with billionaires *and* large numbers of disaffected, precarious people abandoned by traditional political parties in their turn to neoliberal policies and, on the other hand, expansive and inclusionary appeals by unprecedented pro-democracy protests across the world. Both sides claim to be defending democracy.

These varied versions of democracy raise important questions about what democracy is and why it is important. At its most basic level, democracy is the only form of rule that sees people ruling themselves. For people to rule themselves, democracy requires institutions that regulate how it operates and aspirational principles that guide it. In terms of institutional criteria, democracy requires capable and accountable states that develop and implement fair and just laws and public policy that reflect the public's interests, such as economic activity in society's interest, and that support social reproduction, protecting the natural world and all life forms, and creating public institutions that allow for democratic participation. The state must have the capacity to regulate economic activity and discipline corporations to ensure they operate in the public interest, and it must ensure financial accountability of public funds. Democracy also requires states to earn the trust of their publics and build legitimacy for democratic rule (Fraser 2014), which is garnered through democratic practices and inclusive decision making. Equally important is the creation of publics that are organised, engaged, informed and educated in democratic practices.

While public power and states are enormously important in creating and nurturing the conditions for democracy to thrive in political, economic and social spheres, they are not the only actors in a democratic society. It is essential to democratise all sectors of society, including the economy, to upend capitalism and its neoliberal states. To have a caring, democratic society requires extending democracy from the political realm into the economy and social relations. Thus, democracy as a mode of rule is expansive and applies to the entire socio-ecological relations of reproduction. Worker cooperatives and solidarity economy-based cooperative systems internalise democratic arrangements for organising production, distribution and finance, and thus weaken the boundary separating democracy from economic activity. Worker cooperatives are democratic economic institutions that engage in anti-capitalist class *and* boundary struggles. They, thus, represent a crucial emergent transformative possibility.

We now turn to the examples of Mondragón in Spain, democratisation in Kerala and Brazil's Solidarity Economy network to illustrate these issues. We chose these three cases because they all have histories of deeply democratic practices; they relate to public power and the state differently, thus showing plethora conditions of possibility. All the cases move beyond individual enterprises to develop solidarity relations beyond the cooperative with other enterprises and local government.

REDRAWING BOUNDARIES THROUGH A COOPERATIVE SYSTEM: MONDRAGÓN COOPERATIVE CORPORATION

The Mondragón Cooperative Corporation (MCC)[1] is perhaps the most established example in the world of a transformative cooperative system that embeds the economy in socio-ecological relations, operates on anti-capitalist values by placing capital in the service of labour and society, enables solidarity relations among cooperatives and promotes democratic practices not only within the cooperatives, but also in the wider society. In 1956 in the Basque region[2] of Spain, a visionary young priest, Don José Maria Arizmendiarrieta, and five engineers set up Ulgor Cooperative (later renamed Fagor Electrodomésticos),[3] which marked the beginning of the Mondragón experience. Over 70 years, Mondragón has grown into a complex network of approximately 81 cooperatives[4] with 70,000 worker members.

Arizmendiarrieta arrived in the Basque Country in 1941, a few years after the devastating bombing of Guernica[5] in April 1937. He set up the Professional Polytechnical School in 1943, which helped lay the basis for the Ulgor Cooperative. Arizmendiarrieta introduced a radical grassroots Catholicism that emphasised that humanist social relations based on solidarity and people-centred democratic institutions are necessary to preserve workers' autonomy from both capital and the state. The message resonated deeply with the local people as the Basque Country suffered from extremely depressed conditions and dire poverty under Franco's dictatorship in the post-Spanish civil war period. Franco's concerted discrimination and prejudice against the Basque Country helped create the conditions for Arizmendiarrieta's radical ideas, which included collective ownership, people- and community-centred economy, and democratic decision making. It was clear to the Basque people that they could not depend on the Spanish state for any form of support and needed to become self-sufficient. For Arizmendiarrieta, starting a cooperative was only the first step as he envisioned a solidarity society based on humanist values and principles of solidarity and social well-being. These principles have shaped Mondragón for nearly 70 years with commitment to and rootedness in the community of the Basque Country, the centrality of people and their well-being, ecological care, democratic decision making and democratic distribution of surplus. A successful cooperative economy is deeply interwoven into the fabric of the cooperative system.

An Era of Innovation, Growth and Consolidation

In the decades after its formation, Mondragón cooperatives expanded, innovated and became embedded into the political and socio-ecological system of the Basque Country. From the very beginning, Mondragón understood the need to create a diversified cooperative ecosystem if it were to realise a solidarity society. One of the urgent areas to address was finance. Thus, after setting up Ulgor (later Fagor), Mondragón focused its energy on developing avenues to access finance and entrepreneurial skills, which led to the formation of Caja Laboral (in 1959) as the bank and entrepreneurial division that supports cooperatives. Access to capital is essential for survival but is often a massive hurdle for cooperatives. Mainstream banks frequently refuse to provide loans to cooperatives as they do not understand the organisational structure and have an inherent bias against worker-led enterprises. Similarly, state financial support is seldom forthcoming and, if it is, it is often with many strings attached. Thus, in general, cooperatives suffer from dual discrimination – by banks and the state – in terms of access to capital. Mondragón creatively overcame this problem through developing its internal financial systems that provide cooperatives with below-market-rate loans. For example, a cooperative facing financial hardships could secure a loan at eight per cent, in contrast to the market rate of 20 per cent. In the 1990s, when the MCC was formed, the Caja Laboral Popular became a credit cooperative competing with other financial companies. By 2009, the Caja Laboral Popular had €1.366 million invested in Mondragón cooperatives, 1,974 worker members, 394 offices in Spain (mostly in the north of Spain), and it is the second largest finance institution in terms of deposits of credit in the Basque Country. Its insolvency ratio is an impressive 2.9 per cent, which compares favourably to the 4.9 per cent of credit unions.[6]

It is worth pausing on the issue of raising finance as it is so central to cooperative survival. Both Mondragón and ULCCS (discussed in Chapter 4) demonstrate myriad ways of harnessing capital in the interest of labour. While both Mondragón and ULCCS garnered structural power to develop a sophisticated financial system, other worker cooperatives creatively find ways to access finance.[7] For example, Uniforja in Brazil (discussed in Chapter 4) developed a unique approach to accessing funds through the state. When an employee joins Uniforja, the person has three years to become a member. After three years, either the person becomes a full member or they leave. This three-year horizon gives both the employee and the cooperative time to assess whether the person is a good fit for membership in the cooperative. In order to become a member, the worker has to buy a share and pay a membership fee. To facilitate this process, Uniforja officially 'fires' the person, which then qualifies the worker to receive state unemployment benefits. The worker then uses the state unemployment benefits to pay for membership in the cooperative. The use of unemployment benefits to fund membership is a creative and productive use of state funds in support of both the member and the cooperative. As these examples illustrate, cooperatives often find creative and unconventional ways to raise finance in the interest of worker–owners and the cooperative.

Over its first four decades, Mondragón experienced incredible expansion, innovation and consolidation. While industrial cooperatives were (and continue to be) central, the commitment to human and community well-being led to the development of cooperatives in diverse sectors. The founding members recognised the state's failure to provide social provisions to the Basque region and therefore set up a social welfare system, Lagun Aro, to service the town of Mondragón. The sophisticated financial system integrates insurance and pensions with Caja Laboral Popular to provide banking services to the community (for banking and loan making). The interconnections across cooperatives and sectors continued into the 1960s and 1970s, setting the basis for the eventual consolidation into the Mondragón Group. In 1964, Ularco-Fagor formed the first cooperative group, in 1966 Alecop introduced students to working in a cooperative and, in 1969, Eroski was formed by bringing together ten small local consumer cooperatives. In 1974, the cooperatives set up the research centre Ikerlan, which is responsible for designing production technologies, information technologies and energy (for example, solar panels). Otalora Management and Cooperative Development Centre was formed to provide in-service training for managers and cooperative members in cooperative forms of business.

The need for in-house training and research cannot be overstated given that cooperative principles and values are fundamentally different from the profit-oriented capitalist enterprises that send their managers to MBA programmes. Mondragón recognised the need to produce their own managers and leaders with different values to capitalist corporations and to develop technology that kept the cooperatives at the cutting edge without jeopardising their values. In response, Mondragón University was established in 1997. The university not only teaches cooperative principles, values and practices, but also seeks social transformation through participatory learning with a clear objective of human well-being, environmental sustainability and a healthy society (Basterretxea and Albizu 2010).[8] The university is also the innovation hub and centre of research for the Mondragón cooperative system. The investment in education and research has been a defining feature of Mondragón and is reflected in the substantial investment it makes in education. For example, in 2018 it allocated more than €11 million to education and solidarity support to struggling cooperatives (Flecha and Cruz 2011; Santocildes et al. 2021, 86), and by 2024, Mondragón had one university, five technical centres, seven research and development centres, three educational and vocational training centres, and one innovation agent. Building its own institutions, commoning creative labour and collective capacity (such as knowledge) to service the needs of the cooperatives and provide commons public goods reflects its commitment to creating a solidarity society that places humans, nature and the community at the centre. Not only was Mondragón not freeriding on public power and the state but was filling the void left by the state's absence in social welfare delivery and transforming the local socio-ecological relations and political field.

Cooperatives continued to emerge through the assistance of the extensive support system built through Caja Laboral's Business Division, the growth of cooperative associations, initiatives of cooperative development and the Ikerlan Research Centre. While the growth in the number of cooperatives emerging was celebrated, it also meant the needs of Mondragón began to change as the cooperatives required a coherent organising structure that could coordinate the larger cooperative ecosystem. Working in its favour, there were significant changes in the national and geopolitical context with the Basque Cooperative Law (Law 1/1982 of 11 February) coming into effect in 1982[9] and Spain joining the European Economic Community in 1986, which allowed for new developments within Mondragón. As a result, in 1987, the Congress of Cooperatives created the Mondragón Cooperative Group (GCM) and the 1991 Congress formed the MCC.

The dense network of cooperatives and support institutions in education, finance, social welfare, and research and development have ensured Mondragón's continued growth and development with over 80 cooperatives by 2024: nearly 60 industrial cooperatives, two finance cooperatives, one of which is a credit cooperative, six retail cooperatives including Eroski supermarket chain, four agricultural, three educational and training, thirteen research and development cooperatives (including the university), and six services cooperatives. What is particularly interesting is that the dense network of cooperatives that support a wide range of needs of the people, community and cooperatives has not sidelined the central role of the cooperatives in the industrial sector. Rather the growth and consolidation of the Mondragón cooperative system has complimented and strengthened the development of the industrial cooperatives and embedded the system within the broader socio-ecological system.

Success as a Socially Embedded Cooperative System

Mondragón is successful by any measure. It is a successful 'business model' in terms of revenue, dynamism and diversification; it has created jobs, especially industrial jobs, in an era of job losses in the wider economy; it has promoted human and community well-being by embedding economic activity within the socio-ecological system and it has remained committed to its values and democratic practices. For example, the dynamism of the research and development programme is seen in the wide range of sectors that the industrial cooperatives work in, such as automobiles, components, construction, industrial equipment, domestic appliances, engineering and capital goods, and machine tools. In 2013, Mondragón posted that its combined revenue for the Mondragón cooperatives was €12 billion, and by 2023, its turnover was US$13.49 billion, making it the 45th ranked cooperative in the Top 300 World Ranking by the World Cooperative Monitor (ICA and EURICSE 2023).

It is worth pausing on job creation as this is central to Mondragón's vision of human well-being through dignified, secure and well-remunerated work. Between 1976 and 1986, Mondragón increased employment by 3.3 per cent per annum, while Spain experienced increasing unemployment (Solar-Gallart 2024, ebook location 337). Unlike the European and US trend in manufacturing, which saw massive job losses between the 1990s and 2019, Mondragón maintained consistent growth in the number of worker–owners and had an even bigger impact on wider employment. For example, between 2013 and 2018, the cooperatives in the industrial sector created 8,000 new jobs of which 1,589 were worker–owners and 57 per cent were within the cooperatives. The remaining jobs were in downstream industries. This markedly contrasts to the US manufacturing sector which declined by 35 per cent from 19.6 million jobs in 1979 to 12.8 million jobs in 2019, a loss of 6.7 million jobs (Harris 2020, no pagination). It is little wonder that *Fortune Magazine* recognised Mondragón's contribution by ranking it eleventh in terms of 'enterprises that are changing the world' (Cicopa 2020, no pagination).

The number of worker–owners has steadily grown over the last three decades from 23,130 worker–owners in 1990 to 74,061 worker–owners in 2013. This number jumped to 81,507 in 2019. In 2023, there was a decline of 11,000 worker–owners due to two cooperatives – Orona and Ulma – leaving the Mondragón Group. It is worth noting that the drop in numbers was not due to retrenchments, but due to two cooperatives leaving as they wanted more autonomy within their cooperatives. However, they continue to work with Mondragón cooperatives and use its financial and other services. The issue of autonomy relates to the fact that being a member of MCC requires adhering to a number of conditions, including giving 10 per cent of surplus to the solidarity fund to support struggling cooperatives. While losing Orona and Ulma was not what Mondragón wanted, the departure was amicable and they continue to work together. The point here is that Mondragón is one of Spain's major economic actors (fourth largest in the industrial sector and the tenth largest in the finance sector) while growing employment in good jobs. It has achieved this through its commitment to its values and not abandoning its principles.

In contrast to capitalist enterprises that place profit-maximising accumulation as the central organising principle and operate on the basis of organisational hierarchy, transformative cooperatives place human and social needs and ecological care at the centre of their activities, even if they still have to ensure surplus in order to survive their liminal location within and beyond capitalism. The point is that profit-driven pursuits are not the primary goal but rather the means to an end, as they operate in a broader capitalist economy while simultaneously challenging its constitutive parts. Mondragón insists that capital is in the service of labour, rather than the capitalist formula of labour in the service of capital, which ensures human needs and community development remain at the centre of the cooperatives.

While the achievements within the cooperative system are impressive, the real achievement stands out when we look at the impact on the wider socio-economic conditions in the region. The Basque region registers the lowest inequality and highest quality of life in Spain and ranks highly in comparison to the rest of Europe (ESPON 2020; Bizkaia Talent 2019). It has created quality jobs and an entire social welfare system to meet the needs of the people and community.

Value-driven Economic Activity, Economic Democracy and Redistribution

Reflecting the socially embedded vision of Arizmendiarrieta and the five founding members, Mondragón's mission continues to be an innovative socio-economic institution created by and for people in order to create wealth within society through development and job creation (preferably membership jobs in cooperatives). According to the former Director of Cooperative Dissemination, Mikel Lezamiz, the values are continuously being renewed to ensure that the commitment to the social well-being of society remains central.[10] The values include cooperation among worker–owners, participation by worker–owners, commitment to humanist values, ethical management, social responsibility to ensure the distribution of wealth based on solidarity, participatory decision making, involvement in the local community and innovation to ensure constant renewal. These values are married to the ten core principles of the cooperative group: open admission, democratic organisation, sovereignty of labour, instrumental use and subordination of capital, participatory management, wage solidarity, inter-cooperation, social transformation, universality and education.

While some of the values are captured in the International Cooperative Alliance (ICA) principles, Mondragón's principles are rooted in their local experience. For example, wage solidarity has ensured that the ratio of wages within the cooperatives remains on average at 1:5 with most at 1:4 and a few cooperatives going up to 1:6

(Solar-Gallart 2024, ebook location 341; Hodgson 2017). The wage ratio comes into sharp relief when compared to similar management jobs at local capitalist companies whose earnings are considerably higher than Mondragón managers, while the lower wage jobs are remunerated considerably higher (approximately 13 per cent) in Mondragón than their local counterparts. The difference is even sharper when compared to the US. For instance, in 2022 the average wage gap in US companies was 344:1 (Statista 2025), whereas some large global corporations have wage gaps that are in the thousands. According to Oxfam, 'only 0.4 per cent of the world's largest corporations are publicly committed to paying workers a living wage and support a living wage in their value chains' (Amladi 2025, no pagination). Wages of nearly 800 million workers globally have not kept up with inflation with estimates that workers have lost US$1.5 trillion since 2022. While workers have lost dramatically, corporate profits continue to soar. Oxfam reports that the world's richest are growing their wealth at unprecedented levels: 'In 2024, the world's billionaires got $2 trillion richer, growing their wealth by roughly $5.7 billion a day. Their fortunes increased three times faster than in 2023, with nearly four new billionaires minted every week' (Amladi 2025, no pagination). Oxfam goes further to argue that democratically structured corporations reduce inequality: 'if 10 percent of every business in the U.S. was employee-owned, it could double the share of wealth of the bottom 50 percent and the median wealth of Black households' (Oxfam 2024: no pagination; see also Riddell et al. 2024). Going beyond internal wage gaps, another unique Mondragón principle is the inter-cooperative solidarity that discourages competition among cooperatives and ensures inter-cooperation of people, funds and cooperative enterprises. This was demonstrated when Fagor filed for bankruptcy in 2013, and its worker–owners were absorbed into other Mondragón cooperatives (discussed below).

The organisational structure of Mondragón reflects its commitment to democratic decision making and to worker–owners' control, with the Mondragón Group's *raison d'être* to be in the service of the cooperatives and workers, pioneering self-managed democratic decision-making structures for the Mondragón Group and democratic decision making within the primary cooperatives that are part of Mondragón. Reflecting its commitment to the cooperatives and their worker–owners, the Annual General Assembly of the Mondragón Group is constituted with 57 per cent of delegates representing the associated cooperatives and 43 per cent representing the worker–owners. The twelve-member governing board has eight representatives from the associated cooperatives and four representatives from worker members, with the president of the board from the associated cooperatives. Similarly, the way in which wealth is distributed concretises the commitment to workers and the community. The surplus is distributed according to a set formula with 15 per cent allocated to the Inter-cooperative Social Fund (FSI), 10 per cent to the Fund for Education and Promotion (FEP), 50 per cent is dedicated for reserves and 25 per cent is returned to cooperatives. The funds returned to cooperatives are divided into two equal parts between worker members and associated cooperatives, but members can only access the funds when they leave the cooperative. The Funds for Education and Promotion support a wide range of solidarity activities, such as young cooperative entrepreneurs, the promotion of Basque culture and language, welfare, global south institutions, and leisure and cultural activities. The dividends contributed to the Inter-cooperative Social Fund promote solidarity across cooperatives. The transparency in relation to its finances and the distribution of surplus illustrate the central role of human well-being and solidarity. What is noteworthy is that Mondragón has remained committed to its deeply democratic traditions, practices and wealth distribution, despite its growth and complexity.

Democracy beyond the Cooperative and Impact on Society

Thus far we have highlighted the achievements that are largely within the cooperative ecosystem. However, the impact of Mondragón on the wider community of the Basque Country registers in a number of areas, but perhaps most impressively in terms of its low inequality and high quality of life. It is here that we see the way in which Mondragón has broken down boundaries between the political and economic areas. The dense fabric of cooperatives in the Basque region has resulted in the lowest inequality in Spain and the quality of life is one of the highest in Europe. According to the European quality of life index, out of a total of 1,442 provinces in Europe, the Basque Country is in the top four per cent in terms of quality of life (ESPON 2020; Bizkaia Talent 2019). These achievements are especially salient given the history of dire poverty in the region and the lack of national government support after the civil war. Based on the years of experience in democratic practices and structures, Mondragón shows that democracy has positive externalities both for the cooperatives (performance, satisfaction, involvement) and society (greater equality, active citizens). Rather than dealing with the consequences of inequality, the focus is on preventing it through democratic decision making, equitable and transparent distribution of surplus, social welfare system and low wage differentials. The experience of Mondragón shows that democratic organisations generate less inequality as they distribute income, capital and power within the cooperatives, which spills over into the communities in which they are rooted. According to Etxarri (2021, 32), looking at public social protection models, 'democratic organisations (along with other instruments like basic universal income, educational investment, etc.) have become a pre-distributive tool of tremendous reach'. Mondragón is perhaps the preeminent example of such a pre-distributive system with tremendous reach.

Over seven decades, Mondragón has been at the forefront of creating the 'social economy' in the region with the explicit goal of transforming the economy from producing, funding, commerce and consumption to the service of human and community development and, consequently, a more just, socially fair and environmentally sustainable economy (Etxarri 2021, 21-22). The idea of a socially oriented economy gained widespread legitimacy in the Basque Country and is increasingly incorporated into the political and socio-ecological systems. For example, in 2008 through parliamentary mandate, the Basque Social Economy Observatory was founded to bring together and facilitate the work of all social economy entities. While they use the term 'social economy', in our framing it is closer to solidarity economy as it is not primarily focused on ameliorative assistance through services but rather empowers people through work and transforms the economy. This clearly promotes transformative change. What is particularly unique in the Basque Country experience is the central role of the industrial sector and the strong economic and financial actors that have structural power to shape the economy. For example, '2% of [all economic] entities, 5% of added gross value, and 10% of compensated employment in the Basque Country' lie within the social economy (Etxarri 2021, 23). Its footprint spreads across various government competencies and five government bodies: Public Governance and Self Governance; Economic Development, Sustainability and the Environment; Treasury and the Economy; Labour and Employment; and Equality, Justice and Social Policies (Etxarri 2021, 27). The embeddedness of the economy in political institutions has helped deepen the social impact on the wider society with cooperatives accounting for nearly ten per cent of employment in the Basque Country. The achievements in quality of life across a number of indicators further illustrates the point. The Basque Country is among 'three nations with the lowest poverty levels in the European Union, almost two points below the European average' and, in 2023, reduced greenhouse gas emissions by 35.5 per cent, which is significantly better than the EU countries' average of 23.6 per cent (Basque Government 2024, 13). It ranks seventh in Europe on the gender equality index and life expectancy is among the highest in the world at 83.6 years.

The rich tradition of participatory and democratic decision making throughout the Mondragón cooperatives has democratised social relations beyond the factory. While Mondragón does not get involved in politics directly, there is evidence to suggest that the dense web of participatory democratic institutions spills over into the political realm. For example, the Basque Country registers the highest quality government in Spain based on the European Quality Index (EQI).[11] This achievement stands out when we look at the rest of Spain, which has one of the largest regional variations in the quality of government in Europe. The Basque Region's EQI (together with its neighbouring region Navarra) increased in four EQI surveys, while most other regions in Spain dropped in the

EQI over the same period (Charron, Lapuente and Bauhr 2021a). The EQI helps disaggregate national averages and demonstrates a great deal of regional variation within countries. Large variation in the quality of government suggests that local dynamics play an important role. Interestingly, the two regions in Europe that have exceptionally high concentrations of cooperatives – Mondragón and Trentino, Italy – also rank the highest EQI in their respective countries. Thus, the correlation between the dense web of cooperatives and accountable government is very suggestive. The democratic practices honed within the cooperatives nurtures a democratic and collaborative culture, collective sensibilities and trust that are crucial for democracy in society. Mondragón's commitment to human and community well-being reflects its recognition that people live their lives beyond the doors of the cooperative; it is in their communities that the shared bonds, relationships of trust and cultural experiences are developed that bind people to one another, to place and to transformative alternatives that positively impact their lives. Thus, Mondragón's rootedness in the Basque Country has influenced the region economically, socially, politically and ecologically.

While Mondragón is deeply rooted in the Basque Country, it actively supports solidarity relations beyond the Basque Country and Spain. We met many cooperatives in South America and Italy who confirmed the importance of solidarity relations with Mondragón. Through international exchange visits, solidarity relations and hosting scholars, cooperators and activists on study visits of its cooperatives, Mondragón has a strong international network. One of the most publicised solidarity relations is its support for establishing 'union co-ops' in the US. In 2009, it announced an agreement to collaborate with the United Steelworkers Union (USW) to try to establish manufacturing cooperatives (union co-ops) in the US. Directly out of the USW–Mondragón collaboration, the Cincinnati Union Co-op Initiative (CUCI) formed in 2011 as 'a nonprofit union co-op incubator' (Schlachter 2016, 10). By 2016, at least eleven initiatives had been formed and an additional nine cooperatives unionised. The initiatives were affiliated with Mondragón USA, an umbrella nonprofit aimed at supporting union co-ops across the US. These initiatives built on the Union Co-op Committee's work of thinking about how to bring cooperatives and unions together, which started in 2007.[12] Clearly, Mondragón has built solidaristic relations with other entities in the Basque Country, in Spain and globally. It is through its solidarity relations that it has sought to extend cooperative principles beyond its cooperative system.

While it operates within the capitalist market economy, Mondragón sees itself as an alternative with a transformative vision at its core. In fact, its liminal space within and against capitalism has forced it to constantly reflect on what is central. Arizmendiarrieta's original vision of a solidarity society appears to remain an aspirational mooring for the Mondragón cooperatives. Profit making is not the primary goal, but rather a means to an end, which is a solidarity society. Mondragón's insistence that capital is in the service of labour, rather than the capitalist formula of labour in the service of capital, ensures human needs are at the centre of the organisation. While Mondragón is an impressive worker cooperative system by any measure, it has also faced severe challenges, some of which threaten the transformative possibility.

Overcoming Challenges through Value-Centred Practice

Many successful cooperatives face challenges of degeneration, that is, degenerating into a capitalist firm, and some recognise the danger and institute changes to avoid it. Mondragón's experience demonstrates the issue having faced the threat of degeneration for many years operating in the highly competitive sector of manufacturing. In order to survive in the competitive market, Mondragón began expanding beyond the Basque Country in 1989 and opened approximately 140 subsidiaries (75 overseas, 65 in other areas of Spain) with 14,000 employees in subsidiaries.[13] The subsidiaries were enterprises under Mondragón's structure and were not cooperatives in their own right. This raised many questions and some critiques. Is Mondragón another example of degeneration in which a once-emancipatory vision is now replaced by the pragmatism of market logic and expansionary interests? While the danger is certainly present, there is strong evidence to support that Mondragón has not lost its commitment to transformative politics that moves beyond capitalism. It has had to expand beyond the Basque Country and doing so meant that it had to open subsidiaries rather than cooperatives, yet it has nevertheless consciously tried to ensure that four key values drive its expansion: innovation, cooperation, participation and social responsibility. These values contrast markedly with capitalist expansion based on profits, expropriation and exclusion (Flecha and Ngai 2014).

Expanding beyond the Basque Country had many drivers, one of which was pressure from large manufacturing companies. For example, Mondragón opened a factory in Brazil because General Motors pushed them to open a Brazilian plant instead of producing in Spain and shipping across to the Americas. Ironically, opening a subsidiary had a positive ecological dimension, lowering carbon emissions by not needing to ship parts across the long distances of the Atlantic. Similarly, in order to get access to the US market, Mondragón opened a factory in Mexico, which falls within the North American Free Trade Agreement (NAFTA). Through producing in Mexico, Mondragón was able to access the US market on more favourable terms than from its European base. Guiding the expansion programme were a number of non-negotiable principles: they had to minimise exploitation by paying higher than average wages, maintain information transparency (both within the subsidiary and within Mondragón cooperatives), ensure the same style of management as in cooperatives (that is, worker participation in management of the day-to-day running and strategy, worker assemblies, horizontal decision making), create conditions for 30 per cent of property to belong to workers (and within ten years this was to become 50 per cent), and five per cent of profits dedicated to local development in which the workers decide how to spend the money (for example, to build a local school). One key difference is that in the subsidiaries' general assemblies (two per year) and monthly 'collaboration' meetings were for information sharing and not decision making. Decision making power remained with the primary cooperatives in Mondragón. Out of 75 international subsidiaries by 2010, only three had achieved 30 per cent local ownership. Only 50 of the

75 subsidiaries were profitable in 2010, which meant that the Mondragón cooperatives had to heavily subsidise them. Eventually some subsidiaries had to close as the Mondragón cooperatives could not continue subsidising them. Yet, even in closing subsidiaries, Mondragón provided unemployment benefits and tried to soften the hardship caused by job losses. While for critics this experience of expansion represents the degeneration of Mondragón's principles and anti-capitalist visions, in our field visits and interviews it was very clear that the worker–owners and worker leaders within Mondragón were very conscious of their contradictory location and taking seriously the issue of maintaining their values. While they recognise they must remain competitive (one member said: 'we don't create the economy in which we operate'), they are not willing to destroy their cooperative ethos to do it.

This commitment was put to the test in 2014 when Fagor, the flagship cooperative of Mondragón, filed bankruptcy and eventually closed. Fagor's story is instructive as it was severely affected by the Eurozone crisis in 2008 and was unable to regain its previous productivity within the crisis-ridden Spanish economy, which saw many companies fail and led to civil society protests across Spain and the rise of Podemos. Over a couple of years, the inter-cooperation of Mondragón was put to the test as other cooperatives were called on to help Fagor through financial support and to absorb Fagor workers into their own cooperatives. This often meant that other cooperatives had to forgo wage increases or other benefits. After five years of losses and a €850 million debt, Fagor's crisis was too large for the Mondragón cooperatives to absorb. Three cooperatives, including Eroski, which was also under severe economic pressure, vetoed Fagor's request for €170 million in 2013 (Economist 2013). This left Fagor with no option but to file bankruptcy. What is particularly noteworthy is that when Fagor filed bankruptcy it did not retrench worker–owners, but rather the Mondragón cooperative system ensured that 2,000 worker–owners (out of 5,642 jobs including in its subsidiaries) were retrained and placed in other cooperatives or were provided early retirement. Given the 27 per cent unemployment rate at that time in Spain, this was an enormous achievement. For the remaining workers who were not members and mostly worked in Fagor subsidiaries, the cooperative provided unemployment benefits. Lagun Aro, the social services cooperative, proposed the motion that all members pay an additional 1.5 per cent contribution to ensure additional unemployment benefits to retrenched Fagor workers.

Contrary to many critics who argue that these experiences destroyed the soul of Mondragón, what we found is that these challenges made them more conscious of their principles, and the difficulties and importance of maintaining them. For example, one of the reasons that they have not been able to set up cooperatives beyond the Basque Country is that extant cultures vary across local spaces. In its original vision, Mondragón hoped to help set up local cooperatives that could form a global solidarity economy network, as they are acutely aware of the contradictory location in which they operate. However, in their research visits to various countries, they realised that many places and people were not familiar with cooperatives and did not have the commitment required to create them. It had to be nurtured and learnt overtime. Mondragón could not impose its model elsewhere. As a result, it developed a long-term strategy that it hoped would help grow subsidiaries into cooperatives and a short-term strategy that ensured well-remunerated work and high labour standards in its subsidiaries. Mondragón does not have the luxury of operating in a non-capitalist economy or ideal conditions. Rather it is navigating a complex and contradictory location that both promotes radical transformative alternatives within the cooperatives and the surrounding community and makes necessary compromises to survive without undermining its core values. As Erik Olin Wright put it, Mondragón remains 'an emergent form of a *cooperative market economy* rather than simply a cooperative firm within a capitalist market economy' (Wright 2010, 236). In our framing, Mondragón offers a transformative alternative to shareholder capitalism through workplace democracy and emancipatory ideals of a solidarity society anchored in worker cooperatives.

A VIRTUOUS CYCLE: CO-CONSTITUTING PUBLIC POWER, DEMOCRACY AND ECONOMIC ACTIVITY IN KERALA

In contrast to Mondragón's cooperative-led transformative alternatives, Kerala provides an example of state-led initiatives that have helped democratise and invigorate the local political and economic arenas. Through synergistic relations with solidarity economy initiatives and cooperatives such as the ULCCS (discussed in Chapter 4) and Kudumbashree women's groups, the state has facilitated people-centred development that reaches deeply into the fabric of society. In creating the conditions for transformative alternatives, the state has engaged in a long, arduous process over many decades of commitment to deepening democratic and deliberative practices within the political sphere while simultaneously promoting a care economy in the interest of people.

One of the key features that stands out when we look at Kerala's political and economic trajectory is the primacy of human and ecological well-being placed at the centre of development. To be clear, the human-centred development approach is a result of nearly a century of robust civil society claims-making around a range of socio-ecological issues such as social reform, anticaste issues, literacy, anticolonial independence, environmental struggles, political reforms and economic redistributive initiatives. What is unique about Kerala is that the democratic initiatives have largely been at the behest of the Communist Party of India (Marxist) (CPI(M)).[14] Through active participation in representative institutions of government[15] *and* engaging and mobilising civil society, the communists in government helped to create a people-centred democracy that challenges neoliberal corporate power and has achieved impressive social welfare gains (Parameswaran 2005). The successful claims-making politics translated into redistributive gains and human development indicators (literacy, infant mortality, life expectancy) equivalent to first world levels by the 1970s (Sen 1999). For instance, literacy rose from 40.7 per cent in 1951 to 96.2 per cent in 2021, infant mortality[16] dropped from 153 in 1951 to seven in 2021, life expectancy rose from 48.1 to 76.4 years and by 2024 zero hunger was achieved, far above the national averages in all indicators. Similar developments are seen in the quality of housing, low homelessness, sanitation and water, and electrification, where Kerala far exceeds national delivery in all these categories.[17] Perhaps most indicative of its success is that seen in the UN's Sustainable Development Goals, where in 2023/24 Kerala ranked first in India with a score of 79 (out of 100) while the national average was 64 (Hindu Bureau 2024). To put Kerala's achievements in a global perspective, the top-ranking country, Finland, scores 86, whereas the US scores 74 and South Africa 63.[18] These achievements lie alongside impressive growth in per capita income: in 1961 it stood at 259 rupees (US$3.1),[19] which was well below the national level of 306 rupees (US$3.68) and which rose to 216,749 rupees (US$2,604) in 2021, well above the national level of 145,680 rupees (US$1,750). These numbers attest to the redistributive and people-centred development that Kerala has achieved. What the numbers do not tell is that these developments have been at the behest of deeply democratic practices such as public pressure though local initiatives, community mobilisation, active citizen involvement, cooperatives and protest politics, all of which help embed the economy in socio-ecological relations.

Since the 1950s, Kerala has pioneered an inclusive development paradigm that centres on several important redistributive elements, such as wage redistribution, land reform and public goods including healthcare, education including tertiary education, food distribution and other services, and income transfers. The income transfers have been primarily through microfinance and poverty alleviation programmes often involving solidarity economy enterprises, which were significantly scaled up through the democratic decentralisation programme in the 1990s and with the establishment of Kudumbashree (discussed below) (Heller et al. 2007; Isaac 2022; Isaac and Heller 2003; Oommen 2008; Williams et al. 2011). The contrast to the western development model based on economic growth could not be starker. Kerala's democratic landscape is intertwined with development outcomes based on redistribution and human well-being where economic growth is the means to this end, not an end in itself. In other words, Kerala's deep and vibrant democracy curtails corporate power and ensures that human well-being is prioritised.

Yet, it has not been an easy or straightforward road. By the 1970s, a lagging economy and fiscal constraints were threatening the remarkable achievements in human and social development. Rising education levels were not met by increasing job opportunities, which led to high levels of underemployment and unemployment, especially among the educated middle class (13 per cent compared to 6.4 per cent for All-India in the period 2018 to 2019). The economic crisis became acute in the 1990s due to the ASEAN Free Trade Treaty and other neoliberal policies of the national government. By the end of the 1990s, Kerala's commercial crops had collapsed, bringing the economic crisis to a head in the state. Seeing the looming crisis on the horizon, in the mid-1980s the Communist Party sought new ways to grow the economy without compromising the redistributive gains and social development. In this search for generative practices and new ideas, it looked to deepening democracy through democratic self-government and the promotion of local economic development through community initiatives that included cooperative women's groups. It is quite remarkable that Kerala looked to democracy to resolve their fiscal and economic crisis, in stark contrast to many places in the world that turned to privatisation.

Democratic Decentralisation and Embedding the Economy

In 1996, the CPI(M)-led Kerala government launched the *People's Plan Campaign for Democratic Decentralisation*, institutionalising democratic procedures and deliberative processes and devolving approximately 40 per cent of the state's funds to local government institutions. It initiated bottom-up development planning by creating space for democratic participation of the population in local government and local economic development. Beyond the technical dimensions, the campaign shifted civil society from mobilising around redistributive claims-making protests to redistributive generative politics that focused on constructing alternatives through democratic deepening. The campaign anchored development in the nexus of civil society and local government institutions by making them more accountable and responsive to local needs. The campaign created novel institutional innovations for direct participation in local government, such as development committees, beneficiary committees (schools, health, housing, public works), popular monitoring committees and social audits that were crucial for the implementation of plans. Thus, local government institutions became participatory democratic institutions deeply rooted in their local constituencies. The success of the campaign and the long-term challenges are well documented (see Heller et al. 2007; Isaac and Franke 2002; Isaac and Heller 2003; Oommen 2008; Williams 2017; Williams et al. 2011).

For our purposes, the way in which the state invented spaces for economic activity that were deeply intertwined with local government shows how mutually complementary relationships between democratising the political and economic realms helped to create a people-centred socio-ecological and economic ecosystem. Democratising local government bodies gave space for subaltern class interests to come to the fore through the participatory democratic institutions, which provided not just financial support, but also technical, educational and political support. It did not decouple democracy from society but embedded the local state and local economic activity within society and, in the process, helped to improve public sector delivery. In effect, the emphasis shifted from making claims on the state to deliver public goods to being actively involved in the decision-making processes and implementation of people-led initiatives, including initiatives that were economic (microenterprises), developmental (community needs such as roads and schools) and political (village assemblies). The results were impressive as civil society was mobilised and local government institutions re-oriented to create a virtuous cycle between public power, economic and political democracy, and development.

For example, in the first decades of the millennium Kerala reversed the trend towards private schooling and health. Between 2016 and 2021, there were 780,000 new school children in public schools in classes 1 to 10 (many migrating back from private schools), and the number of students in private schools declined. Kerala's education ranks the highest in the country based on the School Education Quality Index (SEQUI) of NITI Aayog, which scored Kerala at 77.6 and looks at learning, access, infrastructure and equity outcomes as well as governance processes. Decentralisation also reversed the trend to private healthcare: in the period 1986 to 1987 only 28 per cent of the population was using public health facilities, which increased to 48 per cent by 2018; the infant mortality rate declined from 15 in 2006 to seven in 2020 (the national average was 32); and the state achieved nearly 100 per cent immunisation rates for many diseases (Isaac 2022; NITI Aayog 2019, 2021). Kerala ranks as the top performing state in the health sector for India (NITI Aayog 2023; Deccan Herald 2024).

One of the most important campaign outcomes in terms of democratic deepening was the growth and dynamism of Kudumbashree women's neighbourhood groups,[20] which span a range of activities including microcredit, small-scale production units,[21] community organising, development discussions about the needs and issues in their communities, and a space for women's empowerment. By 2021 there were 277,000 Kudumbashree across the state, representing 4.3 million households that worked closely with local government institutions through their various activities, including microenterprises. The women's neighbourhood groups were so dynamic that they became a central feature in local government's poverty alleviation programmes. In the mid-1990s, the poverty rate in the state was 25 per cent (25.76 for urban and 24.59 for rural), which by 2011 to 2012 declined dramatically to 6.3 per cent (7.3 for urban and 5.3 for rural) (Government of Kerala 2016; State Planning Board 2024). When measuring poverty through the United Nations Development Programme (UNDP) Multidimensional Poverty Index (MPI), Kerala's poor population dropped from 13 per cent between 2005 and 2006 to one per cent between 2015 and 2016 (UNDP 2019) and is the lowest in India (Economic Times 2021). Kudumbashree played an important role in local economic empowerment. Through democratising institutions in society, Kerala has nearly eliminated poverty, which is similar to redistributive effects seen in the low inequality levels in the Basque Country.

In contrast to Mondragón where manufacturing was central, in Kerala both manufacturing and agriculture have played a minimal role in growing the economy in recent decades. Rather, Kerala developed a care economy that delivers extensive social programmes based on community level economic initiatives that enhance the quality of life of citizens. They continuously innovate on new initiatives. For example, working with Kudumbashree they aim to have one elder club in every ward, universal palliative care and a school for differently abled children in every locality. The state also promotes zero waste, organic waste processing at source and recycling. All of these initiatives are part of a care economy linked to socio-ecological reproduction, many of which are cooperatives and solidarity economy-based enterprises such as Kudumbashree. Thus, one of the important legacies of democratic decentralisation is the local economic activity that is focused on social well-being.

Another important legacy of democratic decentralisation is the strong and capacitated local government institutions that were created through the democratisation processes. The strength, capacity and rootedness of local government has come to the fore in five major crises since 2018: the 2018 Nipah virus, the 2018, 2019 and 2024 floods and the Covid-19 pandemic. The state responded to each crisis by activating civil society and local government institutions and calling on the population to play its part. For example, in the 2018 flood, the adroit coordination of various frontline departments, such as revenue, health, police and local governments, meant the rescue and relief effort began immediately, and daily updates and information were shared through the media. The visibility of local government officials and leaders working in relief camps and rescue efforts reinforced trust in local government. Across the state, volunteers drove creative initiatives such as setting up a call centre for information exchange. In the rescue efforts, a volunteer corps of fisherfolk jumped into action when larger rescue boats could not get to the sinuous backwater areas. An estimated 4,500 fisherfolk with 650 boats rescued approximately 65,000 people stranded deep in the backwaters (Devasia and Varadhan 2018).[22] Local government institutions ran relief camps that provided food, clothing and healthcare to 1.2 million people. The local governments' capacity to act quickly and effectively and the strong volunteer culture are important legacies of decentralisation.

Similarly, the 2018 Nipah virus experience helped prepare them for Covid-19. As soon as Covid-19 was announced, the state's health department acted quickly: before a single case of Covid-19 in Kerala, the health department had already established comprehensive guidelines and training modules for health workers and volunteers. When Covid-19 numbers started to rise precipitously, the state was ready to trace, track and offer support that extended through communities. Within weeks, Kerala flattened the curve and was able to manage the rest of the pandemic without the medical system ever becoming overwhelmed (Isaac 2022, 103). In communities across the state, volunteers assisted health workers, community kitchens fed millions of people,and communities looked after people in need. This intensive support system translated into a very low fatality rate of 0.5, which is a third of India's 1.4 fatality rate.

What is particularly telling is the enormous social relief programmes that accompanied lockdown. The government launched a 20 billion rupee (US$240 million) package, half of which was direct income transfers. Here again, the Kudumbashree microfinance system played an essential role as the government was able to get funds to people quickly. Working with Kudumbashree groups across Kerala, local governments supported 1,000 community kitchens that provided free food to anyone who needed it. At its peak, the community kitchens served 500,000 people daily, and for those who could not come to kitchens, palliative care groups delivered food to their homes. Kerala also ensured that migrants who remained in the state during the Covid-19 pandemic received food, with one study showing that 85 per cent of migrants received multiple meals a day (Diwakar et al. 2022). To ensure that no one went hungry, the government provided food kits and grains that were distributed through the public distribution system to 84 per cent of the population (Lokniti-CSDS 2021, 31).

While Kerala's development trajectory is unique and very rooted in Kerala's traditions, history and class formations, it is also very open to international solidarity relations. It welcomes international scholars and is open to allowing research and studies on its various activities. For example, the Kerala's decentralisation and 'model' of development has evoked widespread interests from scholars, activists, policy makers and movements across the world. Amartya Sen praised its needs-centred approach to development. There is a general curiosity about the world, and a sense of solidarity for progressive initiatives. On one of our field visits to a remote rural community, we met a young woman named after Winnie Mandela (Nelson Mandela's wife and an iconic figure of the South African anti-apartheid struggle). We were struck by this act of solidarity with the anti-apartheid struggle but upon reflection it captures the human solidarity that courses through Kerala society.

The democratic decentralisation initiative in Kerala has clearly had enormous and long-term impact in expected and unexpected ways. Unleashing active citizenry to work with local government to meet the needs of society helped build a care economy that is deeply embedded in the socio-ecological system of the region. While these achievements are impressive in their own right, the state also created more conducive conditions for cooperatives to play a significant role in the economy.

Support for Cooperatives and Value-Centred Growth

It is in this context that the state deepened its support for cooperatives and solidarity economy type initiatives.[23] The role of the state deserves special attention as it illustrates the potential a democratic and accountable state can play in developing synergies with cooperatives and solidarity economy initiatives to the benefit of society. Because cooperatives and other solidarity economy initiatives have different ownership models (worker-owned) and governing structures (democratic) to capitalist companies, they face many disadvantages by working within the capitalist system. Therefore a special support policy environment (including access to credit and other forms of support) from government helps level the playing field. For example, the 1957 government in Kerala introduced a system of preference given to worker cooperatives for government work projects and institutionalised a special scheme for their promotion and regulation.[24] Similarly, the government's 1996 People's Plan Campaign developed a preferential system for cooperatives and promoted ULCCS as a model for the rest of Kerala, recognising it as an accredited agency for local government projects.

The case of ULCSS's public works is worth exploring as it exemplifies economic activity embedded in the socio-ecological relations through government support. For example, between 2016 and 2019, the government passed seven separate Government Orders that facilitated ULCCS public works projects and created a conducive environment.[25] As a result, by 2018–2019, ULCCS was building 836 crucial public works projects, such as highways, rural roads, bridges and government buildings that included rural clinics. During the same period, it built 117 projects for the private sector. Clearly, the special support and incentives received from government did not falsely prop up ULCCS but rather provided it with vital strategic support that facilitated its expansion and diversification while delivering crucial public goods. From the government's side, these supports were simply a component of its general programme of industrial and infrastructure promotion within a care economy framework. The reality is that in normal circumstances the private sector companies, particularly the larger ones, wrest significant concessions from governments and influence policy through myriad ways, often with detrimental effects for public goods. In Kerala, by contrast, the government created a conducive environment for cooperatives to operate.

In contrast to capitalist freeriding on public power and the state, ULCCS prioritised providing the highest quality and fair price public infrastructure projects. Its principle of not wasting public funds[26] and commitment to safe and high-quality public infrastructure, such as bridges, roads and buildings, is baked into its DNA as it remains deeply connected to the place and people of Kerala. Thus, it recognises the importance of public goods for the quality of life of ordinary people. For example, 330 rural roads were constructed between 2018 and 2019, which is suggestive of the government's strong focus on remote rural areas and makes the cooperative's work critical to the quality of life of ordinary Keralites. In other words, its economic activity is deeply embedded in the political and socio-ecological milieu of Kerala. In practice, the cooperative is at the service of society and its worker–owners, effectively overcoming the boundary between the economy and public power that is the hallmark of freeriding of capitalist enterprises.

ULCCS's success registers in its growth, in terms of both projects and workers. In 2019, there were 2,548 worker–owners and an additional 7,986 non-members (3,284 Keralites and 4,702 migrants from elsewhere in India). This massive growth of non-members was a consequence of the cooperative's success, diversification and growth. For example, in 2019 it had 953 projects from various government departments and the private sector across the state and was also starting to build beyond Kerala. The growth necessitated a complex membership structure and while the number of non-members grew significantly, it consciously ensured they received the same material benefits (discussed in Chapter 4). Thus, growth in non-members was carefully managed to ensure that the cooperative's values were not overwhelmed by the growth imperative. For example, when we look at the allocation of net profits, we can see a human-centred ethos at the centre of the cooperative. For example, between 2018 and 2019, 15 per cent of profits was allocated to the Reserve Fund and 15 per cent to Business Loss, whereas 19.5 per cent was for Dividends, 10 per cent for the Common Good Fund, 15 per cent for the Labour Welfare Fund, 0.19 per cent for an Education Fund and 20 per cent for the Building Fund. Taken together, over 45 per cent of the profits were allocated directly to workers (members and non-members). Accountable, transparent and democratic processes have been central to ensuring ULCCS remains a worker-led cooperative with firm roots in its locality. Nevertheless, it also promotes solidaristic relations with other cooperatives in Kerala, India and internationally. For example, it reached out to Mondragón to share experiences and learn from each other.

ULCCS's commitment to embedding the cooperative within the social needs of the broader Kerala society resonated with the goals of the democratic decentralisation campaign, which sought to unleash local initiatives for the socio-ecological development of Kerala. Given the central role in the care economy, local government institutions became a central pillar of local economic and social activity. In effect, the virtuous cycle tamed capitalism through strengthening democracy. If Mondragón shows the transformative role of a cooperative system and Kerala demonstrates the role a democratic state can play in creating the conditions for a care economy and thriving cooperatives and solidarity economy-based activities such as Kudumbashree groups, the Brazilian Solidarity Economy Forum shows the attempts by a social movement to create new values, democratic enterprises and linkages across the value chain based on solidarity and well-being.

CREATING AN ECONOMY BASED ON SOLIDARITY: BRAZILIAN SOLIDARITY ECONOMY FORUM

So far, we have discussed the role of Mondragón's cooperative-led efforts and Kerala's state-society initiatives. In this section, we turn to the movement-led transformative politics of the Brazilian Solidarity Economy Forum that took off in the first decade of the twenty-first century.[27] We have included the Solidarity Economy Forum because of the way in which it combined movement initiatives with state policy to create conducive conditions for people-centred economic activity based on solidarity. Unlike the decades of success we saw in Mondragón and Kerala, the Brazilian case is more instructive for its vision and initial success during the Workers' Party governments. The right-wing government of Bolsanaro was hostile to such creative and transformative initiatives, and consequently significantly weakened the movement, which has not recovered to its former dynamism. Nevertheless, its experience is instructive as it unleashed enormous creativity and dynamism for nearly two decades.

The idea of the solidarity economy was popularised by the Brazilian movement in the 1990s and has been in circulation ever since. The solidarity economy envisions social, economic and political transformation of society through collective ownership, democratic self-management, redistribution, solidarity, reciprocity and worker and popular control of the means of production, consumption and distribution. It is a far-reaching vision, much like Mondragón's founding members' vision of a solidarity society and Kerala's care economy. At its core is an anti-capitalist vision moored in the attempt to remake social relations through transforming the entire edifice of the way in which people produce, consume, distribute and relate to one another, nature, the state and the economy. Like Mondragón and Kerala, democratic participation, ecological care, solidarity, social, gender and racial equity and well-being are central organising pivots around which all activity gravitates.

The Brazilian solidarity economy movement situates itself against a larger critique of capitalism, patriarchy and western ontology and rationalism through a multi-class movement that is based on local economies and democratic enterprises. To achieve this, it built a network of alternative cultural spaces, developed programmes to empower individuals and promoted new social relations, in addition to creating linkages across economic enterprises. One of the notable features of the solidarity economy in Brazil was the density of organisations and institutions involved from cooperatives and solidarity enterprises to faith-based organisations, the labour movement, NGOs, social movements and government bodies.

The idea of the solidarity economy took root in 1996 when the mayor of São Paulo was looking to find a way to deal with the 1.6 million unemployed people in the city. Professor Paul Singer suggested organising the unemployed into a large cooperative of production and consumption with a special currency to exchange among them. He popularised the idea through newspaper articles in which he used the term solidarity economy, drawing on Mondragón's use of the term in 1980s. In response, a number of organisations and initiatives came to the fore who had been working with the principles of the solidarity economy and together consolidated their varied initiatives into a movement, the Solidarity Economy Forum. When Luiz Inácio Lula da Silva (popularly known as 'Lula') became president in January 2003, space was created for solidarity economy enterprises and cooperatives to engage the state.[28]

Institutionalising Relations with the State

In 2003, in response to the solidarity economy movement's demands, the government created a National Secretariat for the Solidarity Economy within the Ministry of Labour, integrally linking the solidarity economy to government and labour. Reflecting their relative movement power, the solidarity economy movement nominated Professor Singer for the Directorship of the Secretariat, which the government accepted.[29] The Secretariat quickly busied itself with creating new legislation to accommodate solidarity economy enterprises, building the movement, setting up a national research project on the solidarity economy and providing support to the newly established Solidarity Economy Forum(s). The Solidarity Economy Forum(s) were a crucial innovation as they democratised communication within the movement and between the movement and government, as well as assisted in developing technical plans and guiding the movement. One reflection of the state's support was that within ten years, over two hundred municipalities and 16 states supported solidarity economy activities. While the Secretariat coordinated solidarity economy activities, it did not dominate the movement and devolved a great deal of responsibility to the forum(s). The Secretariat and Forum(s) worked closely but remained autonomous from one another. Despite this, one of the points of tension was maintaining the relative power balance between the forum (civil society) and the Secretariat (political society), with the forum insisting that its voice was the driving force. The dynamism of the Secretariat and movement-driven forum(s) pioneered state-society synergies that directly and positively impacted on solidarity economy enterprises by creating a conducive environment for their functioning.

With 800 delegates, the first national meeting of solidarity economy enterprises was held in 2004. In just four years, the Solidarity Economy Forum established state forums in all 27 states across the country, with an estimated two million people. By 2017, there were more than 120 local solidarity economy forums and the 27 state forums continued to function. The Secretariat and forums jointly embarked on a massive mapping of solidarity economy enterprises, which revealed that there were mostly producer cooperatives and some consumer cooperatives, some of which were started by companies and others by the labour movement. The joint goal of the Secretariat and Forum was to bring together the consumer and producer cooperatives into an integrated economic network and to create new cultural attitudes about production, consumption and new social relations.

The forums were made up of solidarity enterprises based on criteria that embedded economic activity within socio-ecological relations. To qualify for the solidarity economy, an enterprise had to adhere to the following criteria: engage in economic activity, have associative members (not just family members), be a self-managed, democratic and autonomous organisation with one member one vote, promote cooperation (rather than competition), value diversity and local knowledge, place humans before profits, commit to life-long learning and training, fight for social justice and emancipation, and protect the natural environment. These inclusive and integrative criteria marked the Solidarity Economy Forums starkly apart from boundary-making capitalist principles, which extract economic activity from the communities, nature and the state. By 2017, there were approximately 22,000 solidarity economy enterprises – many of which are cooperatives – and a network of nonprofit, governmental, community, religious and grassroots organisations and university programmes that provided support to the solidarity economy. Solidarity enterprises exist across a range of sectors, including 'community banks, microfinance [institutions], complementary currencies, cooperatives, fair trade, and nonprofit enterprises' (P2P Foundation 2017). Creatively using online tools to foster connections, the enterprises are mapped online, which facilitates horizontal connections across enterprises, expands their linkages, assists to educate and inform consumers and creates 'solidarity economy commerce chains'. This use of mapping to put solidarity economy enterprises into direct contact with one another represents a creative commons, a new space for information sharing and knowledge building through the use of technology. Linked to knowledge and information sharing, the forums established popular education centres in five regions and one national centre.

Incorporating Diversity of Ideas and Organisations

The solidarity economy fosters a plurality of ideas, which is a striking feature of the Brazilian movement, while maintaining common threads that unite them. For example, solidarity economy actors prioritise social justice and happiness over efficiency and profits. Therefore, they accept that collective decisions take longer and human well-being comes before profits. Integrated down-stream and upstream linkages raised interesting debates within the movement and reinforced the point that there is no blueprint. For example, the role of consumer cooperatives versus ethical markets raised questions about transition out of capitalism. Some argued that consumer cooperative markets might be necessary in a capitalist market economy but questioned whether they are always necessary and whether they would be necessary if market relations were based on ethical grounds. Peasant markets, for example, sell their products directly to consumers, which means there is no need for a consumer cooperative. However, in urban areas where consumers are far from direct producers, consumer cooperatives facilitate solidarity economy linkages. The depth of such engagements deeply embedded a transformative vision in which they were building counterhegemonic alternatives.

The range of enterprises participating in the solidarity economy (for example, MST – the Landless Workers' Movement, unions, cooperatives, social movements, NGOs and faith-based organisations) is an extraordinary accomplishment. For example, the Secretariat created a Solidarity Economy Council to ensure that the whole movement was included. It took two years for the Solidarity Economy Forums to discuss the formation of the Council, which it eventually supported. The major point of contention was the issue of the mainstream cooperative federation, the Organisation of Brazilian Cooperatives (OCB), which the Secretariat insisted be included on the Council. The Solidarity Economy Forum saw itself as representing an anti-capitalist perspective, which was not what OCB stood for and therefore the forum was reluctant to include the OCB.[30] OCB began in the 1970s and the main federation of the cooperative movement, with a national office and 27 branches in the states to which cooperatives join.[31] From its early days, OCB was dominated by large agricultural cooperatives that run on capitalist principles such as the German DGRV (discussed in Chapter 3). It was this history that the forum objected to, but from the 1990s OCB began to diversify. By the end of the first decade of the new millennium, OCB represented cooperatives in a range of sectors: infrastructure (electricity cooperatives), transport (cargo and passenger), worker cooperatives, housing cooperatives, consumer cooperatives, agricultural cooperatives, credit and banking cooperatives (rural credit cooperatives and credit union in companies), medical/health cooperatives (such as Unimed), production cooperatives (recovered factories such as a glass factory) and credit cooperatives linked to BankCoob or BansiCred. OCB has 1.2 million members in its consumer cooperatives, which makes it the biggest consumer cooperative movement in Latin America, and approximately six million people (3 per cent of the population) are involved in cooperatives in Brazil. OCB was a major player in the cooperative movement and therefore the Secretariat could not ignore OCB and insisted that it should be part of the Council. According to the Secretariat, OCB's participation in the Council was extremely constructive and the early hesitance on the part of the forum dissipated.

The link to trade unions is worth highlighting as the main labour federation, CUT (Central Única dos Trabalhadores, Unified Workers Central in English), supported the solidarity economy movement in varied ways. In 1999, CUT created a dedicated department, Agencia de Desenvolvimento Solidario (ADS, Agency of Development of Solidarity), that focuses on cooperative development, research and support.[32] The relationship to cooperatives is not straightforward for CUT as cooperative members are not typical employees and cooperatives are not typical capitalist companies. In the recovered factories, such as Uniforja (discussed in Chapter 4), it is easier as CUT already has relations with the workers as former union members and assists in the recovery, but for newly formed cooperatives it is more difficult. To try to overcome this challenge, CUT together with others such as the ABC Metalworkers union, Sorocaba and ABC Chemical workers union, created two separate entities: Unisol and Ecosol.[33]

Unisol began in 2000 as a federation of approximately 230 cooperatives[34] and recovered factories with 11,000 members. Its role was to provide a unified political voice for cooperatives,[35] and provide technical assistance in ten sectors: metallurgy, food, construction/ housing, confection and textile, social cooperatives, recycling, handicrafts, family agriculture, beekeeping and fruit growing.[36] For example, Unisol assisted in factory takeovers when manufacturing companies closed. It helped create production chains where cooperatives exist at every stage of the process. To demonstrate the potential of cooperative production, it created a production chain in cotton from a cooperative that grows the cotton all the way downstream to the cooperative retail outlet that sells the clothing. Unisol's links to CUT are cemented through the requirement that one Unisol board member must come from CUT and another from the Workers' Party (PT), while still ensuring that Unisol maintains its autonomy. ADS provides various forms of support to Unisol and solidarity economy enterprises, such as courses, research, institutional and financial. These productive linkages between CUT and the solidarity economy movement took time to develop and reflect the wide range of synergies that were being forged and the collective creativity across the movement.

Another feature of the Brazilian solidarity economy movement worth noting is its international orientation and its relations with cooperatives and recovered factory movements in Argentina, Venezuela, Italy and Spain. It also actively sought to create solidarity networks through the World Social Forum and promoted working along solidarity relations in production and consumption. For example, Fair Trade Brazil took issue with Fair Trade International when they learnt that Brazilian coffee cooperatives' coffee was being sold in Walmart stores in the US.[37] In an act of solidarity with the workers in Walmart, the Brazilians refused to allow their coffee to be sold in Walmart. Such acts of solidarity reflect a commitment to building solidarity relations in faraway places. Thus, like Mondragón and Kerala, the solidarity economy movement took solidarity relations seriously.

The Brazilian solidarity economy movement found resonance and support across the country, in various sectors, and in a plethora of organisations. Despite its successes, it struggled to withstand President Bolsanaro's assault on various support mechanisms. While it is no longer a thriving movement with synergies to the state, its experience has much to teach us. It is not just survival that makes something worthy of studying, but also what it achieved while it existed and what we can learn from its challenges.

CONCLUSION

The three cases – Mondragón in the Basque Country, Kerala's care economy and Brazil's Solidarity Economy Forum – illustrate varied attempts to remake state–economy relations through democratising the economy and its spillover into the state. Their relations to the state are varied and the relationships are complex and always in flux. Nevertheless, they demonstrate the mutually complementary role of democratising economic activity and embedding the economy within the political sphere. Democratising public power through deep democracy cooperative-economy relations, practices and logics ensures that state power serves socio-ecological reproduction of society and natural relations and not capital's narrow self-serving interests. Our cases show how aggregating democratic power from below through solidarity economy cooperative movement systems and embedding the state tilts power relations away from capital's control of public power. Ultimately, this is not just about local change or prefiguration but about large-scale and macro-level transformation. In addition, the cases demonstrate that competition among enterprises is not a *sine qua non* of economic relations. The zero-sum calculation that underpins mainstream economic thinking is fundamentally at odds with the rationality that governs cooperatives and the solidarity economy. Capitalism's expropriation, plundering and competition were made possible by monopolising national economies and extending outwardly a politics of imperialism and colonialism but are not an essential criteria of economic activity based on people- and nature-centred values. Our cases show that solidarity relations growing out of transformative cooperatives extend into webs of care deep into society and even engulf the state, such that capitalist expansion and its corollary imperial expansion is rendered unnecessary.

Conclusion
Transformative Alternatives in the Age of Planetary Crisis

We live in a time in which the absurd has become normal. Billion-aires build bunkers to save themselves from impending disasters while continuing to accelerate the conditions that are destroying capitalism; their increasing wealth and power means more plane-tary destruction and the last great dispossession of the commons. Climate disasters increase in both intensity and frequency every year, leaving millions precarious, while corporate lobbyists, denialists and weak political leaders continue to influence policy. Biodiver-sity loss and extinction speed up as urban sprawl, car culture and industrial farming march on. Wars destabilise entire regions and thousands are killed, many of whom are women and children, while the global plutocratic class uses every crisis to make a profit. Fragile global food systems feel the shocks with rising prices of basic food stuffs, and local food systems are disparaged, while powerful glo-balised agribusiness earns millions in profits. Market democracies vote into power authoritarian-populist leaders who trade on vit-riolic hate and exclusionary nationalist promises of a better future for the 'insiders', the 'real people' or 'nation'. Democratically elected leaders actively undermine democracy. This certainly looks like the unfolding of the 'end of history'.

Nonetheless, our societies are normalising the convulsive, violent and self-inflicted death of capitalism. The end of endless capitalist accumulation has shown itself with all its horrific symptoms and terrifying consequences, as it plunges us into a planetary scale crisis. In the absurdity of the world lies an important rejoinder: radical and transformative contingency opens the possibility of making a differ-ent world. As Albert Camus (1938: 5) tells us, 'The realisation that life is absurd cannot be an end, but only a beginning.' The beginning in this book is the deep history of human cooperation and dependence on the web of life, including 500 years of resistance to colonialism, imperialism and US-led neoliberal globalisation. Our long beginning gives us a remarkable past to learn from and render visible as we draw on the archive of practices of planetary care that have been with us. In this archive our relationship with water, land, ecosystems, renewable energy, planetary systems, knowledge, public goods and infrastructures, and cultural heritage has certainly been about democratic and ethical care for the commons. Another way of reproducing life has been with us, yet we are accepting and choosing that which is destroying us. The current cycles of resistance are affirming the importance of the natural and social commons and inviting us to return to it. The earth is inviting us to defend, advance and strengthen the commons as life enabling systems. At the same time, worker cooperatives and solidarity economy cooperative systems are showing us how to do this in an emancipatory way, for our times, as part of a richer pattern of the living commons.

We will never know the exact date when capitalism will die but as we amplify planetary care from below there is a chance that capitalism will be eroded, tamed and exited before it destroys us all. The earth is already responding to capitalism and is certainly winning as it erodes it with the raw power of nature. Imperialism and plutocratic power are no match for the planet's power. At the same time, we can work with the earth's shift against capitalism and marshal the capacity, know-how and ingenuity to chart an emancipatory future through transformative politics and at different scalar levels. We had the privilege of witnessing its making over 14 years of research in 15 countries through which we learnt from hundreds of interviewees, including rural communities, waste pickers, factory workers, grassroots women, small-scale peasant farmers, indigenous peoples and radical intellectuals. The doors that opened revealed remarkable and inspiring world making in the nooks and crannies, on the margins and in interstitial spaces. These were not ideal types or blueprints to mechanically follow but intentional, conscious and positive solidarities resisting the encroachments of an avaricious capitalist system, a system bent on destroying natural relations, undermining the reproduction of workers and society, taming public power in its interests and attempting to hollow out sovereignty in the peripheries. The burning desires, the passionate screams, the militant slogans and the transformative socio-ecological practices we encountered reset boundaries. The new transformative political subjectivity and its praxis were saying no and yes at the same time. 'No' to suffering, 'Yes' to systems change, to transformative alternatives and another world. Informed by lessons of 'actually existing socialist' experiments of the twentieth century that were state-centric, de-democratising, anti-ecological and with limited care labour commitments, a new global left has been in formation. The best of humanity has been rising to meet the planetary polycrisis of capitalism and advance care labour. They affirm that capitalism is not the answer; we are working on its end through transformative praxis. New emancipatory utopian imaginaries, new conceptions of constitutive power, poly epistemologies and ethical values are shaping the contemporary subject of history: transformative forces of socio-ecological reproduction. The past and present are being conjoined to constitute the 'not yet' as a bridge into the future. Hope is real and is being made.

While we argue that transformative forces are charting the way through creative, innovative and concrete transformative practices, we are not suggesting it is easy or straightforward. It requires self-transformation that engenders new subjectivities with human and natured values of care and solidaristic relations with others, as well as transforming the structures and systems that have power over us. Patiently navigating these obstacles, building collective capacities and institutionalising change adds up to building power from below. It also means solving the planetary crisis at these frontlines. As our empirical evidence shows, transformative forces have given substance to transformative change by living it and making it – from conscious transformative subjectivity to embedding the economy in socio-ecological relations that build emancipatory regimes of socio-ecological reproduction and advance planetary care from below. The worker cooperatives and solidarity economy-based cooperative systems profiled in this book show us a way forward to create the next world; this is certainly post-capitalist and maybe a democratic eco-feminist socialist world in the making. They are certainly at the forefront of accelerating just transitions beyond the planetary polycrisis. We need to unite around this politics of positive solidarity such that the global left moves beyond its own ideological faultlines to converge more consistently around transformative praxis grounded in experiential, tacit and emancipatory anti-capitalist knowledge. Our societies need to learn from these worker cooperatives and solidarity economy-based cooperative systems engaging in consistent, courageous and powerful world making from below or we can remain trapped in the absurd and, ultimately, perish with capitalism. The choice is ours.

Annexure
Field Research

Country	Interviews	Field visits	Year of interviews and field visits	Workshops with scholars and activists
Argentina	26	9	2008, 2015, 2017	27–29 October 2015, Buenos Aires
Brazil	19	4	2008	
Venezuela	29	10	2008, 2016	
India	99	49	2010, 2013, 2017, 2023, 2024	18-20 September 2013, ULCCS, Kozhikode
USA	22	8	2008, 2009, 2014, 2016, 2017	
Canada	4		2008	
Senegal	11	5	2008, 2011	
Ethiopia	8	1	2008	
Kenya	9	4	2010	
Tanzania	14	4	2010	
Mauritius	17	7	2010	
South Africa	37	23	2008, 2012, 2017, 2023, 2024	Workshop with co-operative scholars and activists, 29 June–1 July 2016, Johannesburg; Permaculture course Goedgedacht Farm, 3–18 December 2022; Agroforestry course, 26–28 April 2024, The Crags; Wild Food Foraging course, 29–30 June 2024, Cape Point
Germany	18	4	2009, 2014, 2017	
Spain	20	5	2009, 2010, 2015	26–30 March 2015, Barcelona and Mondragón
Italy	35	13	2009, 2017, 2019	8–10 June 2017, Padova
Total	**368**	**146**		**5 workshops, 3 training courses**

Notes

INTRODUCTION

1. Onam is the annual harvest and Hindu cultural festival celebrated in Kerala. It is the biggest cultural celebration in the state.
2. Capitalism has had four major periods: mercantile capitalism of the seventeenth and eighteenth centuries, laissez-faire capitalism of the nineteenth and early twentieth centuries, state-managed monopoly capitalism of the twentieth century and neoliberal capitalism since the 1970s. Crises have punctuated these periods of development with some crises becoming a general polycrisis of the entire system.
3. The Mondragón worker cooperative complex, however, attempted to transplant its cooperative model in other countries but did so with limited success. Discussed in Chapter 6.
4. We interviewed Bauen Hotel cooperative owners and leadership in June 2008.
5. We were already alive to limits and challenges facing cooperatives and solidarity economies from over two decades of research, writing and in the case of Vishwas Satgar actively building cooperatives in township communities in South Africa for many years. See Satgar (2007, 2013, 2014, 2019, 2024), Satgar and Williams (2011a, 2011b, 2011c), Isaac and Williams (2017) and Williams (2013, 2016).

CHAPTER 1

1. This has been well documented in the UN Biodiversity and Eco-system Services Conference of the Parties. See www.ipbes.net/news/Media-Release-Global-Assessment. Also see Standing (2019), IPCC (2022), Milman (2022) and Wiseman and Kesgin (2024).
2. See https://cascadeinstitute.org/polycrisis.
3. In both the fourth and fifth Inter-governmental Panel on Climate Change reports this connection was made. It talks about 'human-induced climate change'. There is also a popular literature on the 'Human Age'. The notion of the Anthropocene has its origin in a short essay written by Paul Crutzen, a Nobel Prize winning chemist. His 2002 article is titled 'Geology of Mankind' and was published in

the prestigious journal *Nature.* See Steffen et al. (2011) for further elaboration, and Moore (2015a, 2015b) for a counter perspective named the Capitalocene.

4. See www.weforum.org/publications/global-risks-report-2023.

5. Besides Nancy Fraser's work there is also Ahmed (2010), Panitch and Gindin (2017) and Brand and Wissen (2018), for instance.

6. These premises are derived from the work of Marxist ecology such as Bellamy Foster's *Marx's Ecology: Materialism and Nature* (2000), Paul Burkett's *Marxism and Ecological Economics: Toward a Red-Green Political Economy* (2006) and *Marx and Nature: A Red and Green Perspective* (2014) and, more recently, Kohei Saito's *Karl Marx's Eco-socialism: Capital, Nature, and the Unfinished Critique of Political Economy* (2017).

7. There is substantial literature documenting this in history, anthropology and what can be termed 'commons studies'. See for instance Linebaugh (2014), Polanyi (2001) and Angus (2023).

8. In this regard, see Bowls and Gintis (2011) and LaDuke (2015a, 2015b).

CHAPTER 2

1. In the aftermath of the collapse of the Soviet Union, an avalanche of literature emerged reflecting on the twentieth-century left experience and socialism. Crucial lessons have been drawn from this history for a new global left politics. This section draws on Miliband (1994), Silber (1994), Bronner (2001), Panitch (2001), Harnecker (2015), Rahnema (2017) and Honeth (2017).

2. There is a vast literature in this regard. For instance, see Aronowitz and Gautney (2003), Mertes (2004), Polet and CETRI (2004) and Carroll and Sarker (2016).

3. In this regard we draw on Erik Olin Wright's (2019) thinking on transition beyond capitalism. Unlike Wright who specified four strategies to oppose capitalism in the twenty-first century – smashing, taming, escaping and eroding – we work with three: eroding, taming and exiting.

4. In South Africa, solidarity economy forces have worked with the idea of with, against and beyond the state as they have attempted to deepen the Cooperative's Act of 2005 from below (see Satgar 2019).

5. From the 1860s onwards, Marx in his understanding of primitive accumulation and its impact on the commons, as elaborated in *Capital,* in the First International, in his commitment to peasant communes in

Russia and the Paris Commune, moved away from the state centrism of the *Communist Manifesto* (see Satgar 2022a for this interpretation).

6. A collection of stories from Argentina's worker-run factories brings this to the fore (see Lavaca Collective 2007; Estes 2019).

7. This information is from interviews and field visit with 'Moviemento National dos Catadoras de Recycable' (MNCR) and 'Cooperative of Autonomous Garbage, Paper, and Recyclable Material Collection' on 23 June 2008. At that time, MNCR had 38,000 cooperative members and 400,000 worker–owners.

8. In 2008, we interviewed and did field visits with Orania Coffee Cooperative in Ethiopia and Kilimanjaro Native Co-operative Union (KNCU), Mamsera Cooperative and Moshi College on the foothills of Kilimanjaro in Tanzania.

9. A female worker–owner in the Cheese Board cooperative in Berkeley shared that she was able to plan her work and home time given the flexibility of the labour process and the centring of worker needs. A female interviewee in Eroski, a retail worker cooperative in the Basque country, was excited to share how her self-development was facilitated in the cooperative and included getting the opportunity to learn various foreign languages.

10. In this regard see stories from Argentina's recovered factory movement by the Lavaca Collective (2007) and the important interventions on horizontalism by Sitrin (2006, 2012), which also document political subject formation in the everyday.

11. This process has been carefully documented and curated by Akuno and Nangwaya (2017) of Cooperation Jackson. The solidarity economy initiative in Jackson builds on a long history of African American cooperative economic thought and practice (see also Nembhard 2014).

12. There are various important texts that capture this. Starr (2000) brings out some of the faultiness and key transformative alternatives that have come to the fore. Starr (2005) provides an important guide to the movement manifestos, strategic debates and tactics. Also see Dixon (2014) for his insights into contemporary transformative movements and Van Meter (2017) for how historical resistance has informed the present and how resistance is happening in the everyday.

13. We have written this book from a decolonial eco-feminist Marxist perspective but we recognise that all anti-capitalisms are important as part of transformative or emancipatory praxis. There is a need for convergence and dialogue among these ideological currents to hasten planetary care from below. Ideological rivalries for hegemony detract from this challenge.

14. Both Wright (2000) and Silver (2003) have been trailblazing in developing the foundations for a power resources approach for labour movements. Their contributions highlight structural power (labour's position in the economy system) and associational power (the power arising from collective political or trade union workers' associations). This work has been by augmented with notions of societal power (building coalitions and influencing public discourse) and institutional power resources (labour rights and social dialogue procedures) (Webster and Dor 2023). We argue that this approach can be reframed for transformative movements that champion democratic systemic reforms from below.
15. In 2024 alone, climate change dynamics increased the costs of catastrophes to $320 billion. See Harris (2025).
16. There has been a great deal of excellent scholarship on Xolobeni in South Africa. We also spent three days there in September 2024.

CHAPTER 3

1. There are earlier examples of cooperatives, such as the Fenwick Weavers' Society in Scotland that started in 1761, but the tobacco workers are the earliest recorded example of workers taking over production in a factory.
2. Robert Owen was a utopian socialist and was instrumental in the development of modern cooperatives in England. He started the failed experiment of New Harmony in Indiana, USA and was instrumental in founding Rochdale Society of Equitable Pioneers, which established the famous Rochdale principles for cooperatives. Rochdale Pioneers are considered the prototype of the modern cooperative movement. François Marie Charles Fourier was also a utopian socialist who influenced the 'intentional communities'. William Thompson also a utopian socialist, published *Practical Directions for the Speedy and Economical Establishment of Communities* in 1830.
3. For example, the solidarity economy forums and participatory budgeting in Brazil, the democratic decentralisation in Kerala and Hugo Chavez's 'twenty-first century socialism' all have an important role for cooperative forms of production. Marx and Lenin also saw the potential for cooperatives working together in laying the basis for socialism. See 'Cooperativism and Self-Management in Marx, Engels, and Lenin' in Lorenzo (2013, 63–89). See also Satgar (2014).
4. The banking and credit cooperatives account for more than 703 million of the total one billion membership/clients followed by 122 million in agriculture.

5. The index was developed by the Social Progress Imperative to track social progress in countries around the world (see www.socialprogress. org).
6. For an insightful debate, see Wright's (2016a) 'How to Be an Anticapitalist', Riley's (2016) critique 'An Anticapitalism that Can Win' and Wright's (2016b) rejoinder 'How to Think about (and Win) Socialism'.
7. The social economy literature has grown as cooperatives mainly in the global north have tried to find a role within globalising capitalism and its attendant restructuring of economies and societies. See, for instance, Shragge and Fontan (2000) and Amin (2009).
8. The actual number is likely to be less as some of these are double membership, for example, members of agricultural cooperatives are also members of banking cooperatives and Raiffeisens.
9. We visited and interviewed officials in the DGRV in July 2008 and followed their activities through online research.
10. This information is from interviews with NRECA officials at their head office in Washington, DC on 5 August 2008 as well as desktop research. See www.electric.coop.
11. This framing is very similar to Ashish Kothari's 'Flower of Transformation', which we discovered in the final stages of writing this book, as well as to the values promoted by permaculture. These similarities support the claim that these inter-dependent realms of transformation are similar beyond our cases. See for example, Lulla et al. (2024).
12. While many worker cooperatives own their enterprise, there are cases of diversified ownership models where the state or communities own the enterprise. The point is that a worker cooperative is a collective-owned (that is, worker-owned) and collective-managed economic enterprise, allowing workers full participation as economic actors in their enterprises.
13. In Dow (2003), the entire emphasis is on placing self-management within an incentive-based mainstream economics framework.
14. This information is from interviews with Cheese Board Collective members in August 2017. We have visited the Cheese Board over many years and spoken informally to worker–owners and community members as well as other cooperatives in the Bay area who have direct relations with the Cheese Board Collective.
15. There are other examples that have worker members or worker and consumer members such as Eroski in the Mondragón group in Spain, Cecosesola in Venezuela and the Italian COOP stores. We discuss some of these examples elsewhere in the book.
16. This information is based on a combination of visits to and interviews with members of these cooperatives between 2009 and 2017

and supplemented by online research and communications. In June 2009 we interviewed Willy Street Cooperative members in Madison; in July 2009 we interviewed worker–owners at Rainbow Groceries in San Francisco; in June 2017 we talked to members of Park Slope Food Cooperative in Brooklyn; and in June 2017 we interviewed members and workers at the Community Food Cooperative in Bozeman.

17. For example, NiederKaufungen Intentional Kommune in Germany, which we visited in 2009 and 2014.
18. The information is from interviews with members and founding members, and field visits in Oakland, San Francisco and New York in 2008, 2009, 2014, 2015 and 2017, as well as desktop research. See also www.usworker.coop/en and https://institute.coop/about.
19. See www.usworker.coop/en.
20. In interviews with government officials and cooperatives in Venezuela in 2008, we heard concerns about their fragility and dependence.
21. This information is from interviews and field visits in July 2010 and follow up desktop research.
22. The idea of the solidarity economy was used by Mondragón in the 1980s, and then popularised by the Brazilian movement in the 1990s. Also see Satgar (2014).
23. We visited Timbuktu Collective in July 2024. The information is also from their documents and annual reports.
24. Their net worth was Rupees 57.64 crore in March 2023. Exchange rate converted on 15 September 2024.
25. We visited and interviewed people at Working World in Argentina (July 2010) as well as New York City (June 2017), including the founding director Brendon Martins.
26. Cooperatives might also belong to federations or other structures, but the point here is that they are building forms of solidarity that are outside of these structures.

CHAPTER 4

1. The data are from field visits in January 2010, September 2014 and October 2017 as well as *Building Alternatives* (Isaac and Williams 2017). Some of the material was also in a short popular piece for *Global Dialogues* in 2016. We have maintained electronic communication and desktop research to track its development and we received a comprehensive update in June 2023.
2. For a variety of reasons discussed below, it has innovated on its membership categories. There are approximately 2,000 full worker–owner members.

3. The cooperative is named after the Uralungal hamlet in the Malabar region of northern Kerala.

4. By 2022, it had completed thousands of public projects all within budget and on time.

5. Its workforce includes worker–owners and employees, as discussed below.

6. The cooking team who prepares meals are also worker–owners.

7. Over the four-year period (2015-2018), there were only 38 cases of misconduct (financial irregularity and misbehaviour at the worksite) across the entire cooperative, leading to 35 suspensions. This is less than one per cent of its workforce, and significantly lower than capitalist enterprises. The UK based XpertHR consulting company places grievances at one per every 66 employees, whereas ULCCS is one case per 279 workers. Disciplinaries and grievances on the rise | Editor's choice | Tools | XpertHR.co.uk

8. The cooperative typically has approximately 80 worksites simultaneously across the state.

9. The survey was conducted by ULCCS and included half of its workforce. It was conducted in the evenings and therefore has an over-representation of workers staying at worksites versus those who were at sites close enough to their homes to return home in the evening.

10. The wage was 15,000 rupees and the total emoluments was 22,594 rupees; we converted based on the 11 July 2024 exchange rate of 83.3 rupees to US$1.

11. This reputational issue was repeatedly raised in our interviews and visits with worker–owners and community members on our visits.

12. One of the advantages of the recent diversification process is that ULCCS has been able to offer more skilled job opportunities to local people. For example, a number of aspects of the construction process are now done internally such as architects, engineers and surveyors.

13. There are four categories of membership. 'A Class' members are the full members with an original share value of 30 US cents (25 rupees). Initially the ceiling for the number of shares per member was 20, which was subsequently revised on a number of occasions: it was raised to 40 shares in 1954, through successive upward revisions to 800 shares in 1993, and in 1999 it was decided that an individual could have any number of shares as long as they did not exceed one-fifth of total paid share capital of the cooperative. The value of the A Class share was raised to US$1.20 (100 rupees) in 2008. In the period 2012–2013 there were 631 A Class members with total share capital of US$4.15 million (347 million rupees). The number of A Class members decreased to 580 in 2018–2019. The second category of membership is 'B Class'

for government shares. The share value of government investment in 2012–2013 was US$3.2 million (271 million rupees) and by 2018–2019 government's share capital was US$9.8 million (822 million rupees), registering a massive increase. B Class members do not have voting rights in the cooperative. The third type of membership is the 'C Class' members, which is given to migrant workers, of which there were 699 in 2012-2013 with a total share value of US$215 (18,000 rupees, or 0.18 lakh). Initially the share value of C Class members was US$0.06 (5 rupees) and then increased to US$0.30 (25 rupees). Only one share is issued to each C Class member. By 2018–2019 there was a large increase in C Class members which rose from 699 in 2012 to 1,968 in 2019. The fourth category of membership was created in the 2008 by-laws as 'D Class' members with a share value of US$0.06 (5 rupees) to accommodate depositors. D Class members have no rights in the cooperative other than depositing their savings for a fixed term with the cooperative. In 2012–2013 there were 9,001 D Class members with a share value of US$569 (45,000 rupees). All exchange rates calculated on 11 July 2024.

14. It was 5 rupees (6 cents in US currency) and 25 rupees (30 cents) on 11 July 2024.
15. All the currency conversions were calculated on the exchange rate on 11 July 2024.
16. All data are from field visits to Argentina in 2010, 2012 and 2015 as well as a three-day workshop in Argentina and thereafter desktop research.
17. The 10,000 worker–owners statistic is from a paper presented by Adriana Vitoli at Real Utopias Workshop, 26 October 2015. The 2022 data are from https://geo.coop/articles/self-management-argentina-20-years-after-2001 (accessed on 30 August 2022). All other data are from field visits to Argentina in 2010, 2012 and 2015.
18. The secretary in the balloon recovered factory, one of two in Argentina, used the company's Roller Dex containing all the clients' information to communicate with old clients and keep them committed to the balloon worker cooperative.
19. The Madres (the Mothers of the Plaza de Mayo, *Asociación Madres de Plaza de Mayo*) is an association of the mothers of the children who 'disappeared' during the military dictatorship between 1976 and 1983. In registering their resistance, they hold silent weekly marches in front of the Presidential palace at the Plaza de Mayo in Buenos Aires, which started in 1977 and continues.
20. At that time 12 other factories got definitive expropriation through the City of Buenos Aires government.

21. We had two crucial interviews with Chilavert Publishing Cooperative and spoke at length with Ernesto Gonzales, 18 June 2008 and 14 October 2015.

22. Interview, 14 October 2015.

23. We visited Uniforja in June 2008 and conducted a number of interviews with the general manager and seven worker–owners, and we spent time at the factory watching the production process. In addition to our field visit and interviews, we have conducted extensive desktop research on Uniforja's developments and growth over the years.

24. See https://uniforja.com.br/en/about-us.

25. Uniforja has employees who are not worker–owners. This is a trend we saw in many places with varying reasons linked to local conditions. What we saw in all the cases where worker cooperatives hired employees was a commitment to higher wages and better working conditions than mainstream capitalist enterprises.

26. This practice was especially important in their foundation phase when everyone was new to worker–ownership and collective decision making.

27. The article by Rushe is based on a study done by the Institute for Policy Studies. www.businessinsider.com/?ir=t/these-20-companies-have-biggest-ceo-to-worker-pay-ratios-2022-7?IR=T (accessed 27 August 2023).

CHAPTER 5

1. In 2002, the new Special Law on Cooperatives led them to change their name to 'Cooperative Integration Organization', but they kept the acronym Cecosesola given its long history.

2. Barquisimeto is the capital of the state of Lara in northwestern Venezuela with a population of nearly one million people. It is one of the oldest towns in Venezuela and has a rich history given its central location connecting the western and central parts of the country. It is the centre of a large agricultural region, including the cooperatives in the mountainous areas surrounding the city.

3. This information is from field research and interviews with cooperative members in July 2008, electronic communication and desktop research.

4. In 2022, Venezuela's oil reserves were the largest in the world.

5. Due to the economic crisis in the country, carbon emissions fell drastically to 2.86 tonnes per capita in 2022.

6. These agricultural cooperatives were initiated by liberation theology priests in the 1970s and 1980s. One of the priests continued to live and work in the area, and maintained close relations with the cooperatives.
7. Interview, 3 July 2008.
8. The data for Heiveld Cooperative is from field visits and interviews with members of the cooperative and progressive NGOs that worked with the cooperative in March 2007, April 2008 and October 2015. In addition, we have followed the cooperative's developments and done desktop research.
9. The 2014 poverty rate was 56 per cent, which was 30.3 million people at that time. See World Bank (2025) and Macrotrends (2025). There was no reliable data on poverty rate for 2024 at the time of writing, but the speculation is that the poverty rate had grown due to low economic growth and Covid-19. We erred on the conservative side and indicated that it was 'over 50 per cent'.
10. According to Statistics South Africa (2020), in 2020 the population was 59.6 million.
11. The World Bank (2022) records the average life expectancy in South Africa in 2020 as 64, which is slightly higher than the South African government's number.
12. The per capita greenhouse gas emissions have remained relatively consistently high. In 1990, per capita greenhouse gas emissions were 9.20 tonnes, in 2008 they rose to 10.83 tonnes and in 2019 they dropped to 9.60 tonnes.
13. The farmers are coloured, an official mixed-race category in South Africa, made up of descendants of primarily the Khoi and San, as well as Africans, settlers and former slaves from Southeast Asia.
14. With the support of a local NGO, Indigo, the cooperative also provides gender education. All members understand and support the rationale for the approach to membership and payments.
15. Exchange rate for South African Rand to dollar based on 1 February 2025, which was 1 rand to US$18.69.
16. See www.heiveld.co.za/processing.html (accessed 12 November 2017).
17. Trentino is one of a few provinces in northern Italy that have special Statutes of Autonomy, allowing them a great deal of independence and autonomy from the national government.
18. The information in this section is from field research and interviews in 2009 and 2015, followed up with desktop research.
19. There are two basic laws for cooperatives: (1) a 1977 law that did not tax indivisible surplus (earnings not distributed to members), which allowed cooperatives to recapitalise the enterprises; and (2) a 1983 law that permitted cooperatives to own private companies, which allowed

cooperatives to access capital to invest. From an economic point of view these two laws have been fundamental.

20. Local progressive priests played an important role in organising the formation of cooperatives at this time. For example, Lorenzo Guetti and Silvio Lorenzoni were actively involved in building the cooperatives during this early history.

21. See, for example, https://intrentino.com/en/collections/terre-altre and www.terrealtre.org.

22. See https://intrentino.com/en/collections/caseificio-val-di-fiemme-cavalese.

CHAPTER 6

1. Arrasate/Mondragón is the name of the municipal town where the cooperatives formed and is the home of the Mondragón Cooperative Corporation. The data on Mondragón are from online communications and research, internal documents and field visits between 4 and 14 August 2009 and 20 and 23 July 2010, as well as a three-day workshop at the University of Barcelona in 2010 and a three-day workshop in Argentina in 2015 where scholars presented on Mondragón. We visited five cooperatives and interviewed 15 cooperative members and MCC managers who gave us an extensive overview of Mondragón. The field visits were supplemented with email correspondence and desktop research to remain up to date.

2. The Autonomous Community of Basque Country (commonly referred to as the Basque Country, also known in Spanish as Pias Vasco which includes Bizkaia, Gipuzkoa and Araba) has secured regional autonomy from the Spanish government and was granted nationality within Spain in the Statute of Autonomy of the Basque Country of 1979.

3. As a result of the Euro-crisis, Fagor went bankrupt in 2013 and was bought by the Catalan company Cata for €42.5 million in 2014. Amazingly, the worker members were absorbed by other cooperatives within Mondragón group.

4. Over time, the exact number of cooperatives has fluctuated between 60 and 100 cooperatives due to various factors, including merging cooperatives, cooperatives leaving the Mondragón group and, in one case, due to bankruptcy.

5. The small Basque Country town of Guernica was a hotspot of republican resistance during the Spanish Civil War. Hitler's Germany supported the nationalist forces in the Civil War and, as a favour to Franco, Hitler bombed the town on 26 April 1937, killing thousands of people, mostly women and children as the men were away fighting

NOTES

the civil war. Days after the bombing, Picasso painted his monumental (and perhaps most famous) political work, *Guernica*, memorialising the victims and depicting the tragedy of war. Guernica continues to be a reminder of the horrors of war and cruelty of fascist dictators as well as an anti-war symbol. Within the Basque Country, the bombing of Guernica further reinforced their claims to independence and grievances against the Spanish state.

6. See www.mondragon-corporation.com/en.

7. One of the most creative financing initiatives we learned about was Working World's model to provide working capital to cooperatives. Working World is trying to create 'non-extractive financial infrastructure that shifts economic power to workers and communities' which they call Seed Commons. Working World pioneered its model in Argentina in 2005 and, after investing millions of dollars through a participatory and educational non-extractive finance model, they had a 98 per cent repayment rate. They then opened an office in León, Nicaragua in 2008 and again the model was successful. In 2012, they took their model to New York city, one of the world's centres of finance, and launched their third loan fund, which again has been successful. We spent time with Working World in Argentina in 2008, and did follow-up interviews with Brendon Martin in New York in 2017. See www.theworkingworld.org and https://seedcommons.org.

8. See www.mondragon.edu/en/meet-mu/cooperative-university.

9. The Basque Country law was the first cooperative law in Spain.

10. Interviews, 6 August 2009, 23 July 2010.

11. EQI measures the quality of government and uses the standard definition of Rothstein and Teorell (2008) that looks at the impartiality of government in exercising public power. The EQI includes three aspects in its measurement: 'impartiality (i.e. that the government upholds an impartial treatment of all citizens irrespective of their personal characteristics or connections), corruption (i.e. that there is no abuse of public office for private gain), and quality (i.e. that the public services as perceived as high-quality)' (Charron, Lapuente and Bauhr 2021b).

12. See https://unioncoops.wordpress.com/history.

13. Interview with Lezamiz, 6 August 2009.

14. In 1964, the Communist Party of India split into the CPI and the Communist Party of India (Marxist) CPI(M). See Williams (2008) for further discussion of the causes of the split.

15. Between 1980 and 2019, no party won two consecutive elections, with the Communist-led coalition of the Left Democratic Front (LDF) and the Congress-led coalition of the United Democratic Front (UDF) alternating leading the government. In 2021, the CPI(M)-led front

won a second term, in part due to the way it managed the various crises: Nipah virus, floods and Covid-19.

16. Infant mortality measures how many infants die per 1,000 in the first year of life.
17. While the numbers suggest substantial improvements, there are still many challenges and the need to further enhance the quality of services, including housing, especially for particular communities such as fisherfolk and Dalits.
18. The data are from Sustainable Development Report (2023). Data for Kerala are from Kerala Institute of Local Administration (2023).
19. Per capita income is in current prices, rupee to dollar exchange rate as of 11 July 2024.
20. For more information on Kudumbashree see https://lsgkerala.gov.in/en/kudumbashree.
21. A significant majority of Kudumbashree groups engage in economic activities such as pickling, local vegetable production and so on. While they operate on similar principles of cooperatives, Kudumbashrees do not register as cooperatives, in part due to the onerous cooperative legal framework in India. Instead, they are recognised as Kudumbashree groups and thus avoid the extremely cumbersome cooperative legislation and policy framework that governs cooperatives in India.
22. We also heard these numbers recounted in our field visit in 2023.
23. For a fascinating account of a beedi cooperative see Isaac, Franke and Raghavan (1998).
24. For example, for local government projects, cooperative tenders within 10 per cent of the lowest bid were given preference if the cooperative could match the lowest bid.
25. The government orders are: (1) GO(P) No. 7/2016 of PWD dated 20 February 2016; (2) GO(P) No. 77/2019 of PWD dated 4 July 2019; (3) GO(P) No. 4/2018 Dept of Science and Technology; (4) GO(P) No. 2780/2017 LSGD dated 11 August 2017; (5) GO.Ms.No.189/2018/ H&FWD dated 29 September 2018; (6) GO. No 530/2018/ Tourism dated 19 December 2018; and (7) GO. (Rt.) No. 243/2018/ TSM dated 28 May 2018.
26. In the 100 years of its existence, it has never gone over budget and, with two exceptions only, has delivered on time.
27. The information for this section is from field visits and interviews in 2008 and 2012, which included a crucial interview with Paul Singer on 27 June 2008 and informal discussions with him in July 2012, as well as desktop research.
28. The space within the state withered during Bolsanaro's government.

29. Interestingly, one of the first acts of Tremer's short government was to remove Paul Singer as Director of the Solidarity Economy Secretariat.
30. OCB is a member-driven cooperative that falls between mainstream capitalist and ameliorative types of cooperatives on the cooperative continuum, discussed in Chapter 3.
31. In order to get a sense of OCB given that it is the largest federation in Brazil, we spent a day with them and interviewed OCB representatives in São Paulo (OCESP), Americo Utumi (adviser to the president of OCESP), Edivaldo Del Grande (president of OCESP), 24 June 2008.
32. Information on CUT and ADS is from an interview with Almir dos Santos Alves, 27 June 2008.
33. Ecosol is linked to credit cooperatives and provides a unified voice for workers in credit cooperatives. Unisol and Ecosol are not the only federations providing support to the solidarity economy. Anteag is a national association of workers in cooperatives and self-managed enterprises.
34. Unisol has 35 full-time employees across 12 states. They have Congresses with all members. CUT indicates who they want as their representative. There are six people on the executive board, 33 people on the council (all from the cooperatives) and six on the fiscal commission. The general council meets once a year, sets the direction of the federation and elects the board. Every cooperative has one vote at the annual Congress.
35. These data are from interviews with Uniforja, Unisol leadership and CUT, 25–27 June 2008.
36. See https://unisolbrasil.org.br (accessed 10 February 2018).
37. At the time, the horrendous pay and poor working conditions (no full-time jobs, no medical benefits and irregular hours) of Walmart workers had just come under the spotlight.

References

Acaroglu, Onur. *Rethinking Marxist Approaches to Transition*. Brill, 2021.

Ahmed, Nafeez M. *A User's Guide to the Crisis of Civilisation: And How to Save It*. Pluto Press, 2010.

Akuno, Kali, and Ajamu Nangwaya. *Jackson Rising: The Struggle for Economic Democracy and Black Self-Determination in Jackson, Mississippi*. Daraja Press, 2017.

Albert, Michael J. *Navigating the Polycrisis: Mapping the Futures of Capitalism and the Earth*. The MIT Press, 2024.

Altuna, Gabilondo Larraitz, Aitzol Loyola Idiakez and Eneritz Pagalday Tricio. Mondragon: The Dilemmas of a Mature Cooperativism. In *Cooperatives and Socialism: A View from Cuba*, edited by Camila Pineiro Harnecker. Palgrave, 2013.

Amin, Ash, ed. *The Social Economy: International Perspectives on Economic Solidarity*. Zed Books, 2009.

Amin, Samir. *Re-reading the Post War Period: An Intellectual Itinerary*. Monthly Review Press, 1994.

Amladi, Divya. How Are Billionaire and Corporate Power Intensifying Global Inequality? *Oxfam News*, 20 January 2025. www.oxfamamerica.org/explore/stories/how-are-billionaire-and-corporate-power-intensifying-global-inequality/ (accessed 2 February 2025).

Angus, Ian. *The War Against the Commons: Dispossession and Resistance in the Making of Capitalism*. Monthly Review Press, 2023.

Aronowitz, Stanley, and Heather Gautney. *Implicating Empire: Globalization and Resistance in the 21st Century World Order*. Basic Books, 2003.

Arruda, Marcos. Endogenous Development and a South American Financial Architecture. Paper presented at Beyond Bretton Woods: The Transnational Economy in Search for New Institutions, Mexico City, 15–17 October 2008.

Azkarraga Etxagibel, Joseba, G. Cheney and Ainara Udaondo. Workers' Participation in a Globalized Market: Reflections on and from Mondragon. In *Alternative Work Organizations*, edited by Maurizio Atzeni. Palgrave, 2012.

Azzellini, Dario. From Cooperatives to Enterprises of Direct Social Property in the Venezuelan Process. In *Cooperatives and Socialism: A View from Cuba*, edited by Camila Pineiro Harnecker. Palgrave, 2013.

Bakker, Isabella and Gill, Stephen. *Power, Production and Social Reproduction*. Palgrave Macmillan, 2003.

Barca, Stefania. *Forces of Reproduction: Notes for a Counter-Hegemonic Anthropocene*. Cambridge University Press, 2020.

Basque Government. *7th Voluntary Monitoring Report Multi-level 2030 Agenda Basque Country*. Agenda 2030, Euskadiren Konpromisoa, 2024. https://sdgs.un.org/sites/default/files/vlrs/2024-05/7th_monitoring_report_2023_agenda_2030_engl.pdf (accessed on 17 January 2025).

Basterretxea, Imanol and Eneka Albizu. Management Training as a Source of Perceived Competitive Advantage: The Mondragon Cooperative Group Case. *Economic and Industrial Democracy* 32, no. 2 (2010): 199-222.

Bauwens, Michel, Roc Kranjc and Mayssam Daabul. Commons Economics. In *Digital Capitalism and Its Limits: Technotoopia, Power and Risk*, edited by Vishwas Satgar. Wits University Press, 2025.

Bayat, Assef. *Work Politics and Power: An International Perspective on Workers' Control and Self Management*. Zed Books, 1991.

Biel, Robert. *The Entropy of Capitalism*. Brill, 2013.

Bizkaia Talent. European Quality of Life Index: The Basque Country is among the Best Places in Europe and Is the Spanish State Leader. 2019. www.bizkaiatalent.eus/en/indice-calidad-vida-europa/#:~:text=Job%20offers-,European%20quality%20of%20life%20index%3A%20the%20Basque%20Country%20is%20among,is%20the%20Spanish%20State%20leader&text=At%20the%20European%20level%2C%20Bizkaia,a%20total%20of%201442%20provinces.

Bollier, David. *Think Like A Commoner: A Short Introduction to the Life of the Commons*. New Society Publishers, 2014.

Borzaga, Carlo, and Luigi Mittone. *The Multi-Stakeholders Versus the Non-profit Organisation*. Working paper no. 9707. Department of Economics, Università degli Studi di Trento, Italy, 1997.

Bourdieu, Piere. *Pascalian meditations*. Stanford University Press, 2000.

Bowls, Samuel and Herbert Gintis. *A Cooperative Species: Human Reciprocity and its Evolution*. Princeton University Press, 2011.

Brand, Ulrich, and Markus Wissen. *The Limits to Capitalist Nature: Theorizing and Overcoming the Imperial Mode of Living*. Rowman & Littlefield Publishers, 2018.

Brand, Ulrich, and Markus Wissen. *The Imperial Mode of Living: Everyday Life and the Ecological Crisis of Capitalism*. Verso Books, 2021.

Brand, Ulrich, Barbara Muraca, Éric Pineault et al., From Planetary to Societal Boundaries: An Argument for Collectively Defined Self-Limitation. *Sustainability: Science, Practice, & Policy* 17, no. 1 (2021): 264–291. https://doi.org/10.1080/15487733.2021.1940754

Bronner, Stephen Eric. *Socialism Unbound.* Westview Press, 2001.

Brown, Wendy. *Undoing the Demos: Neoliberalism's Stealth Revolution.* Zone Books, 2015.

Burkett, Paul. *Marxism and Ecological Economics: Toward a Red-Green Political Economy.* Brill, 2006.

Burkett, Paul. *Marx and Nature: A Red and Green Perspective.* Haymarket Books, 2014.

Caffentzis, George. Divisions in the Commons: Ecuador's FLOK Society and the Zapatistas' *Escuelita.* In *Moving Beyond Capitalism*, edited by Cliff DuRand. Routledge, 2016.

Camus, Albert. Review of *Nausea* by Jean-Paul Sartre. *Alger Républicain*, 20 October 1938. Reprinted in *Selected Essays and Notebooks*, translated and edited by Philip Thody.

Carroll, William K., and Kanchan Sarkar. *A World to Win: Contemporary Social Movements and Counter-Hegemony.* ARP Books, 2016.

Chakrabarty, Dipesh. *The Climate of History in a Planetary Age.* The University of Chicago Press, 2021.

Charron, Nicholas, Victor Lapuente and Monika Bauhr. The Geography of Quality of Government in Europe. Subnational Variations in the 2024 European Quality of Government Index and Comparisons with Previous Rounds. 2021a. QoG Working Paper Series 2024:2. Department of Political Science, University of Gothenburg. https://hdl.handle.net/2077/80191.

Charron, Nicholas, Victor Lapuente and Monika Bauhr. Sub-national Quality of Government in EU Member States: Presenting the 2021 European Quality of Government Index and its Relationship with Covid-19 Indicators. 2021b. Working Paper Series 2021:4. The Quality of Government Institute, Department of Political Science University of Gothenburg. www.gu.se/sites/default/files/2021-05/2021_4_%20Charron_Lapuente_Bauhr.pdf (accessed 8 January 2023).

Charron, Nicholas, Victor Lapuente, Monika Bauhr and Paola Annoni. Change and Continuity in Quality of Government: Trends in Subnational Quality of Government in EU Member States. *Investigaciones Regionales-Journal of Regional Research*, no. 53 (2022): 5–23. https://doi.org/10.38191/iirr-jorr.22.008.

Chaudhary, Rajinder. The ULCCS: An 80-Year-Old Construction Labour Cooperative. *International Journal of Rural Management* 1, no. 2 (2005): 263–284.

Chomsky, Noam. *Occupy.* Penguin Group, 2012.

Chun, Jennifer Jihye. *Organizing at the Margins. The Symbolic Politics of Labor in South Korea and the United States.* Ithaca, NY: ILR Press, 2009.

Chun, Jennifer Jihye. Refusing Precarity: Labor Protest and the Politics of Solidarity in South Korea. *The Journal of Asian Studies* 81, no. 1 (2022): 107–118.

Cicopa. Mondragon Corporation Is Ranked 11th in List of Enterprises That Are Changing the World. *Cicopa News*, 2 October 2020. www.cicopa.coop/news/mondragon-corporation-is-ranked-11th-in-list-of-enterprises-that-are-changing-the-world (accessed 17 June 2024).

Claeys, Gregory, and Lyman Tower Sargent. *The Utopia Reader.* NYU Press, 1999.

Cock, Jacklyn. The Climate Crisis and a 'Just Transition' in South Africa: An Eco-Feminist-Socialist Perspective. In *The Climate Crisis*, edited by Vishwas Satgar, Wits University Press, 2018.

Collier, George A., and Elizabeth Lowery Quaratiello. *Basta! Land and the Zapatista Rebellion in the Chiapas*, 3rd ed. Food First Books, 2005.

Cooperazione Trentina. *Trentino Cooperative System.* Powerpoint presentation by Cooperazione Trentina: Federazione Trentina Della Cooperazione, 2006.

COPAC. *Building A Solidarity Economy Movement: A Guide for Grassroots Activism.* COPAC Activist Training Guide, 2010.

De Angelis, M. Commons. In *Pluriverse: A Post-Development Dictionary*, edited by Ashish Kothari, Ariel Salleh, Arturo Escobar, Federico Demaria and Alberto Acosta. Tulika Books, 2019.

De Sousa Santos, Boaventura. *The Rise of the Global Left: The World Social Forum and Beyond.* Zed Books, 2006.

Deccan Herald. Kerala Retains Top Rank in NITI-Aayog SDG India Index 2023–24. *The Deccan Herald*, 12 July 2024. www.deccanherald.com/india/kerala-retains-top-rank-in-niti-aayogs-sdg-india-index-2023-24-bihar-worst-performer-3103489.

Della Porta, Donatella. *Social Movements in Times of Austerity: Bringing Capitalism Back into Protest Analysis.* Polity Press, 2015.

DeSilver, Drew. For Most US Workers, Real Wages Have Barely Budged in Decade. 7 August 2018. www.pewresearch.org/short-reads/2018/08/07/for-most-us-workers-real-wages-have-barely-budged-for-decades (accessed 28 May 2025).

Devasia, Jose, and Sudarshan Varadhan. Unsung Heroes: Fishermen Rescue Thousands in Kerala Foods. *Christian Science Monitor*, 22 August 2018. www.csmonitor.com/World/Asia-South-Central/2018/0822/Unsung-heroes-fishermen-rescue-thousands-in-Kerala-floods.

Diwakar, Dilip G., Visakh Viswambaran and Prasanth M.K. Impact of Covid-19 on Livelihood and Health Experiences of Migrant Labourers in Kerala, India. *CASTE A Global Journal on Social Exclusion* 3, no. 2 (2022): 299–318. https://doi.org/10.26812/caste.v3i2.447.

Dixon, Chris. *Another Politics: Talking Across Today's Transformative Movements*. University of California Press, 2014.

Dorniger, C. The Continuity and Intensification of Imperial Appropriation in the Global Economy. In *The Geopolitics of Green Colonialism: Global Justice and Ecosocial Transitions*, edited by M. Lang, M. A. Manahan and B. Bringel. Pluto Press, 2024.

Dow, Gregory. *Governing the Firm: Worker's Control in Theory and Practice*. Cambridge University Press, 2003.

Dowling, Emma. *The Care Crisis: What Caused It and How Can We End It?* Verso Books, 2021.

DTI. *Baseline Study of Cooperatives in South Africa*. Department of Trade and Industry, 2009.

Dyvik, Einar H. Pay Gap Between CEOs and Average Workers, by Country 2018. 2024. www.statista.com/statistics/424159/pay-gap-between-ceos-and-average-workers-in-world-by-country (accessed 14 January 2025).

Economic Policy Institute. 2025. The Productivity–Pay Gap. www.epi.org/productivity-pay-gap (accessed 27 May 2025).

Economic Times. Kerala's Poverty Index Achievement Reflective of Govt's 'Unwavering Commitment' towards Social Welfare: Vijayan. *Economic Times*, 26 November 2021. https://economictimes.indiatimes.com/news/india/keralas-poverty-index-achievement-reflective-of-govts-unwavering-commitment-towards-social-welfare-vijayan/articleshow/87937185.cms?from=mdr (accessed on 30 September 2023).

Economist. Trouble in Workers' Paradise: The Collapse of Spain's Fagor Tests the World's Largest Group of Co-operatives. *The Economist*, 9 November 2012. www.economist.com/news/business/21589469-collapse-spains-fagor-tests-worlds-largest-group-co-operatives-trouble-workers (accessed 21 January 2018).

Emmolo, Emmilio. 2019. Legal Framework Analysis National Report: Italy. www.coops4dev.coop/sites/default/files/2021-03/Italy%20Legal%20Framework%20Analysis%20Report%20.pdf.

Engels, Friedrich. *The Condition of the Working Class in England*. In *Marx and Engels on Britain*. Progress Publishers, [1842] 1953.

ESPON. ESPON QoL – Quality of Life Measurements and Methodology. 2020. https://archive.espon.eu/programme/projects/espon-2020/applied-research/quality-of-life.

Estes, Nick. *Our History is the Future: Standing Rock versus the Dakota Access Pipeline, and the Long Tradition of Indigenous Resistance*. Verso, 2019.

Esteves, Ana Margarida. The Emergence of the United States Solidarity Economy Network. In *The Solidarity Economy Alternative: Emerging*

Theory and Practice, edited by Vishwas Satgar. University of KwaZulu Natal Press, 2014.

Esteves, Ana Margarida. Decolonizing Livelihoods, Decolonizing the Will: Solidarity Economy as a Social Justice Paradigm in Latin America. Unpublished paper, undated.

Etxagibel, Joseba Azkarraga, George Cheney and Ainara Udaondo. Workers' Participation in a Globalized Market: Reflections on and from Mondragon. *Alternative Work Organizations* 76 (2012): 1–24.

Etxarri, Enekoitz Etxezarreta. Social Economy in the Basque Country: A Shared Narrative. In *Story of Social Economy in the Basque Country,* edited by Santocildes, Marta Enciso, Aitor Bengoetxea Alkorta, Leire Uriarte Zabala and Aitziber Mugarra Elorriaga. 1st ed. Dykinson, S. L., 2021. https://doi.org/10.2307/j.ctv282jg9c.

Evans, Peter. Counterhegemonic Globalization: Transnational Social Movements in the Contemporary Global Political Economy. In *Handbook of Political Sociology: States, Civil Societies, and Globalization,* edited by T. Janoski, R. R. Alford, A. M. Hicks and M. A. Schwartz. Cambridge University Press, 2003.

Fantasia, Rick, and Kim Voss. *Hard Work: Remaking the American Labor Movement.* University of California Press, 2004.

Federici, Sylvia. Re-enchanting the World: Feminism and the Politics of the Commons. *Journal of International Women's Studies* 21, no. 1 (2020): 409–411.

Fisher, William, and Thomas Ponniah, eds. *Another World is Possible: Popular Alternatives to Globalization at the World Social Forum.* Fernwood Publishing, 2003.

Flecha, Ramon, and Ignacio Santa Cruz. Cooperation for Economic Success: The Mondragon Case. *Analysis and Kritik* 33, no.1 (2011): 157-70.

Flecha, Ramon and Pun Ngai. The Challenge for Mondragon: Searching for the Cooperative Values in Times of Internationalization. *Organization* 21, no. 39 (2014): 666-82.

Foster, Bellamy. *Marx's Ecology: Materialism and Nature.* Monthly Review Press, 2000.

Foster, Bellamy and Fred Magdoff. *The Great Financial Crisis: Causes and Consequences.* Monthly Review Press, 2009.

Fraser, Nancy. Democracy's Crisis. Public lecture given at Erasmus University in Rotterdam, Netherlands, upon Nancy Fraser's receipt of an honorary doctorate. 7 November 2014. https://publicseminar.org/2014/11/democracys-crisis/.

Fraser, Nancy. Contradictions of Capital and Care. *New Left Review* no. 100 (2016): 99–117.

Fraser, Nancy. Crisis of Care? On the Social-Reproductive Contradictions of Contemporary Capitalism. In *Social Reproduction Theory: Remapping Class, Recentering Oppression,* edited by Tithi Bhattacharya. Pluto Books, 2017.

Fraser, Nancy. *Cannibal Capitalism: How Our System Is Devouring Democracy, Care, and the Planet and What We Can Do About It.* Verso Books, 2022.

Fraser, Nancy, and Rahel Jaeggi. *Capitalism: A Conversation in Critical Theory.* Polity Press, 2018.

Fridell, Gavin. *Fair Trade Coffee: The Prospects and Pitfalls of Market-Driven Social Justice.* University of Toronto Press, 2007.

FTC. *Statuto Sociale della Federazione Trentina della Cooperazione: Società Cooperativa.* Federazione Trentina delle Cooperative Trento, 15 June 2014.

Gibson-Graham, J. K. Diverse Economies: Performative Practices for Other Worlds. *Progress in Human Geography* 32, no. 5 (2008): 613–632.

Gibson-Graham, J. K., Jenny Cameron and Stephen Healy. *Take Back the Economy: An Ethical Guide for Transforming Our Communities.* University of Minnesota Press, 2013.

Gonzales, Vanna A. A Different Kind of Social Enterprise: Social Cooperatives and the Development of Civic Capital in Italy. *Community Development* 41, no. 1 (2010a): 50–75.

Gonzales, Vanna A. Italian Social Cooperatives and the Development of Civic Capacity: A Case of Cooperative Renewal? *Affinities: A Journal of Radical Theory, Culture and Action* 4, no. 1 (2010b): 225–251.

Government of Kerala. *Economic Review 2002.* Kerala State Planning Board, 2016. https://spb.kerala.gov.in/sites/default/files/inline-files/2002.pdf.

Gramsci, Antonio. The Revolution Against Capital. *Avanti!,* 24 December 1917. Translated by Natalie Campbell. www.marxists.org/archive/gramsci/1917/12/revolution-against-capital.htm. (accessed 5 January 2024).

Gretter, Alessandro, Chiara Rizzi, Sara Favargiotti, Alessandro Betta, Giovanna Ulrici. Trento Social Commons: Community Engagement as Tools for New Physical and Cultural Relationships between Rural and Peripheral Spaces. *Journal of Alpine Research* 106, no. 2 (2018). https://journals.openedition.org/rga/4166 (accessed 11 November 2022).

Grimes, Kimberly M., and Lynne B. Milgram, eds. *Artisans and Cooperatives: Developing Alternate Trade for the Global Economy.* University of Arizona Press, 2000.

Guinness, Katherine, Grant Bollmer and Tom Doig. Billionaires are Building Bunkers and Buying Islands. But Are They Prepping for the Apocalypse – or Pioneering a New Feudalism? *The Conversation,* March

1, 2024. https://theconversation.com/billionaires-are-building-bunkers-and-buying-islands-but-are-they-prepping-for-the-apocalypse-or-pioneering-a-new-feudalism-223987.

Gunn, Christopher Eaton. *Third-Sector Development: Making Up for the Market*. Cornell University Press, 2004.

Hanieh, Adam. *Lineages of Revolt: Issues of Contemporary Capitalism in the Middle East*. Haymarket Books, 2013.

Hardt, Michael and Antonio Negri. *Multitude: War and Democracy in the Age of Empire*. Penguin, 2005.

Harnecker, Martha. *Rebuilding the Left*. London: Zed Books, 2007.

Harnecker, Martha. *A World to Build: New Paths Toward Twenty-First Century Socialism*. Monthly Review Press, 2015.

Harris, Katelynn. Forty Years of Falling Manufacturing Employment. *Beyond the Numbers: Employment and Unemployment* 9, no. 16 (November 2020). www.bls.gov/opub/btn/volume-9/forty-years-of-falling-manufacturing-employment.htm, (accessed 16 June 2024).

Harris, Lee. Catastrophes Cost World $320bn in 2024, Reinsurer Reports. *Financial Times*, 9 January 2025. www.ft.com/content/76d1e4b6-ac70-47c0-82c0-76faca1c22e7.

Helfrich, Silke. Patterns of Commoning: How We Can Bring About a Language of Commoning. In *Patterns of Commoning*, edited by David Bollier and Silke Helfrich. Commons Strategies Group, 2015.

Heller, Patrick, K. N. Harilal and Shubham Chaudhuri. Building Local Democracy: Evaluating the Impact of Decentralization in Kerala, India. *World Development* 35, no. 4 (2007): 626–648. https://doi.org/10.1016/j.worlddev.2006.07.001.

Hickel, Jason, Christian Dorniger, H. Wieland and I. Suwandi. Imperialist Appropriation in the World Economy: Drain from Global South Through Unequal Exchange, 1990–2015. *Global Environmental Change* 73 (2022): 102467.

Hindu Bureau. Kerala retains top spot in the latest SDG India Index Ranking. *The Hindu*, 13 July 2024. www.thehindu.com/news/national/kerala/kerala-retains-top-spot-in-the-latest-sdg-india-index-rankings/article68400190.ece#:~:text=Kerala%20has%20retained%20its%20top,composite%20score%20of%2079%20points (accessed 18 January 2025).

Hodgson, Mary. *Humanity at Work: Mondragon, a Social Innovation Ecosystem Case Study*. The Young Foundation, 5 April 2017. www.youngfoundation.org/our-work/publications/humanity-at-work-mondragon-a-social-innovation-ecosystem-case-study/.

Holloway, John. *Change the World Without Taking Power: The Meaning of Revolution Today*. Pluto Press, 2002.

Honeth, Axel. *The Idea of Socialism*. Polity Press, 2017.

Hornborg, Alf, and Carole Crumley. *The World System and the Earth System: Global Socioenvironmental Change and Sustainability Since the Neolithic*. Left Coast Press, 2006.

ICA. Cooperative Identity, Values, and Principles. 1996. https://ica.coop/en/cooperatives/cooperative-identity (accessed 5 July 2024).

ICA. Cooperatives Facts and Figures. 2024. https://ica.coop/en/cooperatives/facts-and-figures (accessed 27 December 2024).

ICA and EURICSE. 2023. *World Cooperative Monitor 2023 Report: Exploring the Cooperative Economy, 2023*. https://monitor.coop/sites/default/files/2024-01/wcm_2023_3101.pdf (accessed 31 January 2024).

IPCC. *Climate Change 2022: Impacts, Adaptation and Vulnerability: Working Group II Contribution to the Sixth Assessment Report of the Intergovernmental Panel on Climate Change*. Cambridge University Press, 2022.

Isaac, T. M. Thomas. *Kerala: Another Possible World*. LeftWord Press, 2022.

Isaac, T. M. Thomas, and Richard W. Franke. *Local Democracy and Development: The Kerala People's Campaign for Decentralized Planning*. Rowman & Littlefield, 2002.

Isaac, T. M. Thomas, and Patrick Heller. Democracy and Development: Decentralized Planning in Kerala. In *Deepening Democracy: Institutional Innovations in Empowered Participatory Governance*, edited by Archon Fung and Erik Olin Wright, 83. Verso, 2003.

Isaac, T. M. Thomas, and Michelle Williams. *Building Alternatives: The Story of India's Oldest Construction Workers' Cooperative*. LeftWord Press, 2017.

Isaac, T. M. Thomas, Richard W. Franke and Pyaralal Raghavan. *Democracy at Work in an Indian Industrial Cooperative: The Story of Kerala Dinesh Beedi*. Cornell University Press, 1998.

Jackson, Sarah. Here Are the 20 Companies with the Biggest Pay Gap Between CEOs and Workers in 2021, Including Amazon, Apple, Starbucks, and McDonald's. *Business Insider*, 22 July 2022. www.businessinsider.com/these-20-companies-have-biggest-ceo-to-worker-pay-ratios-2022-7 (accessed October 28, 2024).

Jaffee, Daniel. *Brewing Justice: Fair Trade Coffee, Sustainability, and Survival*. University of California Press, 2007.

Kaleido Scoops. 2015. Cooperatives and their Popularity Across the World. www.kalscoops.com/cooperatives-and-their-popularity-across-the-world (accessed 23 December 2024).

Keck, Margaret, and Kathryn Sikkink. *Activists Beyond Borders: Advocacy Networks in International Politics*. Cornell University Press, 1998.

Kerala Institute of Local Administration. Fact Sheet of Sustainable Development Goals Kerala Status. 2023. http://dspace.kila.ac.in/bitstream/123456789/654/1/Fact%20Sheet%20of%20SDG%20Final.pdf (accessed 1 October 2023).

Kioupkiolis, Alexandros and Theodoros Karyotis. Self-Managing the Commons in Contemporary Greece. In *An Alternative Labour History: Worker Control and Workplace Democracy*, edited by Dario Azzellini. Zed Books, 2015.

Klein, Naomi. *The Shock Doctrine: The Rise of Disaster Capitalism*. Allen Lane, 2007.

LaDuke, Winona. *All Our Relations: Native Struggles for Land and Life*. Haymarket Books, 2015a.

LaDuke, Winona. *Recovering the Sacred: The Power of Naming and Claiming*. Haymarket Books, 2015b.

Lang, Miriam, Claus-Dieter König and Ada-Charlotte Regelmann (eds). *Alternatives in a World of Crisis*. Rosa Luxemburg Stiftung Brussels Office, 2018.

Lavaca Collective. *Sin Patron: Stories from Argentina's Worker-Run Factories*. Haymarket Books, 2007.

Lawrence, Michael, Thomas Homer-Dixon, Scott Janzwood, Johan Rockström, Ortwin Renn and Jonathan F. Donges. Global Polycrisis: The Causal Mechanisms of Crisis Entanglement. *Global Sustainability* 7, e6 (2024): 1–16. https://wfabhmdrpib5-u5525.pressidiumcdn.com/wp-content/uploads/2024/01/global-polycrisis-the-causal-mechanisms-of-crisis-entanglement.pdf.

Lenin, Vladimir I. On Cooperation. In *Collected Works*, 4th English ed. Progress Publishers, 1996.

Levitas, Ruth. 2009. The Imaginary Reconstitution of Society: Utopia as Method. In *Utopia, Method, Vision: The Use Value of Social Dreaming*, edited by Tom Moylan and Raffaella Baccolini. International Academic Publishers.

Li, Minqi. *China and the 21st Century Crisis*. Pluto Press, 2016.

Linebaugh, Peter. *Stop, Thief! The Commons, Enclosures, and Resistance*. PM Press, 2014.

Lokniti-CSDS. Kerala Post Poll 2021: Survey Findings. 2021. www.lokniti.org/media/PDF-upload/1622695797_46018800_download_report.pdf (accessed 28 May 2025).

Lorenzo, Miranda Humberto. Cooperativism and Self-Management in Marx, Engels, and Lenin. In *Cooperatives and Socialism: A View from Cuba*, edited by Camila Pineiro Harnecker. Palgrave Macmillan, 2013.

Louw, Rhoda. 2006. Sustainable Harvesting of Wild Rooibos (*Aspalathus Linearis*) in the Suid Bokkeveld, Northen Cape. MSC thesis, UCT.

https://science.uct.ac.za/sites/default/files/content_migration/science_uct_ac_za/841/files/louw%25202006.pdf.

Lulla, Arpita, Iokiñe Rodríguez, Mirna Inturias and Ashish Kothari. A Conversation on Radical Transformation Frameworks: From Conflicts to Alternatives. In *Just Transformations: Grassroots Struggles for Alternative Futures*, edited by Iokiñe Rodriquez, Mariana Walter and Leah Temper. Pluto Press, 2024. Ebook.

Luxemburg, Rosa. *The Accumulation of Capital: A Contribution to the Economic Theory of Imperialism*. Routledge, 2003 [1913].

Macrotrends. 2025. South Africa Poverty Rate 1993–2025. www.macrotrends.net/countries/ZAF/south-africa/poverty-rate.

Magnani, Esteban. *The Silent Change: Recovered Businesses in Argentina*. tESEO, 2009.

Mance, Euclides. The Solidarity Economy in Brasil. In *The Solidarity Economy Alternative: Emerging Theory and Practice*, edited by Vishwas Satgar. University of KwaZulu-Natal Press, 2014.

Marx, Karl. *Capital: A Critique of Political Economy, Volume One*. Penguin, 1976 [1867].

Marx, Karl. *Capital*, Vol. I and III. Progress Publishers, 1996.

Mason, Paul. *Why It's Still Kicking Off Everywhere: The New Global Revolutions*. Verso Books, 2012.

Merchant, Carolyn. *The Death of Nature: Women, Ecology, and the Scientific Revolution*. HarperCollins, 1983.

Mertes, Tom, ed. *A Movement of Movements: Is Another World Really Possible?* Verso, 2004.

Miliband, Ralph. *Socialism for a Sceptical Age*. Polity Press, 1994.

Milman, Oliver. *The Insect Crisis: The Fall of the Tiny Empires that Run the World*. W. W. Norton and Company, 2022.

Moore, Jason W. Putting Nature to Work: Anthropocene, Capitalocene, and the Challenge of World Ecology. In *Supramarkt: A Micro-toolkit for Disobedient Consumers, or How to Frack the Fatal Forces of the Capitalocene*, edited by Cecilia Wee, Janneke Schönenbach and Olaf Arndt. Irene Books, 2015a.

Moore, Jason W. *Capitalism in the Web of Life: Ecology and the Accumulation of Capital*, 1st ed. Verso, 2015b.

Nembhard, Jessica Gordon. *Collective Courage: A History of African American Cooperative Economic Thought and Practice*. Pennsylvania State University Press, 2014.

Ness, Immanuel and Dario Azzellini, eds. *Ours to Master and to Own: Workers' Control from the Commune to the Present*. Haymarket Books, 2011.

NITI Aayog. *The Success of Our Schools: School Education Quality Index.* Government of India, 2019.

NITI Aayog. *Healthy States Progressive India: Report on the Ranks of States and Union Territories.* Health Index Round IV 2019–2020. Government of India, 2021. www.niti.gov.in/sites/default/files/2021-12/NITI-WB_Health_Index_Report_24-12-21.pdf.

NITI Aayog. *Health Index 2023: State-wise List.* Government of India, 2023. www.geeksforgeeks.org/niti-aayog-health-index-2023/.

O'Connor, James. Capitalism, Nature, Socialism: A Theoretical Introduction. *Capitalism Nature Socialism* 1, no. 1 (1988): 11–38.

Oakland Institute. Urgent Alert: Tanzanian Government on a Rampage Against Indigenous People. 2024. www.oaklandinstitute.org/urgent-alert-tanzanian-government-rampage-against-indigenous-people (accessed 22 October 2024).

OECD. *The Co-operative Model in Trentino, Italy: A Case Study Report.* OECD Working Papers, developed with LEED and Cooperazione Trentina: Federazione Trentina Della Cooperazione, 2014. https://ccednet-rcdec.ca/sites/ccednet-rcdec.ca/wp-content/uploads/2022/09/the_cooperative_model_in_trentino_final_with_covers.pdf (accessed 30 October 2024).

Oettle, Noel, and Bettina Kolle. Start Where the People Are: Understanding Enterprise Within Rural Specific Conditions. Paper presented at the Conference on Stimulating Rural Enterprise: Kopaning, 2003.

Oommen, Malayil Abraham. *Microfinance and Poverty Alleviation: The Case of Kerala's Kudumbashree.* Working Paper 17. Centre for Socio-Economic and Environmental Studies, 2008.

Ostrom, Elinor. *Governing the Commons: The Evolution of Institutions for Collective Action.* Cambridge University Press, 2015 [1990].

Owen, Robert. *A New View of Society and Other Writings,* edited by G. Claeys. Penguin Books, 1991 [1813].

Owen, Robert. *The Selected Works of Robert Owen,* edited by G. Claeys. Pickering and Chatto, 1993.

Oxfam. Wealth of Five Richest Men Doubles Since 2020 as Five Billion People Made Poorer in 'Decade of Division'. *Oxfam News,* 15 January 2024. www.oxfam.org/en/press-releases/wealth-five-richest-men-doubles-2020-five-billion-people-made-poorer-decade-division#:~:text=Democratically%2Downed%20businesses%20better%20equalize,average%20wealth%20of%20Black%20households (accessed 2 February 2025).

P2P Foundation. Solidarity Economy in Brazil. 2017. http://wiki.p2pfoundation.net/Solidarity_Economy_in_Brazil (accessed 11 November 2017).

Panitch, Leo. *Renewing Socialism: Democracy, Strategy and Imagination.* Westview Press, 2001.

Panitch, Leo, and Sam Gindin. Class, Party and the Challenge of State Transformation. In *Reflections on the Future of the Left,* edited by David Coates. Agenda Publishing, 2017.

Parameswaran, M. P. *Empowering People: Insights from a Local Experiment in Participatory Planning.* Studies in Local Development 2. Daanish Books, 2005.

Parayil, Govindan. *Kerala: The Development Experience: Reflections on Sustainability and Replicability.* Zed Books, 2000.

Patel, Raj, and Jason W. Moore. *A History of the World in Seven Cheap Things: A Guide to Capitalism, Nature, and the Future of the Planet.* BlackInc, 2018.

Pateman, Carole. *Participation and Democratic Theory.* Cambridge University Press, 1970.

Pinealt, Eric. *A Social Ecology of Capital.* Pluto Press, 2023.

Pineiro Harnecker, Camila. Democracy and Solidarity: A Study of Venezuelan Cooperatives. In *Alternative Work Organisations,* edited by Maurizio Atzeni. Palgrave, 2012.

Pineiro Harnecker, Camila, ed. *Cooperatives and Socialism: A View from Cuba.* Palgrave, 2013a.

Pineiro Harnecker, Camila. Worker Self-Management in Argentina: Problems and Potentials of Self-Managed Labor in the Context of the Neoliberal Post-Crisis. In *Cooperatives and Socialism: A View from Cuba,* edited by Camila Pineiro Harnecker. Palgrave, 2013b.

Piven, Francis Fox, and Richard Cloward. *Poor People's Movements.* Vintage, 1977.

Plumwood, Val. *Environmental Culture: The Ecological Crisis of Reason.* Routledge, 2002.

Polanyi, Karl. *The Great Transformation: The Political and Economic Origins of Our Time.* Beacon Press, 2001 [1944].

Polet, Francois, and CETRI. *Globalizing Resistance: The State of Struggle.* Pluto Press and Tricontinental Centre, 2004.

Rahnema, Saeed. *The Transition from Capitalism: Marxist Perspectives.* Springer International Publishing, 2017.

Ranis, Peter. *Cooperatives Confront Capitalism: Challenging the Neoliberal Economy.* Zed Books, 2016.

Ratner, Carl. Cooperative Economics in Brazil: The UNISOL Cooperative Network. 2015. https://geo.coop/story/cooperative-economics-brazil (accessed 14 January 2025).

Restakis, John. *Humanizing the Economy: Cooperatives in the Age of Capital.* New Society Publishers, 2010.

Rhodes, Rita. *Empire and Cooperation: How the British Empire Used Cooperatives in its Development Strategies 1900–1970.* John Donald, 2012.

Riddell, Rebecca, Nabil Ahmed, Alex Maitland, Max Lawson and Anjela Taneja (lead authors). Inequality Inc. Executive Summary: How Corporate Power Divides Our World and the Need for a New Era of Public Action. Oxfam International, January 2024. https://oi-files-d8-prod.s3.eu-west-2.amazonaws.com/s3fs-public/2024-01/Davos%202024%20Executive%20Summary%20English.pdf, accessed 4 February 2025.

Right Livelihood. Cecosesola. 2022. https://rightlivelihood.org/the-change-makers/find-a-laureate/cecosesola.

Riley, Dylan. An Anticapitalism That Can Win. *Jacobin* 1 (2016): 1–10. https://jacobin.com/2016/01/olin-wright-real-utopias-socialism-capitalism-gramsci-lenin-luxemburg.

Ritchie, Hannah, Max Roser and Pablo Rosado. CO_2 and Greenhouse Gas Emissions. 2020. https://ourworldindata.org/co2-and-greenhouse-gas-emissions (accessed 7 November 2022).

Robertson, Ewan. Venezuela Marks 25 Years Since 'Caracazo' Uprising Against Neoliberalism. 2014. https://venezuelanalysis.com/news/10431 (accessed 30 April 2018).

Rockström, Johan, Will, Steffen, Kevin Noone, et al. A Safe Operating Space for Humanity. *Nature* 461, no 7263 (2009): 472–475.

Rodriquez, Iokiñe, Mariana Walter and Leah Temper. *Just Transformations: Grassroots Struggles for Alternative Futures.* Pluto Press, 2024.

Roelants, Bruno, Eum Hyungsik and Elisa Terrasi. *Cooperatives and Employment: A Global Report.* CICOPA, 2014.

Rothstein, Bo O., and Jan A. N. Teorell. What Is Quality of Government? A Theory of Impartial Government Institutions. *Governance* 21, no. 2 (2008): 165–190.

Ruggeri, Andres. Worker Self-Management in Argentina: Problems and Potentials of Self-Managed Labor in the Context of the Neoliberal Post-Crisis. In *Cooperatives and Socialism: A View from Cuba,* edited by Camila Pineiro Harnecker. Palgrave Macmillan, 2013.

Rushe, Dominic. Wage Gap Between CEOs and US Workers Jumped to 670-to-1 Last Year, Study Finds. *The Guardian,* 7 June 2022. www.theguardian.com/us-news/2022/jun/07/us-wage-gap-ceos-workers-institute-for-policy-studies-report.

Sader, Emir. 2011. *The New Mole: Paths of the Latin American Left.* Verso Books.

Saito, Kohei. *Karl Marx's Eco-socialism: Capital, Nature, and the Unfinished Critique of Political Economy.* New York: Monthly Review Press, 2017.

Santocildes, Marta Enciso, Aitor Bengoetxea Alkorta, Leire Uriarte Zabala and Aitziber Mugarra Elorriaga. *Story of Social Economy in the Basque*

Country, 1st ed. Dykinson, S.L., 2021. https://doi.org/10.2307/j.ctv-282jg9c.

Satgar, Vishwas. Cooperative Development and Labour Solidarity: A Neo-Gramscian Perspective on the Global Struggle Against Neoliberalisation. *Labour, Capital and Society* 40, no. 1–2 (2007).

Satgar, Vishwas. Challenging the Globalised Agro-Food Complex: Farming Cooperatives and the Emerging Solidarity Economy Alternative in South Africa. In *Beyond Capitalism: Building Democratic Alternatives for Today and the Future*, edited by Jeff Shantz and Brendan Macdonald Jose. Continuum Press, 2013.

Satgar, Vishwas, ed. The Solidarity Economy Alternative in South Africa: Prospects and Challenges. In *The Solidarity Economy Alternative: Emerging Theory and Practice*. University of Kwazulu-Natal Press, 2014.

Satgar, Vishwas. The Climate Crisis and Systemic Alternatives. In *The Climate Crisis: South African and Global Democratic Eco-Socialist Alternatives*, edited by Vishwas Satgar. Wits University Press, 2018.

Satgar, Vishwas, ed. With, Against and Beyond the State: A Solidarity Economy Through a Movement of Movements. In *Cooperatives in South Africa: Advancing Solidarity Economy Pathways from Below*. University of Kwazulu-Natal Press, 2019.

Satgar, Vishwas. Marx, the Commons, and Democratic Eco-Socialism. In *Marx Matters*, edited by David Fasenfest. Brill, 2022a.

Satgar, Vishwas. Epidemiological Neoliberalism and Covid-19 in South Africa. In *Socialist Register 2022: New Polarizations, Old Contradictions*, edited by Greg Albo, Leo Panitch and Colin Leys. Merlin Press, 2022b.

Satgar, Vishwas. Crises, Socio-Ecological Reproduction, and Intersectionality: Challenges for Emancipatory Feminism. In *Emancipatory Feminism in the Time of Covid-19*, edited by Vishwas Satgar and Ruth Ntlokotse. Wits University Press, 2023.

Satgar, Vishwas. *A Love Letter to the Many: Arguments for Transformative Left Politics in South Africa*. Jacana Media, 2024.

Satgar, Vishwas, and Ruth Ntlokotse, *Emancipatory Feminism in the Time of Covid-19: Transformative Resistance and Social Reproduction*. Wits University Press, 2023.

Satgar, Vishwas, and Michelle Williams. Cooperatives and Nation Building in Post-Apartheid South Africa: Contradictions and Challenges. *In Hidden Alternatives*, edited by Anthony Webster, Linda Shaw, John K. Walton, Alyson Brown and David Stewart. University of Manchester Press, 2011a.

Satgar, Vishwas, and Michelle Williams. The Worker Cooperative Alternative in South Africa. In *New South African Review 2: New Paths, Old*

Compromises? edited by John Daniel, Prishani Naidoo, Devan Pillay and Roger Southall. Wits University Press, 2011b.

Satgar, Vishwas, and Michelle Williams. *Cooperatives and Worker-ownership in South Africa.* In *New South African Review 2*, edited by John Daniel, Prishani Naidoo, Devan Pillay and Roger Southall. Wits University Press, 2011c.

Schlachter, Laura Hanson. Stronger Together? The USW-Mondragón Union Co-op Model. Unpublished paper. Department of Sociology University of Wisconsin-Madison, 2016.

Scholes, Bob, Francois Engelbrecht and Coleen Vogel. Climate Change: Effective Action Based on Enhanced Understanding. 2020. https://emancipatoryfutures.co.za/future (accessed 28 May 2025).

Sen, Amartya. *Development as Freedom.* Alfred A. Knopf, 1999.

Senato della Repubblica. Constitution of the Italian Republic. 1947. www.senato.it/documenti/repository/istituzione/costituzione_inglese.pdf (accessed 12 November 2022).

Shragge, Eric and Jean-Marc Fontan, eds. *Social Economy: International Debates and Perspectives.* Black Rose Books, 2000.

Silber, Irwin. *Socialism What Went Wrong? An Inquiry into the Theoretical and Historical Sources of the Socialist Crisis.* Pluto Press, 1994.

Silver, B. J. *Forces of Labor. Workers' Movements and Globalization Since 1870.* Cambridge University Press, 2003.

Sinwell, Luke. *The Participation Paradox: Between Bottom-Up and Top-Down Development in South Africa.* University of Johannesburg Press, 2023.

Sitrin, Marina. *Horizontalism: Voices of Popular Power in Argentina.* AK Press, 2006.

Sitrin, Marina. *Everyday Revolutions: Horizontalism and Autonomy in Argentina.* Zed Books, 2012.

Solar-Gallart, Marta. The Cooperative Market Economy: The Promise and Challenge of Mondragón. In *Engaging Erik Olin Wright: Between Class Analysis and Real Utopias*, edited by Michael Burawoy and Gay Seidman. Verso, 2024.

South African Government. People of South Africa. 2021. www.gov.za/about-sa/people-south-africa (accessed 7 November 2022).

Southall, Roger. *Liberation Movements in Power: Party and State in Southern Africa.* University of Kwazulu-Natal Press, 2013.

Standing, Guy. *The Plunder of the Commons: A Manifesto for Sharing Public Wealth.* Pelican, 2019.

Starr, Amory. *Naming the Enemy: Anti-corporate Movements Confronting Globalization.* Zed Books, 2000.

Starr, Amory. *Global Revolt: A Guide to the Movements Against Globalization*. Zed Books, 2005.

State Planning Board. *Government of Kerala Economic Review 2023*, vol. 1. Government of Kerala, State Planning Board, January 2024. https://spb.kerala.gov.in/sites/default/files/2024-02/ER_English_Vol_1_2023.pdf.

Statista. Household Poverty Rate in Venezuela 2023. 2023. www.statista.com/statistics/1235189/household-poverty-rate-venezuela (accessed 23 October 2024).

Statista. South Africa: National Poverty Line 2024. 2024. www.statista.com/statistics/1127838/national-poverty-line-in-south-africa (accessed 23 October 2024).

Statista. Aggregated CEO-to-Worker Compensation Ratio for the 350 Largest Publicly Owned Companies in the United States from 1965 to 2022. 2025. www.statista.com/statistics/261463/ceo-to-worker-compensation-ratio-of-top-firms-in-the-us/#:~:text=In%20 2022%2C%20it%20was%20estimated,key%20industry%20of%20 their%20firm.

Statistics South Africa. Mid-Year Population Estimates 2017. 2017. www.statssa.gov.za/publications/P0302/P03022017.pdf (accessed 13 November 2017).

Statistics South Africa. 2020 Mid-Year Population Estimates. 2020. www.statssa.gov.za/?p=13453 (accessed 27 May 2025).

Stavrides, Stavros. Emancipatory Commoning? 2016. https://onlineopen.org/emancipatory-commoning (accessed 2 February 2025).

Stavrides, Stavros. Emancipatory Commoning as a Process of Collective Inventiveness. Opening keynote of the Cinema of Commoning Symposium, 5 July 2024. https://cinemaofcommoning.com/2024/09/30/emancipatory-commoning-as-a-process-of-collective-inventiveness (accessed 1 February 2025).

Stefania, Barca. *Forces of Reproduction: Notes for a Counter-Hegemonic Anthropocene*. Cambridge University Press, 2020.

Steffen, Will, Jacques Grinevald, Paul Crutzen and John McNeill. The Anthropocene: Conceptual and Historical Perspectives. *Philosophical Transactions of the Royal Society A* 369, no. 1938 (2011): 842–867.

Sustainable Development Report. Rankings. 2023. https://dashboards.sdgindex.org/rankings (accessed on 1 October 2023).

Thompson, Peter, and Slavoj Žižek, *The Privatization of Hope: Ernst Bloch and the Future of Utopia*. SIC 8. Duke University Press, 2014.

Thompson, William. *Practical Directions for the Speedy and Economical Establishment of Communities, on the Principles of Mutual Co-operation, United Possessions and Equality of Exertions and of the Means of Enjoyments*. Strain and Wilson, 1830.

UN. 2014. *Measuring the Size and Scope of the Cooperative Economy: Results of the 2014 Global Census on Co-operatives*. United Nations Secretariat Department of Economic and Social Affairs Division for Social Policy and Development, 2014. www.un.org/esa/socdev/documents/2014/coopsegm/grace.pdf (accessed 24 December 2024).

ULCCS. Survey of ULCCS Workers. Unpublished document, 2014.

UNDP. *Global Multidimensional Poverty Index (MPI): Illuminating Inequalities*. United Nations Development Programme, 2019.

Van Meter, Kevin. *Guerrilla's Guide to the Commons*. Irene Books, 2017.

Vieta, Marcelo. Autogestion: Prefiguring a 'New Cooperatitivism' and the 'Labour Commons'. In *Moving Beyond Capitalism*, edited by Cliff DuRand. Routledge, 2016.

Wainwright, Hilary. A New Politics from the Left: The Distinctive Experience of Jeremy Corbyn as Leader of the British Labour Party. In *Reflections on the Future of the Left*, edited by D. Coates. Agenda Publishing, 2017.

Wainwright, Hilary. *A New Politics from the Left*. Polity Press, 2018.

Webster, Anthony, Alyson Brown and David Stewart. *Hidden Alternatives*. Manchester University Press, 2011.

Webster, Edward with Lynford Dor. *Recasting Workers' Power: Work and Inequality in the Shadow of the Digital Age*. Bristol University Press, 2023.

WEF. *The Global Risks Report 2023*, 18th ed. World Economic Forum, 2023. www.weforum.org/reports/global-risks-report-2023/.

Williams, Glyn, Binitha V. Thampi, D. Narayana, Sailaja Nandigama and Dwaipayan Bhattacharyya. Performing Participatory Citizenship: Politics and Power in Kerala's Kudumbashree Programme. *The Journal of Development Studies* 47, no. 8 (2011): 1261–1280.

Williams, Michelle. *The Roots of Participatory Democracy: Democratic Communists in South Africa and Kerala, India*. SG Distributors, 2008.

Williams, Michelle. Alternative Production and Consumption Relations? Fair Trade, the State, and Cooperatives in the Global South. *Journal of Contemporary African Studies* 31, no. 1. (2013).

Williams, Michelle. *The Solidarity Economy and Social Transformation*. In *The Solidarity Economy Alternative: Emerging Theory and Practice*, edited by Vishwas Satgar. University of KwaZulu-Natal Press, 2014.

Williams, Michelle. Uralungal: India's Oldest Worker Cooperative. *Global Dialogues* 6, no. 1 (March 2016).

Williams, Michelle. Practicing Democratic Communism in Kerala, India. In *The Socialist Register: Democracy*, edited by L. Panitch and G. Albo. Merlin Press and LeftWord Books, 2017.

Williams, Michelle. Democracy as a Transitional Compass: Women's Participation in South Africa and Kerala, India. *Globalizations* 17, no. 2 (2020): 338–351.

Williams, Michelle, and Vishwas Satgar. Emancipatory Alternatives: Worker Cooperatives and the Solidarity Economy. In *Große Transformation? Zur Zukunft moderner Gesellschaften: Sonderband des Berliner Journals für Soziologie*, edited by Klaus Dörre, Hartmut Rosa, Karina Becker, Sophie Bose and Benjamin Seyd. Springer, 2019.

Williams, Richard. *The Cooperative Movement: Globalization from Below.* Ashgate, 2007.

Wiseman, Wendy A., and Burak Kesgin, eds. *Lost Kingdom: Animal Death in the Anthropocene.* Vernon Press, 2024.

World Bank. Life Expectancy at Birth, Total (Years). 2022. https://data.worldbank.org/indicator/SP.DYN.LE00.IN?locations (accessed 29 October 2024).

World Bank. Global Poverty: Poverty and Equity Data Portal. 2025. https://pip.worldbank.org/country-profiles/ZAF (accessed 17 January 2025).

World Population Review. South Africa. 2022. https://worldpopulation review.com/countries/south-africa-population (accessed 7 November 2022).

Wright, Erik Olin. Working-Class Power, Capitalist-Class Interests, and Class Compromise. *American Journal of Sociology* 105, no. 4 (2000): 957–1002.

Wright, Erik Olin. Compass Points: Towards a Socialist Alternative. *New Left Review* 41 (September–October 2006).

Wright, Erik Olin. *Envisioning Real Utopias.* Verso, 2010.

Wright, Erik Olin. How to Be an Anti-Capitalist for the 21st Century. *Journal of Australian Political Economy* 77 (2016a): 5–22.

Wright, Erik Olin. How to Think about (and Win) Socialism. *Jacobin* 4 (April 2016b): 1–12. https://jacobin.com/2016/04/erik-olin-wright-real-utopias-capitalism-socialism (accessed 29 October 2024).

Wright, Erik Olin. *How to Be an Anti-capitalist for the 21st Century.* Verso, 2019.

Wright, Erik Olin, and Michael Burawoy. Taking Seriously the Social in Socialism. Unpublished draft chapter, 2004.

Wynberg, Rachel. How Justice Can Be Brought to South Africa's Rooibos Industry. *The Conversation*, 22 November 2016. https://theconversation.com/how-justice-can-be-brought-to-south-africas-rooibos-industry-68693 (accessed 23 October 2024).

Wynberg, Rachel. Making Sense of Access and Benefit Sharing in the Rooibos Industry: Towards a Holistic, Just and Sustainable Framing. *South African Journal of Botany* 110 (2017): 39–51.

Acknowledgements

Working on a book over so many years allowed us to engage with many amazing people, cooperatives, cooperators, movements and initiatives across 15 countries who generously shared their experiences and ideas with us. While we cannot name all of them as there are too many to count, we are deeply grateful to everyone we met and interacted with for their generosity of spirit and commitment to sharing time and experiences with us. This book is first and foremost a creation reflecting the experiences of those attempting to build transformative alternatives and create relations of care for each other and the planet. We thank all of them for their work and for sharing with us.

On this long journey, a few stand out for the connections we formed over multiple engagements and for their generosity during the research. Thanks to Erik Olin Wright, Melissa Hoover, Brendon Martins, Anne Reynolds, Laura Hanson Schlachter; to Iñaki Santacruz Ayo, Martha Solar, Theresa Sorde Marti, and Ramon Flecha for organising the workshop in Barcelona and research trips to Mondragon; to Rodolfo Elbert and Julián Rebón for hosting the workshop in Buenos Aires; to Devi Sacchetto and Mimmo Perrotta for hosting the workshop in Italy. Special thanks to T.M. Thomas Isaac for years of engagement and for hosting us at the three-day cooperative conference in Kerala.

Much of the fieldwork and research for the book as well as participation in two World Social Forum meetings was funded by the Rosa Luxemburg Foundation, the most progressive and visionary foundation that remains committed to planetary emancipation. The Emancipatory Futures Studies (EFS) Project at Wits University funded the open access publication, fieldwork in 2023 and 2024, and writing retreats. The 'Producing Alternative Green Futures' research project at Wits University (funded by the Independent Research

Fund Denmark (DFF), Project no. 1127-00212B) provided support for copyediting.

Thanks to our excellent copyeditor Alexis Grewan and our postgraduate student Joanne Morrison for her wonderful work on our diagrams and the reference list, to Sinovuyo Boltina for her research assistance and collating references, to Jane Cherry for her research support, and to the many conversations over the years with the Cooperative and Policy Alternative Centre (COPAC) Team past and present: Jane Cherry, Awande Buthelezi, Charles Simane, Andrew Bennie and Qhawe Mahlalela. We are grateful to a global network of friends, some of whom read drafts of chapters along the way: Jackie Cock, Peter Evans, Sarah Mosoetsa, Rachel Sherman, Sumangala Damodaran, Mandla Radebe, Tanya Turneaure, Bill Carroll, Hilary Wainwright, Roger Southall, Niveditya Menon, Aditya Nigam, Asanda Benya and Isabel Hofmeyr. Thanks to our family for all their support: Barbara and Richard Williams, Tina Daoussis and Scott Aldas, Ujala Satgoor, Kirun Satgoor, Lexi, Tasso and Gavin Daoussis, and Vedika, Prasanth, Mihir, and Vihaan Gokool.

Thanks to our commissioning editor at Pluto Press, David Shulman, and the rest of the Pluto team who supported us in the process: David Castle, Melanie Patrick (for the cover design), and Dave Stanford. A special thanks to Veronica Klipp from Wits University Press for her support in publishing the book in South Africa. We are grateful to our academic departments of Sociology and International Relations at Wits University for the collegial homes they have provided and to a number of colleagues including Jacqui Ala, Tatenda Mukwedeya, Thabang Sefalafala, Pulane Ditlhake, Sam Kariuki, Mbuso Nkosi, Bridget Kenny, Kezia Lewins, Ran Greenstein, Warren McGregor and Michelle Small. Thanks also to our wonderful administrators at Wits: Ingrid Chunilall, Gloria Bowes, Yurisha Pillay, Laura Bloem, and Josephine Mashaba.

Our very dear friend and mentor, Michael Burawoy tragically died just as this book went into production. Michael was our strongest supporter and fiercest critic over all the years of the book. His feedback in October 2024 on the introduction led us to completely rewrite the introduction and restructure some chapters. We have dedicated the book to him, as well as three other amazing scholar activists who shared our journey but who have also passed on: Paul Singer from Brazil, Martha Harnecker from Cuba and Chile, and Erik Olin Wright from the USA.

Index

fig refers to a figure; *n* to a note; *t* to a table